More praise for *Bad Girls*

"Sussman makes no pat pronouncements about 'what it means' when women, bred for compliance, misbehave. . . . Then come the tales of glorious, even dangerous, badness, or rebellions both classic and creative. . . . Bottom line, when it comes to bad girls, you want good stories, well told." —*New York Times Book Review*

"Devotees of secondary-school reveries will love *Bad Girls: 26 Writers Misbehave*, a book verifying, at least for me, that my high-school pals must have been correct when they insisted that girls also wrote graffiti on bathroom walls." —*Wall Street Journal*

"The confessions provide titillating insight into what some women do when radically embracing life." —*Philadelphia Journal Register*

"A lively assortment with enough variety to hook a wide range of readers." —*Publishers Weekly*

"Ellen Sussman recruited 25 women to write short, intensely per-sonal pieces about how it happened to them. All are accom-plished writers. Their notion of being 'bad' greatly varies from girlhood misdeeds to unhealthy relationships to feelings of guilt. . . . Good girls or bad, they are trying to make sense out of the world, and themselves." —*Palo Alto Weekly*

"Affairs, one-night stands, forgery, self-destructiveness, risk-taking and lies—these essays about bad girls cut deep into the heart of what it means to grow up, what it means to become a woman liv-ing life in all of its radical fullness. Certainly these terrific essays are marked by confusion and pain, but running like a trip wire through every single one of them is a hint of wildness, a glimpse of joy." —Dani Shapiro, author of *Black and White*

"*Bad Girls* is a witty, sassy read . . . in turn, both hilarious and heartbreaking. The perfect summer book for smart readers."
    —Amanda Eyre Ward, author of *Forgive Me* and *How to be Lost*

Bad Girls

26 WRITERS MISBEHAVE

Edited by Ellen Sussman

W. W. Norton & Company New York London

To the memory of my mother,
who really did dance on a table at a wedding

My thanks to Sally Wofford-Girand, my agent; Jill Bialosky, my editor; and Neal Rothman, my in-house counsel, first reader, last reader, one-man support team, husband, and bad boy.

Contents

Introduction

ELLEN SUSSMAN

I once drove to East Hampton with my first husband to meet hotshot clients of his who had invited us to their summer house for a weekend. My husband was a corporate attorney—I was a writer and college teacher. The clients were advertising executives. We met them at the door of their luxurious home, got the very grand tour, and walked through the back door so they could show off their ocean. I took one look, threw off my clothes, and ran naked into the waves.

I behave badly to set myself apart. To test myself. To push myself. To prove something. To shock someone. To get attention. To get a reaction. I behave badly because I can. Because I won't get caught. Because I will.

Every time I come close to being a good girl the bad girl in me goes wild.

I'm not alone. There are a lot of us acting badly out there.

I gather these writers' essays here because I want to peek behind the curtains. I want the naughty rush of witnessing bad behavior. I want the comforting shoulder rub of recognition. I want the smarter-than-me insight into what makes us so bad. Not that I'm about to change my bad-girl ways.

Maybe I just want a little company. I'm a bit of a loner. (I wonder if most bad girls are.) But I'm not going to miss this party.

My first memory: I'm standing on the stage. I'm two or three, and I can feel the smallness of me on that stage. My eyes burn against the bright lights—out there, somewhere, is a sea of people. There's a hum of noise and then silence. I look straight out into a black space that is filled with everyone I know and I recite:

There was a little girl
Who had a little curl
Right in the middle of her forehead
When she was good
She was very, very good
And when she was bad
She was horrid!

I kidnapped my Brownie Scout troop.

I let a twenty-one-year-old boy teach me almost everything I ever needed to know about sex when I was fourteen.

When a massage therapist let his hands wander, I went back for more.

At twenty-four I married a good boy. I wonder now if my own untamed desires frightened me. I had some vision of adulthood and it looked different from me. I just couldn't figure out how to get from here to there.

I met my husband after a wild night in Cambridge, out at a bar with a group of friends, during which time I asked, "Has anyone had group sex?" No, no one had. "Let's," I said. The good boy wasn't there—he didn't enter the scene until the next morning. But during the night the group in "group sex" dwindled from four to three to two—and I ended up sleeping with a guy who had been my best friend's date. In the morning we emerged from his room and saw my future husband sitting at the kitchen table. I was introduced; he frowned and glared and ate Cheerios. He and I didn't start dating until a year later, but I have to wonder: Did he think, Now, there's a bad girl I'd like to tame? Did I think, Now, there's a good boy who will rein me in?

To no one's surprise the marriage didn't work. When I think back on my marriage I recall this: We're driving home from a party. It's two or three in the morning. The streets are empty, the streetlights shimmer in the dark, the car is warm, the music is loud. I'm buzzed from too much wine or pot. He's driving; I'm coasting in my postparty haze. He turns down the radio. My chest tightens. My eyes close. Because in a minute he'll tell me what I did wrong—what I said or how I said it or what I did or how I did it. I don't want to hear it. I want to imagine the face of the man I danced with, the hand that slid around my waist, the whisper in my ear.

At forty-five I married a bad boy. Well, he's my kind of bad boy: He loves sex and he loves a bad girl. He's got an odd combination of bad-boy credentials: He drives a pickup truck and a Jaguar, he builds furniture now that he's done practicing tax law, he takes me to bed after we've done the Sunday crossword puzzle. He knows how to rewire a circuit, fix the plumbing, frame a house, tile a bathtub. Who needs married-lady fantasies when at the end of the day I get to bed the electrician, the plumber, the builder, the tile guy? Maybe I'm an odd combination of bad girl:

I want to celebrate sex, march naked along the beach, and talk dirty at a dinner party; at the end of the night it's now my husband's hand that snakes around my waist, his voice that whispers in my ear.

I asked twenty-five women writers to write about being a bad girl.

They told me:

I'm always a bad girl.
I'm never a bad girl.
I can't write about it because I have kids.
I have to write about it because I have kids.
I've changed.
I'll never change.
I love being a bad girl.
I hate being a bad girl.

There's a kind of energy that gets generated when bad girls hang out together. It's here. These pages bristle with danger. The writers are digging deep—bad behavior lives in our souls. And what they bring to the surface reveals truths about our psyche and our society. By lurking in the shadows they bring to light our fears, our passions, our desires.

Some of these writers luxuriate in a lifetime of bad behavior. Are bad girls born or made? Some of the writers examine how one wicked moment in their lives revealed the delicious power of being bad. What is that power? Where does it come from? Where does it take us? Some of the writers regret their misdeeds, some revel in them. Is bad behavior a fall from grace or a triumph? The answer is yes.

As I collected these remarkable essays I was struck by some of the similarities:

> A good Jewish girl like Elizabeth Rosner can rebel against Orthodoxy as well as any of the Catholic girls like Madeleine Blais, who recounts her days at Ursuline Academy, where "occasions of sin lurked everywhere."
>
> Bad girls grow up to be good girls. Sorta. Many of them spend a lot of time looking back into their darkest memories, sometimes with glee, sometimes with horror. Lolly Winston says it for many of us: "I miss my inner bad girl."
>
> When a girl doesn't fit in, as many of us found in our lives, sometimes she makes a spectacle of herself (like Susan Cheever in her "triumphant" return to her old school), rather than slink off into a corner.
>
> Bad girls aren't victims. We don't act out because we were abused or unloved. We act out because we want to or have to.

The ways in which we act out are astonishingly different— from Maggie Estep's affair at age fifteen with a middle-aged married horse thief to Roxana Robinson's sly signing of a parental permission slip for a friend in boarding school. Is one worse than the other? Hardly. Just ask Roxana's father, the Quaker headmaster of another school.

Some of the bad-girl behavior is delightful, as in Ann Hood's essay on lying, and some is terrifying, as in Jennifer Gilmore's exploration of bulimia. Some is spirited, as in Tobin Levy's sexual pursuits, and some is revengeful, as in Kate Moses' account of her outrageous adventure at age fourteen with a very bad-girl mom at the German Club Independence Day picnic in Anchorage,

Alaska. My own idea of a bad girl has twisted and turned, reshaping itself into something that catches us off guard, that knocks our socks off, that crawls under our skin. How appropriate that a bad girl won't allow herself to be easily defined.

And, not surprisingly, bad-girl writers don't follow the rules. The shape and style and format of these essays often challenge the very nature of the genre. Daphne Merkin bumps up against a barrier in trying to write about the penises she has known: Good girls don't talk about that. Determinedly she penetrates (so to speak) that hallowed territory with intelligence and wit. Michelle Richmond takes a hilarious approach in a letter to a TV producer begging to get a part on a reality TV show by proving what a badass she really is. Caroline Leavitt's account of her affair as a young woman with her sixty-year-old trailer-trash ballet teacher is written with the immediacy and vividness of a short story. Susan Casey delivers an episodic account of her wild trip to Baja in what she calls "Skipping Christmas: *Postcards from the Underworld.*" Kaui Hart Hemmings delivers an author's questionnaire instead of an essay, and through this unconventional format, shows that the bad girl has some trouble adjusting to motherhood. "I want to bring my old, bad self into my new good-girl life, what with the playdates and the casseroles and antibacterial wipes."

The range of writers in this collection shows us that bad girls are young and old, married and single, city girls and country girls, living conventional lives and living on the edge. They act out in a confessional (Mary Roach), at writers' conferences (Kim Addonizio), at work (Laura Lippman), while speeding down a country road (Susan Straight), at their father's funeral (Pam Houston), in the middle of the night on the ninety-ninth floor of the partially completed World Trade Center (Katharine Weber), by writing a book about her affair with J. D. Salinger after too many painful years of silence (Joyce Maynard). When they find themselves living with a good boyfriend and his perfect daughter, what do they do? They teach the girl to use the word "fuck," a powerful girl tool if there ever was one (Elizabeth Benedict).

Enter at your own risk. There's dangerous territory ahead. The ground shifts beneath you. The currents carry you away. There's the harsh smell of wildfire, the hiss of a snake, the bubbling cauldron, the wild winds of the mistral. But don't go there alone. Take my hand. We'll go there together.

Lying

ANN HOOD

*W*hen I walk into Bendel's on Fifth Avenue in Manhattan, a beautiful woman swoops down on me. "You want to try Mally?" she asks.

I've come for the sweater sale, but here in the atrium women are getting makeovers. Tall blonds in lab coats are applying shimmer on eyelids, gloss on lips, contours on cheekbones. It's impossible to resist the fawning, the shiny pink-and-green cases opened like treasure chests, the possibility of metamorphosis. Who needs a new cashmere sweater when a new self is possible?

"Yes," I murmur, "I want to try Mally."

Mally herself, also gorgeous, flits around the room. She is a makeup artist to the stars. "You like Jennifer Lopez?" whispers the blond Brazilian urging me onto a stool. "Mally does Jennifer Lopez."

I smile and nod. Mally does J-Lo and me. Mally pauses and stares into my face. She opens compacts and tubes. She tells me I'm beautiful. She moves on.

"So," my makeup artist says as she evens out the redness on my face, "where do you live?"

"Third and A," I tell her. This is a lie. I haven't lived in Manhattan for thirteen years. I came into the city from my home in Providence for a meeting with a magazine editor. But would a woman who has to catch a six o'clock bus back to Rhode Island be sitting in Bendel's with Mally?

"I live right there too!" she gushes. "Fifth and A! We're neighbors!"

"How about that?" I say, hoping she doesn't ask for specifics. Third and A is where my cousin Tony *used* to live before he left the city three years ago for the Berkshires.

But she doesn't. She is too busy curling my eyelashes with an instrument of torture I have not seen since the 1980s. Then she strokes on mascara, and I am suddenly a person with luxurious lashes, cheekbones, full lips. I stare at myself in the mirror, startled.

"You go to the woman on Ninth Street and get a Brazilian wax," she whispers gleefully. "You know who I mean, right?"

I nod knowingly, the way a person who really lives in that neighborhood would.

"Your husband will go wild tonight," she says.

"Oh, I'm not married," I lie. A woman who looks like I do right now, her face covered in Mally makeup, on her way home to the East Village and a Brazilian wax, wouldn't be married. She would have a boyfriend, someone sultry and temperamental. "I live with someone," I add. "An actor." Long ago I *was* in love with an actor, and as far as I know, he still lives somewhere in the East Village— with his wife.

"I bet he's famous." She giggles. "Right?"

Actually the old boyfriend now teaches ESL, but I say, "Well . . . ," in a way that tells her he is, indeed, very famous. Then I pay way too much for a concealer system with setting powder, adjustable coverage foundation, Citychick Smoky eye kit, and Shimmer, Shape & Glow face defining system in Love Is Deeper. We exchange email addresses; I invent a gmail account because certainly the person I say I am would have a gmail account. I forgo the sweater sale and instead spend the next hour trying on Diane von Furstenberg wrap dresses that I can't afford, admiring who I am pretending to be in the dressing room's triple mirror. Then I head for Port Authority and the bus ride back to who I really am.

I come from a family of liars. My grandmother, Mama Rose, lied to cover up her misdeeds. After putting a curse on our neighbor across the street for slighting my aunt, Mama Rose claimed the woman had put a curse on her first. After I told my mother that Mama Rose had served me a hamburger and given my brother a steak for dinner one Saturday when she babysat us, my grandmother lied and said I was inventing things again. After slapping my hand in anger, Mama Rose grabbed her own hand, and collapsed onto a chair, crying, claiming I had slapped her. Her lies were defensive moves, aimed at protecting herself. My grandmother did small mean things all the time; then she smiled sweetly and lied. Her lies made her seem nicer, kinder, victimized, even sympathetic.

She claimed that all seven of her daughters were liars. And she was right. Some of them lied to get other people in trouble. Some of them, like their mother, lied to cover up their own wrongdoings. Some of them simply lied for effect. They all knew they lied, and frequently fought about the lies. When one of my aunts talked about her high school graduation, the rest of them called another aunt to verify that in fact she had dropped out of school in the tenth grade to work making artificial flower displays. When another aunt bragged that she made the best polenta, she was forced to make it for everyone the very next Sunday; it was, of course, a dismal failure because she had no idea how to make polenta. In fact they lied all the time about recipes, leaving out ingredients when they shared them, and inventing others altogether.

The lying wasn't purely a female pursuit. For example, Mama Rose's son, my uncle, told lies about fights he had. He once told us that he had beat up a salesman at Sears, for selling him a faulty washing machine. He also told everyone that he punched out a mechanic for not figuring out what was wrong with my uncle's car. And he regularly bragged about slapping the faces of random people: neighbors, waiters, my cousins' teachers. He loved telling these stories, and my relatives, crowded into my grandmother's kitchen, enjoyed hearing them. As a child I used to wonder why he never got arrested for beating up so many people. Wouldn't the police come after someone decked a salesman at Sears? My father, an honest Midwesterner, finally explained that all these stories were lies. He chalked up my uncle's stories to aftereffects of World War II.

The war itself was fertile ground for lies. My uncle claims to have stormed Omaha Beach, walked across Italy, liberated Auschwitz, spent a great deal of time in London, and traveled up and down the Rhine. In truth he was wounded almost immediately and spent the war recovering stateside. A machinist by trade, he tells my son stories about building the Newport Bridge, how terrifying it was to be so high above the water painting it, and the tragic tales of the people who died during its construction.

Another lie he loves telling is how he studied art at the Rhode

Island School of Design. Like most of my aunts and uncles, he was actually forced to drop out of school and go to work after their father died. But he tells long stories about RISD and his time there. One morning shortly after my first wedding, in New York, one of the guests, a friend of my new mother-in-law's, called for my uncle's phone number. "Why do you want to talk to my uncle?" I asked her. "Why, he's going to paint my portrait!" she said. "He told me that he teaches painting at RISD now, but he still does some portraits." "Uh-huh," I said. I didn't want to embarrass my uncle by telling her the truth. Instead I told her I'd have him call her when his schedule opened up.

A sure sign that one of my relatives is about to lie is that they raise their right hand and say, "Honest to God, I'm not lying."

After I graduated from college I lived in Boston with five other women. In college, I wore Izod shirts and khaki pants, went to keg parties, and spent spring break in Fort Lauderdale drinking cocktails with names like Sex on the Beach, working on my tan, and kissing boys. Now I wanted to be someone different, some-one worldly, someone sophisticated.

The first thing I did was to assume a Boston accent—a little bit Kennedy with a hint of Rhode Island. Although I grew up mostly in Rhode Island, I actually spent the formative years of my child-hood in Virginia. My father had a Southern accent; my mother a strong Rhode Island one. They kind of neutralized each other, and my brother and I were accentless. Until I decided that sound-ing as if I was from Boston might make me more interesting. Once, long after I had abandoned my own pretense, I met a man who spoke with a fake British accent. I went along with it, empa-thetic to his need to present a better self. Isn't someone from England mysterious? Doesn't someone who "pahks her cah in

Hahvahd Yahd" somehow better than a girl who sounds like just about everybody else? Eventually, out of exhaustion, I dropped the accent.

But I couldn't let go of the hope that if I lied people would simply like me better, admire me more, envy me, even. Whenever one of my roommates talked about a restaurant, a movie, a book, I said I had eaten there, seen it, read it. I hated not knowing what was cool or popular or interesting. "You've done everything," one of my roommates sighed one afternoon. "You're so lucky." I shrugged, worrying that I didn't feel guiltier about lying so much. I had, in fact, done hardly anything at all.

Slowly, of course, I did accumulate experience. I moved a lot. I traveled a lot. I didn't have to lie so much about the things I had done, because I had finally done some interesting things.

It would seem that my lying was linked to immaturity, and so would fade away as I got older. But instead it took a new turn. I lied about how much things cost or where I bought them. Once I found a sweater at Urban Outfitters in Harvard Square, and whenever someone admired it I told them I got it at a vintage store in New York. The Prada shoes I paid seventy dollars for at a secondhand store I tell people I bought for forty dollars. Sometimes I tell them that even if they don't ask. "Prada shoes," I say, showing the inside label. "Forty bucks. Can you believe it?"

When I lie about these things, I become a person who gets the best deals, who knows where to shop, who finds things. In her short story "Harvest," Amy Hempel writes that she received four hundred stitches as the result of a motorcycle accident. Later she confesses that it was actually only three hundred stitches. "I exaggerate . . . because it's true—nothing is ever quite as bad as it could be."

Or, in my case, quite as good. I have had my share of bad luck, catastrophe, even tragedy. I don't need to make these things any worse than they really are. No, what I strive to do is make what is simply good great. I want the things I do well to seem fantastic. I want to be the best bargain hunter, the coolest mom, the wisest friend.

Take cooking, for example. I am a good cook. A really good cook. And I read cookbooks and cooking magazines for fun, clipping recipes, making notes, marking pages. One afternoon before a dinner party, I found a recipe for garlic bread that involved putting Parmesan cheese, unsalted butter, garlic, and lemon zest into a food processor, then smearing it on the sliced bread and baking at a high temperature. The result was memorable: crusty bread baked to a golden brown, garlicky with a hint of lemon.

"Did you invent this?" one of my guests asked as she swooned over her third piece.

It had not occurred to me to take credit for creating the actual idea of the bread. Wasn't finding the recipe and making it enough? But once she planted the notion, I jumped on it.

"I just threw some things in the food processor," I said.

"Lemon?" she asked. "Who would have thought of it?"

Me, I told myself. And her. "Me."

I never lie about things that matter. I have never said "I love you" to someone I don't love. I never lie when I write nonfiction. The only lie I've told my kids is that there is a Santa Claus. I do not lie about matters of the heart. Or matters of the soul. I am a person friends turn to only when they want to hear the truth about the man they love, the work they've done, or a choice they have to make. I do not sugarcoat the truth. I am not swayed by romanticism. I am practical, a realist. I call a spade a spade. If a friend gets a bad haircut or wears an unflattering skirt, I say nothing rather than lie.

Yet I lie all the time when it doesn't matter.

I am sitting on an airplane heading to Los Angeles to visit a friend. Why do I tell my seatmate that I live there, in LA? Why do I tell her, when she asks, that I write for television?

In the line at the post office, waiting to buy stamps to mail my bills, why do I say I am visiting the city where I live? Why do I add that I actually live abroad? In Rome?

Why do I tell the person on the bus that I've been married three times? Isn't twice enough?

The jeans I bought on sale at J. Crew I say I bought in London.

The Betsey Johnson skirt I paid too much money for I claim I got marked down for fifty bucks!

Look at this deal I got!

I know the best places to eat, to shop, to travel, to go!

I am cool! I am confident! Don't you wish you knew what I know?

*H*ere is the truth: I do find bargains. I have traveled to many places, lived in many cities. Here is the truth: Many people find me interesting. I have many friends. I really do have stories to tell, things that really happened, events that can keep you spellbound.

But somewhere deep inside me, I am not interesting. I am not cool. I am the new kid in first grade wearing all the wrong clothes, saying all the wrong things; I am the twelve-year-old girl standing in a shopping mall not knowing what to buy; I am the teenager who chose the ugliest green-plaid-and-floral prom dress; the college kid who didn't understand that blue jeans were better than outfits that matched perfectly: belt, socks, handbag; the girl whose first car was a white Firebird with a baby blue racing stripe and white interior, who drove it home and realized that she had just paid three thousand dollars for the ugliest car on the block.

I pulled it off that day at Bendel's. I really could be a person living on Avenue A with a famous actor. I really could afford a four-hundred-dollar dress. When someone believes me, when they look at me with admiration or even awe, I feel I am important. That person believes I could live in Rome? Manage a high-powered job? Set style trends? Be this special, this unique, this fascinating? I put on new identities not for the people I lie to, but for me. Over time my lies have gotten smaller, more harmless, more inconsequential. I have learned that there is no shame in saying that I have not heard of that painter or this writer, and that people will happily, even eagerly, tell me what they know. I have learned that the best way to find bargains and unusual things is to ask the person who has them.

But that younger self still lurks inside me. Here I am, in line at the grocery store, telling the woman waiting behind me that the skirt I bought at the Gap comes from a specialty shop in London. I pick up my groceries and smile at her, in that way that only someone as unhip and ordinary as I would smile. And in that moment I am special. Even now, after all this time. I lie.

Bad Dancer

CAROLINE LEAVITT

*I*t's a sultry summer night, and my husband, Tom, is in the kitchen, cooking shrimp curry for twelve. Everyone's buzzing around him, and though we've only been in Akron for six months, I'm already used to the hum. My friend Abby is laughing, leaning closer toward him, dotting his shoulder with the tip of her finger. My mother, visiting from Boston, ruffles his gleaming black curls. "My gorgeous son-in-law," she sighs. I wander toward Leslie, an East Coast transplant like me, whose unhappiness at being in the Midwest matches my own and has bonded us. Her baby's fussing on her lap, her whining cries growing louder. Tom looks over, turns the heat down on the curry, and goes and gets his guitar. He sits down by the baby, plays a few chords, and the baby stops crying. "Works every time," he says. Leslie kisses the air in gratitude, but with her eyes closed, as if her lips are right on his. And he's up again, talking to my friend Sara, asking her how law school is going. "If you need help you just call me," he tells her. "I can put a good word in at my firm for an intern-ship, too."

Leslie readjusts the baby on her lap. "You're so lucky," she says. "Tom's so nice. Can't you talk him into giving my Bobby lessons?"

Tom gives my mother an impulsive hug and then jumps up to check on dinner. When Leslie rises to change the baby, my mother plops down in her seat. "Sweetheart, what a dinner party this is turning out to be," she says. "Everyone loves Tom."

"Yes, they do," I say carefully.

Tom is guiding everyone to their seats, clowning a little, hand-ing them their napkins with a flourish that makes them laugh.

"You're so lucky to have him," my mother tells me.

"Sometimes I feel like I don't have him," I say quietly. "He works every night and weekends." I try to think of the last time we went to a movie or out to dinner. I try to think of the last time we made love.

"Well, he's a lawyer, he's busy." My mother's voice lowers even more. "If I were you I'd keep very close to him, because other women are going to try to snatch him right up."

Something snakes up along my spine. "Mom—" I say sharply. "How do you think I feel when you say that? It's like you're telling me I'm not good enough for Tom. You're my mother. Aren't you on my side?"

"I'm just trying to protect you," she says, stung. Then she tells me it's time to eat, that everyone is going to the table. My appetite has vanished.

*W*hen everyone leaves, the house is blanketed in quiet. My mother's insisted on staying in a hotel, something she never gets to do, so it's just Tom and me.

"Great party, wasn't it?" I say, resting my head against Tom's shoulder.

Tom bends away from me, gathering the dishes. "Yep," he says, "It was."

"Want to watch a video?" I ask. "We can snuggle on the couch."

He stacks and fits dishes into the washer, then notices we're out of dishwasher detergent, and even though I tell him to leave it, that it'll wait until tomorrow, he shakes his head. He insists on going out for a box. Two hours later he comes back, flushed and happy, the detergent in his arms. "I took the long way home," he says. "It was such a gorgeous night." I think about the way Abby had draped herself on him at the party. I think of Leslie asking if Tom could give her husband lessons on how to behave. I think, too, about what my mother said.

"Where else did you go?" I said.

"Jesus, not this again." His voice tightens. His face grows dark. He opens the refrigerator and gets a bottle of water and drains it. Then he places his hands on my shoulders. "We're *married*," he says. "Why are you so insecure?"

"I'm not," I insist and try to loop my arms around his shoulders, but he's already turning from me. "I just want to know where you went."

"What did I do that makes you this way? Wasn't I nice to your friends? I cooked dinner! I played the guitar!"

"And you took two hours for a five-minute drive—"

He throws his arms up. "I'm not having this discussion," he says abruptly. "I'm tired."

We go to bed, both of us tense and angry, and almost instantly he's sleeping. I lie awake, turning from side to side, trying to get comfortable. In the morning, when I wake up, he's already gone to work. I hate myself, but I go through the pockets of the clothes he wore last night.

There's nothing there. There never is.

---

*F*ast forward. It's a year later. I'm twenty-three and sitting outside a freezing dance studio with Jack, who is fifty-nine and my ballet teacher. He's an old fifty-nine, with a balding head and lanky hair, dentures, and a squint, and even a bit of a potbelly. He's got a little boy and a young wife. I suspect he doesn't bathe that often because he says the pipes in his house are always freezing in the winter, breaking in summer, and, too, because he often wears the same clothes three days in a row. Sometimes, when I get close, I see the grease sparkling in his hair. All he does is teach ballet.

*A*nd I'm sleeping with him every chance I can get.

*I*t starts innocently, with Introductory Ballet for Adults, the class he teaches. I sign up because the nights are too long, too lonely and empty for me, and because ballet is something I've always wanted to do, and because it'll tone my body, and maybe Tom will want me more. My friend Leslie is taking one class with me, hiring a sitter to do it, insisting this is the thing that will get her back in shape. I take all three classes offered, one right after another. I'll be gone four nights a week from six until ten, and that suits me just fine. When I tell Tom, he nods. "Good," he says. "It'll keep you out of trouble."

The class is in an old converted gym. There are twenty of us, all women, and we stand at the bar, young and middle aged, all of us awkward in our new tights and leotards and soft pink ballet slippers, our hair pulled back into sloppy buns. And then Jack strides in, a gnome in a tight white T-shirt and black tights, and some of the women titter. "That's the teacher?" Leslie whispers. "Oh my fucking God."

He plants his hands on his hips and surveys the class. "You're all too old to be good dancers," he says gently. "But I'll make dancers out of you anyway."

He tells us that he himself didn't start until he was in his twenties, that when he saw he wasn't good enough to get into a company, he went on to get a degree in dance so he could teach. "I dance for my own pleasure," he says. "And you will, too."

Confidence rises from him like heat from a summer sidewalk. When he passes the mirrored wall, he turns and looks at himself with such a sunny smile and a wink that I am enchanted. "He thinks he's the cock of the walk," Leslie says.

"Before you can dance, you have to learn how to stand properly. You," he says, pointing at me. I come forward, and he stands behind me. I smell his sweat. I feel his whole body behind mine. His breath is against my ear. He takes both my hands and draws them out horizontally, nudges his knee between my legs so my stance is wider, and then he crouches down before me and takes each of my legs in his hands and turns them outward. Even though he's the teacher, even though he's nearing his sixties, his touch is both paternal and provocative, and I inadvertently shiver. When he lets go of my legs, I stumble.

It doesn't take me long to love class. I love the clothes we all begin to wear, the T-shirts that we tear the necklines from so they hang low, the woolly leg warmers, the rainbow of leotards, and the pretty wispy skirts tied around our waists. I love the music, the way my muscles are slowly appearing, how strong I'm getting. I make friends, too, besides Leslie: Robin, who teaches second grade and has coffee with me sometimes. Anne, who works for a bank and sometimes sees a film with me. I go to class exhilarated and come home exhausted, and when Tom sees me in my ballet gear, the only thing he says is, "I'm glad you're keeping busy."

Every day before we start our warm-ups, Jack has another

story, and they're all always about why you shouldn't give up, or how society imposes rules to fuck you up, or most often, about how talented he is, how amazing. He tells us that both his parents were alcoholics, that his father drove him to the local orphanage and left him there, and when Jack ran crying after the car, his father refused to stop. He tells us he taught himself photography and won prizes for his pictures. "Anything is possible," he keeps telling us. "And I'm proof of it."

I practice every day. I get a portable chrome ballet barre from a mail-order place, and set it up in our living room, and I spend an hour doing pliés and turns and stretching. I get to class early every time, so I can practice there, as well, with the huge wide mirror, and suddenly, Jack begins coming early. "I'll warm up, too," he says, and takes his place at the barre. While we work I concentrate on my positions, my stretches. I try not to look at him, because if I do I'm afraid I'll forget how to speak. He begins to ask me questions. What do I do? How do I do it? I tell him about growing up in Boston; I tell him I'm a novelist writing my first novel; I tell him that my father died when I was very young. I talk for what feels like hours, and when I finally glance over at him, to my surprise, I see that he's stopped practicing, that he's leaning along the barre, staring at me, and his eyes are glinting with interest.

*I*s it my imagination that he begins to touch me more in class? I feel him staring. He comes over while I'm trying to do an arabesque, my left leg high up behind me. When he adjusts my arms, I feel a pulse of heat from his hand that makes me suddenly dizzy. As soon as class is over, I can't wait for it to start again. I can't stand leaving the dance studio, and the only reason I want to go to sleep is so I can wake up and get back to class. And back to Jack.

We have two weeks off class. I don't know what to do with myself. I can't write. I can't think. I go to the movies, one after another, and sit in the dark and when each movie is done, I have no idea what I've been watching. All I see, all I feel is Jack. When I get together with Leslie, with my friends, I become so restless, I make excuses why I have to go home. I write pages and pages and tear them up. I practice pirouettes for hours until I can do three, one right after the other, and when I'm finished, my limbs feel like noodles.

I get out my watercolors, and all that last week I begin sending him cards. Sweet anonymous cards I paint and don't sign. A figure leaping into the air, and inside I write, "My life feels like a grand jeté now."

When class starts up again, the first thing Jack says is, "Someone's been sending me cards! Who's doing it? I want to know!"

Leslie nudges me. "Yeah, you are!" she laughs, and I laugh back as if this is the most ridiculous thing I have ever heard. I feel a flush up my shoulders. "Like anyone would send him anything," I whisper back, and Leslie winks at me. Later, after Jack and I are sleeping together, he'll boast to me about those cards. "I sent them," I tell him, and his face falters. He's disappointed.

Six months after I've started ballet, I sell my first short story. The *Michigan Quarterly Review* is going to pay me fifty dollars! I call Tom, who puts me on hold to take another call, and I hang up without telling him. Instead I run to class. I tell Jack, who whoops and lifts me up. "I've always been a catalyst!" he exults, and when the whole class is assembled, he announces, "We have a star in our midst," and he tells them all, and I feel so happy I could explode.

In class, because I've been practicing hard, because I'm so

elated, for the first time I can do four pirouettes. I can hold my arabesque for ten seconds longer than usual. I never want class or this feeling to end.

"Do you need a ride home?" Jack asks when class is over. He says he just has to stop at his office, then he asks me if I would like to come upstairs with him, and I say yes. His office is dark even with the light on. I'm not thinking. Every cell is sprinting forward. As soon as we're upstairs, he starts telling me that when he was in his twenties, he worked for a Chinese man, Sam Yee, and his wife, Anna Yee. When Sam went to take the printing jobs out, Anna would appear, and it was Anna who taught him Chinese sex secrets. "We did it in a chair," Jack says. "She had this way with silk ropes, with feathers. She taught me the right way to breathe— very important in making love."

I don't know what to say, but it doesn't matter, because I can't speak, I can't breathe properly. Jack turns to me and then pushes my head down, pulls his tights down so his penis bobs against my mouth. I look up at his face, but his eyes are closed, his mouth half open, and I finally take him in, and then out, and a few minutes later, he jerks himself away from me. "Not yet," he says.

He turns me roughly around, so I'm facing a table, not him. The edge of the wood cuts into my hip. Then he bends me down and tugs at my jeans. "I would have thought you knew enough to wear a skirt," he says. He scissors my legs apart and then enters me roughly, and when I try to move against him, he says, "Wait—" and then he pulls out and pushes himself in again. I twist around so I can see his face, his eyes wide open watching me, and he smiles and then thrusts harder and grabs my breasts. "Oh—" he cries, making a sound like a cat, and then abruptly he pushes me away from him, so he splashes onto the floor.

I stand up and wipe my mouth. Sperm is leaking from me onto my thighs. My pants are squishy with it, and my breasts hurt where he grabbed them. "Tissue," he whispers and hands me one. I daub at my pants and pull them on, zip them up. I straighten my blouse, my hair.

Unfaithful. I've been unfaithful. And the sex was horrible.

"What?" he says. "You look unhappy."

"What about Dr. Chang's sex secrets," I say. "The silk ropes."

"We're in my office," he snaps. "Do you see any silk ropes?"

All I want to do is get out of there and never come back, but when I walk to the door, Jack takes my arm. "Caroline," he says, and this time his voice sounds desperate to me, and I turn toward it. "I'm almost sixty. This is my last chance to fall heedlessly in love."

Then he cups my head in his hands, and all my anger flows out of me. I rest my head on his shoulder.

I make him drive me home. "Stop the car," I tell him. We're a block away from my house. I don't want anyone to see me. It's late, dark outside, and I run to the house and open the door, flooding our place with light. I notice there's a small dot of semen on my blouse, and I take the blouse off and stuff it in the trash. And then I think again about what I've done, and I cry and cry and cry so hard that it takes me a half hour to realize that Tom isn't home. That I don't know where he is, that he hasn't even left me a message. And that I can't stop thinking about Jack, that I crave the attention Jack's giving me. That I heard him say the word "love."

I tell no one. No one. Certainly not Leslie, but that's easier now, because she's stopped coming to classes. She's too busy with the baby, and she says Jack is too creepy. Certainly not the other women in the class who make casual fun of Jack when he stands in front of the mirror and talks about how young he looks, how he's not like the other fifty-year-old men, how brilliant his kids are, how perfect his wife. "So many women want me," he boasts one day, and the woman next to me laughs. I giggle too and roll my eyes and I wonder if it shows, if people know that something is up, and I'm both alarmed and thrilled and sickened. It's a relief to have a man no one is after instead of Tom, whom everyone is.

One day my mother calls me up and in the middle of a conversation about what I'm cooking Tom for dinner, she blurts, "I wouldn't stay with anyone who had an affair. It's a horrible thing to do to a marriage." Since she thinks Tom is so perfect, I'm sure she means me.

"I wouldn't either," I tell her, and then I hang up.

That evening, when I'm leaving Jack's class, a car beeps and it's Tom's partner, a guy named Phil who does cocaine and has a young, breasty girlfriend. "How funny to see you walking out here alone," Phil says, and then he shoots me a look. "It's as if you're having an affair or something."

"Oh, sure," I say, laughing.

*J*ack and I have been seeing each other for two years when he invites me to his home for lunch. I imagine it's just the two of us, but he blinks. "No, no, you misunderstand," he says. "My wife, Janey, will be there, and the kids, Don and Bobby. We'll have a spread. I insist on a spread because I was so deprived as a kid." I'm so caught up in the innocent way he says this that I don't for one moment think what I'm doing is wrong. I get in his car, and he buckles me in his seatbelt so we're close, and then he drives on the highway.

There's a sign, Gold Gate, and then my mouth drops open because there's a row of squat little trailers set on a series of scrubby green lawns. The tarry road loops and curls around them, and on one end there's a row of plastic chairs. I hear a radio in the distance, the snap of grease on a grill. I look at him, astonished.

"We were able to buy our own place for less than ten thousand," he says proudly, rubbing my thigh. "You and your husband ought to think about a trailer park." I stare at him to see if he's kidding, but he isn't.

His trailer is on the far corner, painted red with blue shutters. There's a jump rope wriggled on the lawn like a snake. I can hear music, something from *Jacques Brel Is Alive and Well and Living in Paris.* "Jacks Breel," he says. And I don't correct him.

We walk inside, and it's all wood paneled, with what must be his paintings everywhere. They're all bright abstract blobs of color, with a chaotic design. "It's big, isn't it?" he says proudly, but it's like a railroad flat, a long corridor of rooms. There's a long wooden table in the center of the room, but it's not set for lunch. There are no plates or glasses, nothing brewing on the stove. "Janey!" he calls, and he takes his hand from my back and I flinch, and suddenly there she is, pushing her long, curly brown hair from her face, a baby balanced on the hip of her flowery blue dress. Behind her a little boy tumbles in, all blond bangs and lashy eyes and a freckled face. He's got a cowboy holster over his jeans, with two little fake silver guns, and he jumps right on Jack. Jack. "Daddy's big boy," he says.

Janey ignores the hand I hold out. She doesn't even look at me, but she's staring at Jack. "Jack, I need to see you outside," she says. Her voice is broad and flat and Midwestern.

Jack touches my arm. "Watch the kids for a second." It's not a question.

Jack takes the baby from Janey and desposits him in my arms, a bundle of warm sleepy baby. "He'll doze," Jack promises, and then he follows Janey outside and suddenly I'm alone in his trailer with a baby who's not mine and a little boy who's staring at me. "Want to see me jump?" he offers, and I nod. He spins around. "Pow, pow, pow!" he says, grabbing a toy gun from the holster and pointing it at me, so I flinch. "Don't do that," I say. The baby stirs and begins to whimper, and I look around for a bottle, and can't find any. "Look at me!" Don cries, "Watch me!" and he's twirling around crazily, and the baby begins to scream, stiffening and thrashing in my arms. Sitting down on the couch doesn't help.

I look around the room for a bottle, a pacifier, for anything to calm this baby. I glance at my watch. They've been gone an hour already. Where could they possibly be? Are they fucking in the back of Jack's car? Is she serving him with divorce papers? The baby is still screaming when the door slaps open and Jack and Janey both walk in, not touching, Janey's face tense and quiet. As soon as Janey takes the baby, he calms, and I stand there, my hands flopping at my sides, ridiculous. "I tried to find a pacifier," I whisper.

"We don't use those. They buck the soft palate," Janey says.

"Who's hungry?" Jack asks, clapping his hands together. I wait until Janey is in the kitchen and then I whisper to him, "I should leave—"

"And insult Janey?" he says. "She's cooking already."

"Can I help?" I ask, and though I think I am whispering, Janey lifts her head and stares at me. "No, thank you," she says pointedly.

Lunch is baked beans and salad and sweet corn shucked from the cob, and different cheeses and crusty breads, the whole huge spread Jack insists on, and no one's eating much except for him. "This is delicious," I say, and Janey studies me. "It's just baked beans from the can," she says. I keep up a patter all through lunch, all through the apple sauce dessert, but almost no one else is talking. "Isn't my family wonderful?" Jack asks me. "I am one lucky man." Janey bends toward me and, without touching me, takes my plate away. "Let me help with the dishes at least," I say. But she acts as if she hasn't heard me.

When I leave, she doesn't say thank you for coming, or how nice it was to meet me, or how she hopes she'll see me again.

$\mathscr{J}$ack and I don't talk on the way home. He puts on the radio, a country station, and sings, but he can't carry a tune, and he's off the beat. He traces my knee with his finger, gliding it up to my thigh, and I press my legs together. He tries to wedge his hand into my blouse, and I jerk away from him. "What is it with you?" he says, annoyed. He beeps the horn at another car. "I love you," he says. "But I will never leave my wife or my family. That's why you had to meet them."

"I wish I hadn't."

"I explained it to you." He's as patient as he is when he tries to show the class how to do a grand jeté. "I can't be tied down. Janey knows that."

I swallow. My mouth is dry, and my eyes are burning. "I thought you said this was your last chance to fall heedlessly in love." I can't believe I'm saying the words.

He takes my hand, and I let him. "It is. And I am."

"Are you sleeping with anyone else beside me?"

He hesitates before he answers. He slows the car, a block away from my house, the way we always do. "Did you think I'd be a monk?" he asks. And then I throw open the door, even before he's stopped. I tumble, scraping my knee, and I hear him shout my name, just once, and I keep going.

$\mathscr{A}$s soon as I get home, the phone's ringing. I pick it up, and I hear breathing, and I think Jack must have stopped at a pay phone. "I love you," he says, and I hang up. And when the phone rings again I don't pick it up again. I stop going to class. The loneliness I've felt with Tom is nothing compared to the loneliness of this. I don't care if my husband doesn't come home until three in the morning or not at all. Tom's not the one I love now. And the way Tom hurts me is nothing compared to this.

I get mail and when I open it, it's one of the cards I've sent Jack. Inside is a note: "The woman who wrote this can't harden her heart to me." I rip it into pieces.

That night I clean the whole house, scouring every room. I buy two hundred dollars' worth of groceries. I chop vegetables and braise carrots and fillet fish and then I shower and wash my hair and put on my favorite black dress. I'm not doing this for Tom, I'm doing it for me, and I'm just putting daisies in a vase for the table when Tom comes home. He stares at the flowers, and then he sits down heavily.

"Are you okay?" I ask, and he shakes his head.

"I'm not happy," he says and I hear the fish snapping and burning in the pan, but I don't move.

"I haven't been happy for a very long time. Surely you know that."

"I don't," I whisper. I wait, terrified that Jack's name is going to be the next thing he says, but instead he is talking about himself, how it's not another woman, that there's just something missing between us, some kind of necessary glue. He gets up—the considerate Tom everyone knows—and shuts off the burning fish so the smoke alarm won't go off, so there will be something to eat if either one of us ever has an appetite again. "I want a divorce," he says.

He urges me to stay. "This is your home," he tells me, even though we both know it's not. And in any case, it isn't about

Akron. I'm leaving him, and I'm leaving Jack. I committed the crime and arranged the punishment, too, and now I tell myself, Well, you're getting out on parole.

I start a whole new life in New York, even signing up for a ballet class at Carnegie Hall, but after a few months, I drop out. It's not the same without Jack. Every once in a while Tom calls me. He hasn't started divorce proceedings yet, and sometimes he talks as if he wants me back. "I just want to make sure you're okay," he says.

"Why wouldn't I be?" I ask him, though the truth is, I'm struggling.

One evening I'm at home when the phone rings, and I listen while a woman tells me that she's been Tom's lover for three years, that she just wanted me to know. "You have to give him up," she tells me. "All he does is talk about you." I hang up the phone. I feel so sick I go into my tiny bathroom and I have the dry heaves so terribly that for days afterward my throat is raw. I can barely speak. And then, because there's really nothing else to do, I pick up the phone to call a lawyer, to file for divorce.

It's twenty years later. I'm in Manhattan now, a whole different person with a whole different life. I'm blissfully remarried to a man who is funny and smart and adoring, and we have a young son. I'd no sooner think of being unfaithful to my husband than I would imagine hurling myself off a building. To my surprise I'm having lunch with Leslie, from my dance class, my first friend in Akron. She's come up to the city to see her daugher—the baby!—graduate college and even though we've long lost touch, she calls me spur of the moment. We're talking over old times and our husbands, laughing about how lucky we've become, how happy, how we left our old selves behind. "Remember Jack?" she asks, reaching for a French fry, and I suddenly stop breathing.

"Sure I do," I say quietly.

"God, remember how dirty he was? How he never shut up about all his stupid accomplishments?"

I haven't seen or heard from Jack in twenty years. He'd be in his seventies now. Surely too old and creaky limbed to be teaching ballet anymore. Surely retired. Surely still with Janey because who else would be there for him now, an aging man with no power or money?

"Is he alive?" I reach for my water and take slow, careful sips.

Leslie waves for the waitress. "God, who knows?" she says, and then she changes the subject, she starts talking about her daughter's piercings, how many there are, how wild she is, and how that worries her. She asks if New York City is safe, if she should get her daughter a guard dog, or a bodyguard, and both of us laugh. And then, as we're about to leave, she whispers, "I've never told anyone this, and if you do, I'll deny it to my grave. But I had an affair with Dirty Jack."

I can't move. "You didn't," I say. I remember her mocking Jack in class. I remember her dropping out, saying she didn't give a fuck about ballet and wanted to spend time with her baby.

Leslie nods. "It's the one humiliation of my life. But at least it made me stay with my husband. You did well for yourself, leaving Tom. But me—well, I'd have done worse. Staying was the only thing I could have done."

I could have made her feel better by telling her about me and Jack, and confiding in her about Tom's philandering and how the only solution to feeling so terrible about myself seemed to be Jack. I could have told her I understood. I could have asked her details, filled in the blanks about Jack's past. I remembered, too, her at my dinner party all those years ago, when her baby graduating from college really was a baby. I remember the way she gushed over Tom, the way she told me she wished he could give her husband lessons on how to behave. She kissed the air. When she said good night to Tom, she draped herself around him like a bedsheet.

I could tell her what my mother had once said about infidelity. How it's the only sin in a marriage.

Instead I touch her hand. "How terrible for you," I say gently. "I'm so sorry," and then I pat her shoulder.

She scribbles her phone number on a piece of paper and folds it into my hand. "I don't expect you to remember it after all this time," she says.

She's going uptown, and I'm headed to the Village, so we hug and she promises to call me, first chance she gets. Or, she says, I can call her.

"Don't forget!" she shouts after me.

I watch her walking up Madison, her long coat swinging. We don't have anything in common anymore. She was my friend, but now she's part of a life that doesn't exist for me any longer, and I take out my cell phone to call my husband, to ask him if he wants to meet me for a movie, if he's got any thoughts about dinner later. "Maybe we'll just go to bed early," he says, and I hear his wink on the phone. I tell him I love him, and I'm still talking to him, smiling, when the paper with Leslie's number floats out of my hand, and I don't stop to pick it up.

The Thrill of a Well-Placed "Fuck"

ELIZABETH BENEDICT

I'm teaching E. to swear, because she aims to be perfect, and I'm afraid for her."

I wrote this on the bottom of a concert program six years ago and stuffed it into a box of scraps and photographs in my bookcase. Until I found it the other day, I had nearly forgotten how deliberate I had been back then, making sure she heard me swear when I spoke—swear enough but not too much—and how delicate an operation this was.

At the time Emily was the thirteen-year-old daughter of my beau, who lived most of the time with her mother. She was an immensely serious violinist, a straight-A student, a reserved, sweet-tempered, self-described perfectionist who routinely stayed up until two in the morning doing homework and got up a short time later to wash her hair and get ready for school. She spent every Saturday, from nine until six, at a Boston music conservatory. Our weekly time with her was from six o'clock until early Sunday afternoon, when she returned to homework, rehearsals, and hours of daily practice.

The pressure she lived with broke my heart and often left her exhausted and depleted, but it was impossible to argue with the dazzling skill and depth of her performances, on stage and in the classroom. Still, the pursuit of perfection in every part of life made me fearful, because I know how tempting it is for teenage girls to believe in the p-word, and how much damage it can do. I felt the only influence I might have for those few hours a week was to be as relaxed and imperfect as I could be. I tried to set a standard for chilling out after her grueling week, not ramping up.

I made plentiful dinners with desserts of ice cream and cookies—no diet-plate specials on those nights. When I told stories about the parts of my life that Emily didn't see—I was a New Yorker who traveled to Boston on a regular basis to see her father—I tried not to censor myself too much when "damn" and "shit" wanted to spring from my mouth, though I always (almost always?) held my tongue when the f-word beckoned. We watched a thousand movies and as much junk TV as her tired eyes permitted. And once—or was it twice?—I regaled her with the tale of my most dramatic academic failure.

At the end of my senior year in college, the day after I won the poetry prize and second place in the prose prize, I learned I had flunked geology—the science requirement I had taken pass-fail. When the professor called me to her office a few days before graduation and cried, "*What* were you thinking when you got a 57 on the midterm?" I coolly and honestly replied, "That I would do better on the final." (I got a 49.) I told the story as a standup routine—Emily laughed at all the places I hoped she would—and a lesson in making choices about what matters. Flunked geology *and* lived to write six books. I wanted her to know that she could be a great violinist even if she got a B– in calculus—her B– was my F—but I never said it in so many words.

One of the movies we viewed several times was Emily's and her father James's favorite, *Get Shorty*, which they had been watching together for years, and whose "fuck"-filled lines James loved to repeat. "They say the fucking smog is the reason the fucking sunsets are so fucking beautiful." "Take me to the fuckin' airport." "What's the difference?—e.g., i.e., fuck you." But he used the f-word rarely in his own conversation. In her presence I followed his lead—and hers. On rare occasions she would quote from *Get Shorty* when it was under discussion, but never with gusto, never seeming to enjoy the badness or fun of having an excuse to say "fuck"—not, at least, in front of us. Back then, when she was annoyed or distressed, all I ever heard her mutter was "Shoot."

Because James's language around her was so squeaky clean, I remember one of his rare embraces of the f-word. He'd received an honor at work and was showing it to Emily: His name and a tribute to him had been engraved in stone on a front step of the school he had run for twenty years. We were excited and proud. "How does it make you feel, Dad?" she asked. It was the fall of 2001, and she was fourteen years old, delicate, beautiful, still sweet tempered.

"Like I really can't fuck up now."

We laughed, and I secretly admired his judicious use of the word. This notably sexual, warlike word, in this context, wasn't sexual, wasn't aggressive, and best of all, it was self-mocking and funny. It was up there with the fucking smog and the fucking sunsets.

I come from a family (Jewish and top-heavy with anger), a city (New York, where mouthiness is a virtue and a necessity), and a culture (writers and artists, many of us childless) where the f-word is said often in work and in play without a second thought, in concert with some of George Carlin's other "Seven Dirty Words." I was somewhat surprised to find myself—in the middle of my middle age, after a marriage and a divorce—in the environs of Boston, in a family from a very different culture: reserved (read WASP), musical, not prone to anger or flippant, loose-lipped self-expression. And a family raising a classical musician, hardly a pursuit where challenges to authority and individual peccadilloes are welcomed. Just being there had the effect of sharpening my hearing, making me hyperaware of nearly every sound that each of us made—especially the loud notes, the offnotes. Especially my own. It was as though I'd moved in with a troupe of ballet dancers and felt my essential clumsiness in every step I took.

On the split screen of my experience, on one side I saw my angry, chaotic family of origin, where personal boundaries barely existed, where conflict, shouting, and swearing were the daily soundtrack. On the other side, many decades later in *echt* New England, I was happily consorting with soft-spoken Yankees who disagreed mainly about which recording of Beethoven's late string quartets is best. I was moved to clean up my act, particularly around Emily. At the same time I felt a countervailing instinct to show her a way to be a powerful woman in the world without relying entirely on good-girl definitions of poise and restraint and burdensome ideas about perfection. I wanted her to know that it's okay—no, better than okay: fun, smart, witty, necessary—to swear now and then, to blow off steam, to make a point, to express a feeling that's deep and raw and hard to hold in. Children cry to release their tension; adults swear. I never discussed the issue with her. I simply said the words when they came to me and hoped the message would get through, a message similar to the bumper sticker I occasionally see on older-model cars: WELL BEHAVED WOMEN DON'T MAKE HISTORY.

As committed as I was to passing on that lesson, there were times I came face-to-face with the very different reality of Emily's life—and her talent. When I watched her in orchestra rehearsals, where she spent most Saturdays, I was perplexed by the degree of discipline she and her hundred young orchestra mates exhibited. How could they bear the regimentation, pressure, and impeccable behavior required of them? Weren't their parents concerned they were being stifled?

I kept my puzzlement to myself. I grasped the operating principles. Young classical musicians *need* team spirit. They *need* discipline. If they don't follow the rules, obey the conductor, and do what the teacher says, the show does not go on. I knew that if these young people weren't cut out for this, they wouldn't be there. If they were grumpy misfits and malcontents—a type I clearly identified with—they would be doing what such young people often do: smoking cigarettes, writing poetry, becoming writers.

There were times, now long ago, when managing my internal conflict felt like a high-wire act. There were a few tense instances when I wished we lived among the perennially pissed-off New Yorkers I knew so well, to whom letting it rip comes easily, and for whom the word "fuck" is a form of punctuation as common as a comma. For whom "fuck" is merely a way of italicizing an idea or a burst of outrage, straightforward shorthand for rage, frustration, even joy ("Wow, I can't fucking believe it!"). But there were many more times than I could ever have imagined when I felt enveloped in blissful sanity and heavenly music, when I was exposed to a language I could never learn, and to another way of being a family. On Sunday mornings, the mornings after our ice cream binges and movie festivals, I would often see James and Emily at the dining room table in their pajamas, listening to CDs, rapt as they analyzed a passage from Shostakovich or swapped observations about key changes in the third movement of the Archduke Trio.

"I think that was a diminished seventh," he'd say.

"No, it was a minor second," she'd answer. "Didn't you hear the key change after the violin came in?"

As fluent as they are in music, they don't always have the vocabulary for what needs to be said. Not long ago I sat across a room from them during an awkward spell, when something fraught rumbled beneath the surface. The words and feelings—probably frustration, anger, a little guilt—seemed caught in their throats, unable to move. I could see they were afraid to hurt the other's feelings or reveal too much of their own, and it was painful to watch them struggle. "Too bad you're not Jewish," I said finally. "You could just scream and swear for a while and get through this." I offered some sample dialogue for each of them—including a few hard-edged words they would never say to one another. They smiled. They looked relieved. Even I could hear that the key had changed.

I'm not often reluctant to say the f-word, but I do feel a flicker of hesitation in admitting how fond of it I am. Its bite, punch, hard and soft edges, its infinite possibilities, its abilities, still, to make others take notice. One criticism often made of swearing—mostly by those in charge of children—is that it makes the swearers lazy with language. Instead of building young people's vocabularies, permission to swear keeps them overly reliant on five or ten words. I certainly don't object to that objection, but I wish it routinely came with a forward-looking notice, the way discussions with children about sex often do: *You'll be able to do this when you're a grown up.*

How hard would it be to say to kids: *When you're older, you might find creative, appropriate ways to use these words—especially when you're angry, when you need to make a point or get someone's attention?* How difficult would it be to frame the children's future usage as a reward for enduring childhood, for having to learn all the vocabulary words that aren't prohibited, and a privilege of adulthood, like voting? There is an art to swearing—albeit a lowly one—but the more eloquent the speaker is with the other words, the more of an impact she can have when using the bad words.

Former U.S. poet laureate Robert Pinsky loves jokes. "Do you know how they say the alphabet in Jersey?" he asks. "Fuckin' A, fuckin' B, fuckin' C, fuckin' D . . ." "Do you know why women fake orgasms? Because they think we fuckin' care."

"Fuckin'" = toughness, tough-guyness, brawn. In an instant, in two syllables, the distinguished poet becomes Tony Soprano, Marlon Brando in *The Wild One*. The word is transformative, it's theater. The drama is heightened because the word is spoken by a man whose life is devoted to language and meaning, to the high art of sculpting with words.

If Robert Pinsky can become Marlon Brando when he says "fuck," who do I become when I say it? One of the guys, but a tough guy, not a girly man; a swaggerer, not a poet. One of the tough dames: Moll Flanders, Molly Bloom, Mae West, Lauren Bacall, Barbara Stanwyck, Lana Turner, Auntie Mame. One of the naughty girls: Marilyn Monroe, Betty Paige, Holly Golightly, whose naughty expression in *Breakfast at Tiffany's* (the novel) is "Oh, balls," but whose bad behavior is far more baroque than that.

That little word goes a long way. It's something of a prop, like a cigarette in the days when cigarettes were signs of suaveness and sexuality. It's an off-the-shoulder dress, from the days when an unexpected patch of female flesh was provocative. It's a pair of elevator shoes that adds a few inches of height to a short man. It can be an attention grabber, a burst of strength, an announce-ment of sex, swagger, bravado, desperation, rebellion, high emotion, low language skills, or lazy thinking. It's the most elementally human utterance, the activity from which each of us springs. It's offensive, it's passé, it's funny when very proper people say it, and tedious when it's said too much. And there is nothing quite like it. I can't think of when I said any of these things, but each suggests a drama, a cast of characters, a film-noir plot, a gripping dilemma. *Who the fuck do you think you are? What the fuck are you doing? There's fuck all to do around here. Fuck it, fuck that, and while you're at it, fuck you.*

"Can I hold your violin?" I asked Emily one night when the three of us were on a vacation together at the beach. It was the summer she was sixteen.

"You never held it?"

I shook my head. I wouldn't have touched it when she wasn't present, and I had no reason to when she was. But that night I was curious. The case was open on her bed, the blue velvet cloth half covering the body. I'm sure I'd held a cheap violin when I was much younger, but it had left no precise memory.

I perched on the edge of the bed as she casually reached for it and handed it to me, this instrument that was an extension of her body, connected by this time to her nervous system, every aspect of her development, the core of her identity. She practiced for four hours a day and some weeks rehearsed for or played two or three concerts. By then she had performed 150 times in settings large and small, been on tours to Europe and Latin America with her youth orchestra, and played a benefit at Symphony Hall in Boston.

"Tilt your head a little," she said. "Hold the bow like this." I know that people spend years of their lives learning how to hold a bow. I know that violinists think that playing the piano is laughably easy. Itzhak Perlman said that a beginning pianist can play something as soon as she sits down, even if it's "Twinkle, Twinkle, Little Star," but that it takes years to learn the most basic violin. "Put your fingers on the neck," Emily said. "Put this finger here and this finger there. Now move the bow over the strings very gently."

A scratchy sound came out. Then another. I'm not sure if they were significant enough to be called "notes," but I was surprised that they were not screechy and horrible. In fact the tentative responses coming from just below my chin took my breath away, not because I had produced something beautiful—I hadn't—but because of the vibrational nature of the sound and its proximity to my ear, my head, my upper body. The sound and its closeness to me had a sensual, human quality, as elemental and startling as a baby's cheek on one's shoulder, a lover's whisper in the ear. I had spent all these years watching, listening, and admiring Emily from a distance—even when I saw her play in her father's living room—without a clue as to the intimacy between herself and the violin. It had to be—now I understood that it was—completely intoxicating.

"What's wrong?" Emily asked.

It was difficult to say. "I get it now. I understand what makes you want to play."

It crossed my mind that I could take lessons, not with the aim of being good but to continue having that feeling. For a few minutes it seemed like a distinct possibility. I handed the violin back to her. It was lighter than a lot of books I read. It seemed magical, nearly human. Before it had just been her instrument, a fragile, beautiful thing that in a real sense ruled her life. Now I understood her connection to it in a deeper way.

"It's an amazing feeling," I said. That hardly did it justice.

"Yeah," she said, pleased. "It is."

As she returned to practicing, filling the room with sounds so rich, full, and accomplished that they brought tears to my eyes, I remembered the story I had heard so often. When Emily was six, two women gave a violin concert at her school. She had never played an instrument or been urged to by her parents, though they came from musically sophisticated families. Emily describes the experience in nearly mystical language. The music penetrated and transformed her. She went home and announced to her mother that this was what she wanted to do. What she was meant to do. And so the incredible journey began.

Saturday in the country. We're inside a screened-in shed for a weekend of concerts at this summer-long chamber music festival where Emily is performing with conservatory students like herself and recent graduates. This afternoon they play Mozart, Beethoven, and Brahms in the blistering summer heat, bearing up as the sun bears down on the shed.

After her freshman year in conservatory, she's a straight-A student and a celebrated musician, with a list of prizes, honors, and appearances as long as this page. In the last few years, in the midst of these accomplishments, she's learned how to relax, hang out, explore new cities, and make many new friends. She doesn't call herself a perfectionist anymore, except when it comes to playing music. In her first year away I heard her say the f-word three times—once in despair, once in anger, once for the hell of it—and it pleased me perversely to know that she knows the useful word is hers to do with what she wants.

Unlike Emily and her father, when I listen to the music, I can't hear the key changes or easily remember the themes. But my ear is much better than it used to be. This Saturday as I listen, my thoughts drift to the subject of swearing, the matter of perfection, the challenge of growing up. I'm not sure how Emily would mark turning points in her evolution from full-time to part-time perfectionist, but I'm sure she remembers our planning for a family splurge when she was seventeen, two weeks in Italy, one of them with her best friend. Emily didn't know whether to bring her violin and asked her teacher what to do. I held my breath waiting for the answer, hoping she would be able to enjoy Italy to the fullest. "You know what she said?" Emily reported, sounding surprised. "She said, 'Are you kidding? Absolutely not!'" Perhaps this was one step on her way to learning that there is more to being excellent than working around the clock, that time off can be as nourishing as focused concentration.

I know how important balance is, and relaxation, and letting one's hair down, but when I sit in the shed listening to piece after piece, in the presence of such dazzling talent and dedication, I have to laugh at my good intentions. What does it feel like to reach young adulthood, having acquired a mastery as children and teenagers that few adults ever achieve? I have no idea. None whatsoever. I'm remembering how important it was to me that I let Emily hear me swear all those years ago, when she was trying so hard to be well behaved and perfect all the time, and I'm smiling at my folly. I swear like a sailor, and she plays the violin like an angel. Perhaps there's a connection: These young artists don't need to swear to get attention, to feel tough and powerful, to have an excuse to swagger. Why would they want to be someone else for even a minute—Marlon Brando or Marilyn Monroe—when they can make such beautiful music being exactly who they are?

I Am Badder than Omarosa

An Open Letter to Mark Burnett's Production Assistant

MICHELLE RICHMOND

I've been waiting for a phone call. I've been waiting a very long time, or what passes for a long time in the mind of the terminally impatient. I've been waiting exactly twelve hours. The phone call I'm waiting for, sadly, isn't from the National Book Award Committee or from some venerable institution of higher learning at which I am vying for a coveted professorial position. It's from the casting crew of *The Apprentice*, for whom I recently auditioned at a dingy talent agency in downtown San Francisco.

Of course the call never comes. Of course I will not be the next Apprentice. Nor will I be the next Survivor, or the next half of a two-person wonder team on *The Amazing Race*. I will not even be the next contestant on *The Biggest Loser*. It occurs to me now that my audition strategy was all wrong. I shouldn't have presented myself as a devoted mother, an earnest writer of obscure literary fiction, an enthusiastic teacher. Enough with the girl-next-door act. If I'm ever to have my fifteen minutes of fame and my shot at public humiliation with a pot of gold at the end of the line, I should confess to the producers all the ways in which I am bad.

Let's face it: To the bad girls go the spoils. As it is in life, so it is in reality television. It wasn't Omarosa's fine business sense that landed her gigs on *Oprah* and *Passions* after she was canned by Trump. Nor was it Jerri Manthey's exacting execution of the downward-facing dog that earned her a *Playboy* cover following her disgraceful exit from *Survivor*. Omarosa and Jerri became famous for one reason only: They were down and dirty, mean and nasty, the kind of girls you don't want to meet at the office or, worse, at your husband's office party. Omarosa and Jerri and their ilk would probably argue that their apparent reprehensibility is a matter of unfair editing, that in truth they spend their spare time knitting ecofriendly rice-bowl cozies for homeless widows, but we all know the truth: These women forged lucrative if not exactly respectable careers out of being bad.

To this end, and in advance of the next round of reality television open calls, I am making a list. In order that the list may be quickly digested and neatly summarized by the poorly paid and likely hungover production assistant who stands between me and Mr. Burnett, it will follow the easy-to-read bulleted format. Let it be known that this list should serve as a representative but in no way exhaustive sampling of my forays into the bad.

(Note to production assistant: Should the task of vetting my application prove overly daunting, I have organized the bullets into categories of badness. Please note that the final category, "Bad Things I Have Not Yet Done but Would Gladly Do for a [Reasonable] Fee," is constantly expanding and very much open to suggestion.)

Sexy and/or Sexual Badness

- For a couple of years in high school, I was an enthusiastic member of an overzealous Southern Baptist youth group. It was not beneath me to give a guy a hand job in order to persuade him to attend a Contemporary Christian rock concert. My target audience: track-and-field boys. My message: Religion can be fun!

- I once worked for Dollar Dial in Knoxville, Tennessee. Under the alias Charity Strong, I sold subscriptions to *Sesame Street* and *Popular Mechanics*. I bombed with *Sesame Street*, but when it came to *Popular Mechanics*, I was salesperson of the month for five months running. It might have had something to do with the Charity Strong voice—breathy, sleepy, very southern. I was frequently known to veer from the script and more than once was called into my supervisor's office for using unethical sales techniques, which I cannot divulge here, as they form the basis of my work-in-progress, *Get Rich Slow: A Raunchy Salesgirl's Guide to the Male Psyche.*

- I arrived at the initial interview for yet another telemarketing job—this one in Atlanta—without the proper identification. Unable to produce a driver's license, I proffered instead a wallet-size photo I'd had taken for that year's Christmas card: me in black fringe and leather, standing beside a repentant-looking Santa who has been bound and gagged. A couple of months later my boss would willingly find himself in a similarly compromised position on the floor of his office in a high-rise in Buckhead. In the interests of protecting my former boss's reputation, it should be noted that he was not wearing a Santa suit.

- Speaking of binding and gagging, I own a number of items from Good Vibrations, some of which may or may not involve straps, fringe, and padlocks. The male chastity belt is highly underrated.

• Ten years ago I met an alarmingly attractive man named Kevin in an orientation course for graduate students at the University of Arkansas. For six days I tried to get his attention, to no avail. At two in the morning on the seventh day I found myself standing outside his first-floor apartment. It was a hot night, and his bedroom window was open. Because I am not one to ignore a clear instance of divine intervention, I climbed through the window and crawled into his bed. "Hi," he said, as if this sort of thing happened to him all the time. I suddenly felt the need to set parameters. "Let's get one thing straight," I said. "I'm going to sleep with you, but I'm not going to *sleep* with you." The next morning I asked if he had a girlfriend. He did. "Good," I said. "I have a boyfriend." Five years later we were married. The conundrum being, of course, that once you are a wife you are expected to be good, but the only way you get to *be* a wife is by being bad.

Social Badness, of or Relating to My Failure to Act as a Productive Member of the Community

• On a number of occasions I have fraudulently taken General Mills up on its Goodness Guarantee, which states, "If you are not satisfied with the quality of this product, a prompt refund or adjustment of equal value will be made."

• At the end of each semester I tell my students that if they would like to receive my comments on their final papers, they must submit a self-addressed, stamped envelope. I say this with the full knowledge that most of them are either too poor or too ill coordinated to provide a self-addressed, stamped envelope, thus significantly reducing my workload.

• My cell phone has a permanent outgoing message that says,

"This cell phone user is either out of the area or has been disconnected. Please do not leave a message unless you are Mark Burnett or Mark Burnett's assistant."

Cultural Badness, Most of Which Pertains to Television

- If I'm flipping channels and a Britney Spears video comes on, I watch it, start to finish. I am particularly fond of the early pom-poms-and-knee-socks extravaganza. I have also been known to sit in rapt attention through entire Whitney Houston interviews and Lindsay Lohan exposés. I've yet to turn away in horror from a celebrity crash-and-burn story—the more drugs and bulimia, the better.
- I own all seven seasons of *Bewitched* on DVD.
- The last time I caught a show on Broadway, *Rent* had just opened.
- I prefer In-N-Out to any restaurant at which sprouts are featured prominently on the menu. I prefer Krispy Kreme to In-N-Out.
- I have TIVO. I've had TIVO since long before most folks even knew it existed. I'm on the lifetime plan. In the beginning I made an effort to record only art films and *Frontline*. These days, however, I've succumbed to my own worst tastes, and can often be found scrolling through the "Now Playing" list, debating whether to watch *Hell's Kitchen, Magnum P.I.* reruns, or *Vacation Home Search*.
- If there were only two men left on earth—Vince Vaughn and Bill Gates—and I had to procreate with one of them in order to ensure the survival of the human race, there would be no contest.

Bad Beginnings, or How I Came to Be Bad

- Kindergarten, Greystone Christian School, Mobile AL 1975: A boy named Roland sticks his hand in the fish tank, which we are not allowed to do because, according to Mrs. Hoyt, it will result in certain painful death for the fish. Until this point I've been considered the shyest girl in the class—so shy that I have on a couple of occasions peed on the floor rather than ask Mrs. Hoyt if I can go to the bathroom. But when Roland sticks his hand in the fish tank, his rebelliousness so excites me that I step forward and land a big wet one on his mouth. Roland begins to cry. This for me is a defining moment—the moment I realize the awesome power of a kiss.

- The summer of 1978: During a family trip to Six Flags over Georgia, inspired by a made-for-TV movie starring Carol Burnett, I make a sign that says "Help! Kidnap!" and put it in the window of our Buick station wagon. I proceed to ham it up for passing cars, crying and showing signs of terrible distress. My parents in the front seat have no idea what's going on. It's all fun and games until, just outside Atlanta, a state trooper pulls us over. He won't even approach the car, but instead stands back and gives instructions for my dad to come out with his hands up. Within ten minutes we're surrounded by squad cars, sirens blaring, guns held aloft. It turns out somebody took my plea for help seriously, and there's been an APB out on our car from Alabama to Atlanta.

- 1982, Dauphin Way Baptist Church, Wednesday night prayer meeting: I am sitting in the balcony with Jimmy, a blond boy whom I love. The pastor is miles away, at the front of the church, praying into the microphone. The lights in the church are low. The choir is singing "Have Thine Own Way," and Jimmy stretches out his hand, palm up. It hovers above my lap. It occurs to me that he would like for me to hold his hand, but I've never held hands with a boy before and don't know how to go about it. We are supposed to be praying, but I am thinking of Jimmy's beautiful hand, tiny blond hairs just beginning to form at the base of the wrist. I am twelve years old in a church in Alabama, and I am thinking, quite plainly, about having sex with Jimmy—despite the fact that this is something I have never done before and wouldn't know how to do. The shape of his hand hovering there is enough to plunge me into erotic bliss.

Bad Things I Have Not Yet Done but Would Gladly Do for
a (Reasonable) Fee
- Grand larceny
- Counterfeiting
- Gerrymandering
- Anything involving Vince Vaughn and/or Benicio del Toro.
- Anything involving chocolate, preferably from Joseph Schmidt, preferably in combination with bad acts to be committed with Vince Vaughn and/or Benicio del Toro.

Should the aforementioned acts of badness not prove bad enough, I will be more than happy to provide you, Mark Burnett's production assistant, with further evidence of badness. Should you still find yourself questioning my ability to capture an audience's attention with lewdness, perversity, random acts of selfishness, and general bad attitude, please see the attached list of references, which include but are not exclusive to my parents, past boyfriends, in-laws, members of various law enforcement agencies, and a certain former employer who, following a life-altering bout with bondage, has revamped himself, for better or worse, as a submissive. Should you remain unconvinced after reviewing the not inconsiderable supporting materials which accompany my application, I offer one last, desperate incentive: I am willing and able to engage in questionable relations of the fiduciary and/or sexual variety with Mark Burnett's production assistant, provided that said assistant can provide documentation supporting his/her position of influence in the murky underworld of reality television.

Forgive Me, Father,
but You're Kind of Cute

MARY ROACH

*I*t was a standard three-compartment confessional, with a priest's cabinet in the center and one on either side for the kneeling penitents— one confessing, one on deck. From the outside it resembled an antique armoire, and as a child I believed that's what it was. Every few weeks I'd watch my mother step inside the priest's armoire and pull the door closed behind her. I pictured her hiding amid the spotless white robes and the purple ponchos with gold embroidery. Some of them were fringed with silken tassels, tassels even finer than the ones on the fezzes in the Shriners' parade. I had an urge to reach out and riffle them with my finger as the priest passed our pew in the opening processional. I was jealous of my mother. I, too, wanted to play inside the armoire.

When I was seven years old my mother told me that soon I

would be old enough, but she didn't call it playing in the armoire. She called it confession.

The challenge to the young penitent is figuring out what is a sin and what is merely an irritation to one's parents. I knew that singing—shrieking, really—the Oscar Mayer theme song over and over in the car on the way home from school made my mother's nostrils flare and my father's knuckles go white on the steering wheel, but was it technically a sin? My mother could lose her composure over what seemed to me to be utterly random and trivial matters. I once left the honey jar open on the kitchen table. Though I had not meant to (the child's all-purpose excuse), she flew into an exasperated rage. *"It'll draw ants!!"* The decibel level alone suggested that this was, at the very least, a venial sin. But how to confess such a thing?

"Forgive me, Father, for I have sinned. It's been five weeks since my last confession. I drew ants."

While Catholicism keeps a checklist of mortal sins, venial sins are nowhere spelled out. A mortal sin is one for which your soul is condemned to hell when you die (and here I pictured a sort of glow-in-the-dark Wiffle ball bursting through my chest wall and plummeting through a dark tunnel based loosely on the laundry chute at Matt Duroche's house). Based on some of the sins that made the Mortal roster, it seemed to me that most of the things I had done in my short life had the potential to be venial sins. If skipping church on holy days is a mortal sin, then trading a Ring-Ding for the healthful, vitamin-fortified Space Food Stick that my mother packed in my lunch or pulling down my underpants in front of Matt Duroche out behind the bandstand must surely have approached the ranks of the venial. But I wasn't about to tell a priest these things. They were too embarrassing.

The trick was to find an appropriate generality for each sin, thereby sparing oneself the humiliation of fine detail. If the sin was, say, "I found a Girl Scout badge on the playground and sewed it onto my sash, even though I have not completed any of the requirements for the Hospitality Badge and I know that the badge belongs to Cindy Peters," the apt confession would be: "I was dishonest." Week after week I confessed the same three or four bland, amorphous sins, as did, I suspect, all my friends: "I was dishonest, I swore, I disobeyed my parents." No details were ever offered up. How dull it must have been for the parish priests. How much livelier their job had they gotten to hear little Mary Roach kneel down and confess that she'd called her brother a fucker or belched at the dinner table.

I am lucky to have grown up in the late twentieth century, when the priest, at least in my parish, simply listened and took you at your word. He did not ask follow-up questions ("Was it the forced, intentionally drawn-out variety of belch, or was it the kind that slips out despite one's best efforts to suppress it?"). When you stopped talking, he would—following a pause to be sure you were finished and not merely considering the phrasing of the squalid grotesquerie you had saved for last—quietly deliver the penance and the absolution and set you free to sin some more.

This was not always the case. Confession in earlier centuries entailed a fearsome grilling. In a university library near my home there is a copy of a handbook for priests, originally printed in 1634, called *A Guide to Confession Large and Small*. The guide provided novice priests with suggested scripts for the confessional box. The scripted questions for breaking Commandment Five, the honoring of one's mother and father, begin in a straightforward manner ("Did you honor your father and your mother, your elders, the old people and the ancient ones?") but quickly devolve into an accusatory barrage: "Did you once lose respect for your father and your mother? When you were drunk did you beat them up, hit them, kick them or mistreat them in any other way, pulling out their beard or hair as you always are accustomed to do when you are drunk?" The least of it being that the priest seems to be implying that the penitent's mother has a beard.

The sin of fornication eats up a lot of ink, particularly when the penitent is a woman:

Did you touch yourself, having as the object of your desire some man, in such a way that you completed and consummated the carnal act?
Answer: Yes, Father/no.

Did you commit a carnal act with another woman like you, or she with you?
Answer: Yes/no.

When your husband had carnal access with you (being drunk), was it in the common vessel [i.e., the vagina] or did he commit the unspeakable and abominable sin, switching parts [i.e., anal sex], and you did not stop him?
Answer: Yes, Father/no.

Have you used lewd words to provoke women?
Answer: Yes, Father/no.

I can't say for sure, but it would seem to me that celibacy was taking a toll on the author of the *Guide*. Based on historical accountings of the day, that toll played itself out in rather disquieting ways.

On the same shelf as the *Guide* was a scrupulously sourced Oxford University Press book called *Sexuality in the Confessional: A Sacrament Profaned*. The author, Stephen Haliczer, combed the Inquisition files of sixteenth- to nineteenth-century Spain, documenting the disquieting tango of sex and confession. One writer at the time counseled that "the confessional was a place where the priest could expect to experience erection and ejaculation while hearing the confessions of female penitents." Particularly with the sort of explicit probing encouraged in the *Guide*. As the ejaculation was involuntary, this writer pointed out, it wasn't considered sinful.

It was not all involuntary. Haliczer tallied sixty-three cases of priests accused of masturbating during confession. Some of them weren't especially subtle about it:

> Shortly after she began her first confession with Fray Gines de Carranza [the complainant], saw him throw himself down in his side of the confessional and begin "making disgusting movements as if he were a woman engaging in the sex act." After ejaculating, he regained his composure and without saying anything, helped her to complete her confession. Horrified, . . . she turned instead to Antolin Cavallero, another friar in the same convent. Unfortunately, the result was the same, and she saw him masturbate through the confessional screen "with great filth and lewdness." After trying still another friar and finding that he kept rubbing his member during confession, she decided to abandon any attempt to find a confessor from among the Mercedarians.

The screen installed in the wall between priest and penitent suggests, but does not deliver, anonymity. The priest, it seems, always knows who's in there. My friend Patrick Cooke told me a story about his brother Will. Sometime in Will's preteens, he committed what he believed to be an onerous sin and felt a pressing need to confess it. As head altar boy he didn't want the priest to know it was him. He counted on the screen to conceal his identity and, as an added safeguard, disguised his voice. "He attempted a thick French accent or something," recalled Patrick. Will slipped into the confessional and spared the father no detail. "Whereupon Father gave him his penance and ended by saying, 'Oh, and Will, please go back and turn out the altar lights before you leave.'"

Part of the problem, sexuality-wise, was the box itself. Ironically the confessional was introduced, in part, to put a stop to hanky-panky—consenting and non—between priest and penitent. Confession used to be said in the open, with the priest sitting on a bench or chair, and the penitent kneeling before him, offering, says Haliczer, "alluring possibilities to a confessor bent on seducing his penitent." And, let's be fair, vice versa: The author details the case of the wife of a local blacksmith, caught with her hands under the habit of one Alonso Guerro. The church hoped that separating confessor and penitent in their own stalls, like hockey players in penalty boxes, would put a stop to physical contact. Which it did—except that the screen had a tendency to go missing. Writes Haliczer, "One of the nuns, Sor Eugenia de Santa Teresa, even removed the screen herself and then raised her habit so that [the priest] could see her thighs."

Even if the barrier remained intact, the box often failed as a sexual deterrent. For the confessional introduced two sexually volatile elements to the atmosphere of confession: privacy and darkness. Haliczer cites the example of a nun and prior who used her weekly confession to set the time and place of their next tryst.

As a hormone-beset pubescent, I was not immune to the suggestive elements of the confessional box. Whispering in the dark, secluded from view, with a strange man, nay a *forbidden* strange man, is, I'm sorry, a recipe for impure thought. There were times, sitting in mass—right there under the baleful eyes of the Savior—

that I fantasized about seducing a priest in the confessional. It was not my own priest. Father Gallagher was a warm, portly Friar Tuck sort of figure, well into his sixties. I have a memory of Father Gallagher, after the mass, standing by the door and giving my mother—she was in her seventies at the time—what was probably the warmest, most genuine hug she'd received in all her uptight Germanic-born, New England–raised days. (Whereupon, as we descended the steps, she whispered to me: "He knocked off my hearing aid!")

Needless to say I did not confess my confession-themed lust to Father Gallagher. How could I?

"Forgive me, Father, for I have sinned. I had sexual fantasies involving a priest in a confessional box. Not you, Father. Not that you're not attractive in your way. And it wasn't a real priest. Does that help? It was Father Damien in *The Exorcist*."

What is it with the Jesuits? Father Damien. Jeremy Irons in *The Mission*. It's that long suffering, chiseled-cheekbone scholarly and omnipotent yet vulnerable and deeply human thing. When I was in my early twenties, I had a European roommate named Catherine. One Christmas Eve, bored because the bars were closed and there were no parties to go to, Catherine suggested we dress provocatively and sit in the front row at Midnight Mass at the Jesuit church in our neighborhood and make eyes at the priests. As we were to everything back then, we were late to Midnight Mass. The downstairs pews were filled, and the usher sent us to the balcony. You could barely see the alluring or possibly-not-so Jesuits down on the altar. Catherine left at "half-time," as she put it, but I stayed. It was not snowing, as it always was in my memories of Midnight Mass back home, but it was beautiful anyway. Candles burning and the pillars candy-striped with pine boughs. The organ music went right in through the holes of the wiffle ball in my chest and buoyed it toward the ceiling. Sitting there, I imagined trying to summarize this nitwit escapade for confession. The acute embarrassment I felt in simply pondering how to word it was, I realized, perhaps the point of confession. Whether there exists the kind of God who can hear and absolve a million penitents at once, there is surely value in saying one's missteps aloud, and in thinking about them beforehand. Confession forced me, on a regular basis, to take a look at the silly, selfish, peevish person that I was and, hopefully, to set the course a few degrees to right. I don't go to mass anymore, but there are days when I pass a church and see people lined up for confession, and I think, Do you some good, M. Especially the church near the park with the brooding Jesuit with the graying temples.

Forgive me, Father.

The View from the Ninety-ninth Floor

KATHARINE WEBER

*W*hen my friend Philip asked me if I wanted to see a great view of the city, a view he had discovered, a view nobody else knew about, it was an attractive, typical offer. An adventure, presumably something a little risky, on that cold winter night, something very us. I was eighteen, he was nineteen, and we weren't boyfriend and girlfriend because we had something even better, even closer—a friendship that had skipped that awkward romantic step and gone instead straight to comfortable, sexless, old-married-couple bickering and overfamiliarity, and a pact that if all else failed, we would marry each other by age forty.

Philip, who hailed from Mercer Island, Washington, was a precociously talented graphic design student at Cooper Union, living in a tiny walk-up studio apartment on Fifth Street in the East Village. He had a girlfriend who worked as an assistant to a famous fashion designer. Their relationship was inexplicable and beside the point. Beside my point, and also, it seemed, beside Philip's. Neither of us took her very seriously. Our secret nickname for her was "Goo-Goo Eyes," the name by which she was known to us before we knew her real name, Laura, because Philip's older sister had observed her clear infatuation across the room at a large party in the East Village where Philip, his sister, and I had stood in the corner drinking bad sangria (I am not sure I know of any other kind) and making ironic comments about everyone else.

Laura was almost glamorous in a wholesome Midwestern way. She shopped for "grosheries" and made casseroles with cornflakes on top in the invariably teensy, filthy ovens in her various apartments. She moved frequently, from one claustrophobic Village apartment to another, and I was often enlisted to help, because I had an old Volkswagen Squareback with sufficient cargo space to transport her rolled mattress, her milk crates, and her old-lady-plaid suitcases from one dodgy little studio to the next.

Moving was something Laura did the way other people buy shoes. She stayed in the tiny, quaint, street-level Gay Street apartment only a week, disliking the way sightseeing groups habitually peered in and studied her through the window as she lazed in her bed, which about filled the room, unless she kept the curtain closed, depriving herself of daylight. Laura seemed inexplicably happiest in a nondescript postwar building populated by secretaries and flight attendants. It was one more thing for Philip to be condescending about, her preference for a higher level of ordinary comforts over decrepit yet intriguing architectural features. I was condescending, too, worldly and weary as we packed her up to move once more. Our mutual condescension for Laura was one of the many strange threads that bound Philip and me together. Sometimes it just felt fun, being the two of us, being smug and superior to everyone else, including Philip's girlfriend, proof to me that our relationship was more intense, more intimate, than was theirs. Sometimes this gave me an uneasy feeling, as if we had been getting away with something that was about to come to an abrupt halt at any moment.

I was working in an architecture office on Fifty-seventh Street by day, ghostwriting text for a book for a famous big-ego architect known equally for his white buildings and for his unwillingness to share design credit with his staff, and I was taking night classes at the New School, working slowly toward a college degree I never did obtain. I was an independent eighteen-year-old, proud to the point of obnoxiousness about my independence and precociousness. Having left my suburban New York home at sixteen (a freshman year of college after eleventh grade having been my ticket away from a very unpleasant family life), I was now living on my own (in a somewhat nicer apartment than Philip's, since my bathtub was in the bathroom and not the kitchen), on Waverly Place, just west of Washington Square.

I had the place to myself at this point, since the departure of a difficult roommate who wrote her initials obsessively on everything in the apartment that was hers, including certain eggs, though she always denied eating my unmonogrammed sardines and Triscuits, which she devoured as fast as I could replenish my (monogrammed) side of the pantry shelf. When she moved out, she absconded with a particularly good can opener I had pilfered from my ancestral domicile, and my bathmat—thefts she justified in a subsequent phone call because, she explained, she had reason to believe that I had written a troublemaking letter to her mother with details of her nonstandard sex life.

My own situation had its nonstandard aspects, because at the time I was involved in a strange obsessive romance with a charming and unreliable poet of thirty-five who arrived in and disappeared from my life at unexpected intervals, and I would not have written any kind of letter to her mother about her various oddly effeminate boyfriends, not that I liked any of them. The loss of the bathmat, which was only moderately fluffy, though it did match my towel, was a small price to pay for the end of the endless cycle of irritating heartfelt discussions that seemed to circle around boundary issues and eating disorders without ever really landing anywhere or resolving anything.

Philip and I began our mystery expedition after ten on that frigid January night. Of course he had not told Laura a thing about this outing, which made it a little bit of a conspiracy, and all the more appealing. The night was the kind of cold that encases everything in its glittering skin, the kind of cold that forms sharp, icy specks that hurt your lungs in a satisfying way when you draw a deep breath. We walked south, through Little Italy and then through Chinatown, and as we trudged farther downtown and the streets grew less well-lit and less populated, I asked Philip to give me a hint about where we were heading, but he wouldn't tell me anything. I granted him this power. Sometimes I was the one with the power, as when I revised all his writing, and knew more about history and politics, or, one time, when I was able to provide soothing unguents to extinguish the blistering itch of the strange case of poison ivy all over his ass. We knew each other with an ease and familiarity neither of us had with anyone else. We had few secrets. But Philip was in charge of secret expeditions. I was wearing a parka and gloves. My nose was going numb, however, my thighs were frozen in my jeans, and my feet were frozen in my ridiculous Frye boots, which I wore incessantly in those years. Who didn't?

We stopped at a construction site near Wall Street that occupied an entire city block, and we slipped through a gap in the plywood fence with which Philip seemed familiar. It was a giant pit, a vast excavation in preparation for some immense construction project. We climbed down to the bottom, which took a long time, picking our way in deep frozen muddy ruts, and finally we were in the center of this earthen bowl, gazing up at the mostly dark office towers that rimmed the site.

"This is the view a cockroach has in your kitchen sink!" Philip shouted into the darkness, wheeling around, his arms extended, a cheerful twirling cockroach. Was this it, then? I tried to appreciate the drama of the setting, tried to see it through his eyes. We had come a long way for this big pit of nothing. No, not at all, we still had a distance to walk. A little trap. Had I no faith?

We climbed out, sliding on the frozen muddy bulldozer ramps. It was now that much later, and colder, and darker. We trudged on. I trusted him that this was worth my while. At this point I had absolutely no idea where we were or where we could be going. Perhaps we were headed for the very southern tip of Manhattan, perhaps the South Street Seaport and one of the tall ships sometimes docked there. Perhaps we were going to walk over a bridge to Brooklyn. It was already a long night, and my sense of time was frozen along with everything else. I couldn't be bothered to fish out my watch from under my parka. I wore a small silver pocket watch on a chain in those days, an affectation with which I was briefly experimenting at the time. (I dropped it precipitously the day I met a weird girl who not only also wore a pocket watch on a chain just like mine, she also wore a deerstalker cap and smoked a meerschaum pipe. Yikes.)

I had no idea we had arrived at our destination, many blocks later, until Philip steered me to a halt at the edge of a walled-off construction site. I couldn't see what it was because we were standing so close, and I had had no sense of the dark site as we approached. The only signs around us now were those identifying the various construction companies and engineers, and safety warnings, and numerous severe No Parking exhortations.

Philip now told me he had been here the night before, and had discovered a way into the site. I followed him as he went first, wriggling through a gap in a chain-link fence which he held for me as I wedged myself through, gallantly covering the spiky wire that had snagged his parka with his gloved hand so as to protect mine. Knowingly Philip then proceeded to flip aside the loose edge of a piece of plywood, and together we squeezed through a second barrier. There were very few lights, but my eyes adjusted to the darkness as I followed Philip's confident shape ahead of me. Now we were entering a building, making our way up an unfinished dark concrete stairway, a flight, another flight, another flight, the stairs lit only every few floors by a single bulb dangling here and there from snaked orange plastic electricians' work lamps.

"Where the hell are we?" I asked at about the twentieth floor. Philip grinned over his shoulder. We kept going up, and up. The stairwell was enclosed, though unfinished, and I could only sense that we were in a modern office tower under construction. A very tall office tower. Another flight and another. We settled into a wordless rhythm. It was hypnotic, exhausting yet exciting, dangerous. The air was raw with the fresh concrete of the stairwell, raw steel, freshly cut lumber. At about the fiftieth floor, the partitions weren't completed, there were stacks of drywall piled high on every floor instead, and then, after a few more flights there were no partitions at all, not even stacks of drywall.

We stopped climbing and picked our way across the open floor that ended at infinity, at nothing, it ended in the sky, it ended with all of Manhattan pressing against the cold air. I drew back, though we were a good twenty feet from the edge, discovering a fear of heights I hadn't known about. There was only a bracing of some low steel beams crossed by simple planks to mark the edges, to mark the difference between standing here on the fifty-somethingth floor and falling through space, sailing away into New York City.

"What is this? Where are we, seriously?"

"Look over here," Philip said, steering me into a turn. I didn't want to leave the safety of the vast middle of the space, and he didn't fight me. He swiveled me all the way around, in place. It was almost like dancing. We were alone in our world. I saw the skin of another building close by, like a twin of this building. "What is this? Where are we?"

"It's the World Trade Center," Philip said. "Look, there's the other tower. This is the South Tower. The other one's already finished, so we can't get in. I mean, we probably could, but it would be a felony breaking and entering. This is still a construction site, so if they catch us here we're just dumb kids wandering." We stared at the other tower, black except for a dim light deep inside here and there.

We resumed our climb. Would it be that different higher up? This view was the view. Philip said he thought we couldn't get to the top, we couldn't get to 110, but he thought we could get to something like ninety-nine or one hundred, and it would be worth it. By about the seventieth floor (floor numbers were spray-painted on some of the concrete surfaces every so often) the rawness of the construction meant that the building's skin was incomplete, and the sides were open to the frigid night air. Thick plastic sheets flapped in the wind where they weren't completely tacked to the beams they shrouded. My lungs were burning, and I was gasping for air. My feet were numb from the cold of the concrete stairs, a cold that radiated right through the soles of my absurd cowboy boots. My feet were blistering. I never wore those boots again after that night.

It was nearly three in the morning when we got as far as we could go, when we ran out of finished stairs. We thought we were on the ninety-ninth floor, but there were only some scribbled markings here and there to indicate floors at this point, and we might have been off in our count. Climbing higher would have meant balancing on open scaffolding.

Bad Girls

The climb had taken almost three hours, and we had been slowed by a sudden freeze—no movement, don't make a sound—for several paralyzing minutes somewhere in the eighties, when we thought we heard footsteps coming up below us. There was a single guard, Philip said, presumably responsible for making some kind of rounds, but possibly he spent his nights dozing in some overheated hut at ground level. It felt as if we were the only souls in the entire structure, which moaned eerily when the wind blew through the unfinished gaps. Standing there, trying not to gasp for air, listening for the footsteps of the guard who may or may not have been below us on those stairs, I listened to the primeval sound of the night wind forcing itself through the interstices of the building, like a magnificent version of the note you can play when you blow across the top of your soda bottle. I want to hear that note again. I have never heard that note again.

Reaching the ninety-ninth floor didn't feel like a particular triumph so much as the end of something endless. I was limp with fatigue. My hands were shaking. My teeth chattered with cold as we gazed at the frighteningly vast view of glittering, magnificent New York, punctuated by steel beams and flapping plastic. It was a higher up view than anyone else's. It was something strange and thrilling, being up here where nobody was supposed to be. It was very us. We knew things nobody else knew. We were a pair, Philip and I, and at this moment we were truly looking down on everyone else, from here to infinity. I knew I would not do something like this again, glad as I was to have done it.

Philip hugged me. I hugged him back. "I knew you could do it," he said.

"You knew you could talk me into it," I corrected him, "and I have blisters that you should feel guilty about."

"We should come back here," he said.

"Yeah, sure, for our wedding when we're forty," I agreed.

"Deal," he said. We held each other closer and more seriously than we ever had before. It suddenly felt real, no longer a game, a shtick. We were on a precipice and needed to take a step back. Neither of us said anything more. The moment passed and we moved apart.

From that moment on we kept moving apart until we hardly spoke from one month to the next. Two years later I would marry the man to whom I am still married thirty years later. We live in Connecticut, and Paris, and Ireland, we have two daughters older than I was on that night. Laura and Philip came to our wedding, and then I never saw either of them again, until I ran into Laura, just once, on First Avenue, pushing a prosperous stroller that held a sleeping blond child. She was married to a banker, hadn't worked in years. Laura told me she had thought of me not so long before our chance encounter, when she had glimpsed my old boyfriend, the charming and unreliable poet. He was wearing the uniform of a garbage man, riding the back of a garbage truck, swinging down to empty trash cans and then swinging back up. She laughed triumphantly when she told me about Jack's fate. Neither of us had heard from Philip in some twenty years. We both knew that he had become something of a name in urban planning on the West Coast and that he never married.

Does he remember that night? Did he think of it as I did, in the days after September 11, 2001, when the news was filled with so many images of that stairwell? Does he recall it the same way, the night we stood so close together, gazing down at the city, the night our friendship or whatever it was culminated in that private, secret, triumphant ascent? The arduous, cold, and dark descent lay ahead of us, but for that moment, we had everything worked out, we knew so much, we had our lives ahead of us, and we were, it seemed, on top of the world.

Executrix

PAM HOUSTON

I was in Greencastle, Indiana, when I got the call. I was sitting in my dreary hotel room on a dreary Sunday morning in February, wondering how I was going to kill the hours until my reading that night. I was about one month into a three-month book tour of independent bookstores and universities to promote my novel *Sight Hound*. I was dogless and friendless and stuck for a week in the part of the country that gives me hives.

I glanced at my ringing cell phone, saw the 610 area code with an unfamiliar number, and knew it couldn't be good news. I only knew a few people in the 610 area code. One was my father, who was in an assisted living center called Country Meadows in Bethlehem, Pennsylvania. Another was the social worker who called me three years before to tell me that my father's dementia had progressed to the point where assisted living was required.

Another was a woman, about my age, who had taken to visiting my father at Country Meadows and then calling me up and telling me about him. Her name was Cheryl, and my father reminded her of her father, with whom she failed to reconcile before he died. Cheryl was doing important work with my father, she always said, and I never knew whether she was calling me in hopes of bringing about some reconciliation between my father and me, or if she was suggesting that I might find some other woman's father, somewhere farther down the line, that I could forgive on *his* daughter's behalf.

I let the call switch over to voicemail, and when the little bird chirped, I called in to let the message play back. My father's lawyer identified himself and then, without any hesitation, told me my father had died from a massive heart attack during dinner at Country Meadows the night before. He left his number and asked me to call him. I snapped the phone shut and watched the rain hit the hotel room window and felt the slippery-scratchy polyester bedspread underneath me. This was the moment some very essential part of me had been waiting for all my life. What did I feel? I hadn't the slightest idea. I picked up the phone to call the lawyer.

It had been twenty-six years since I moved out of my father's house. First to college in Ohio, then to graduate school in Utah, most recently to a teaching job in Davis, California. I went, each time, as far west as my imagination would allow. From the last day of my senior year in high school I never asked my father for anything. No money, no shelter, no food. We endured one another semiannually while my mother was still alive, and after she died in 1992, we continued to endure each other biannually in her honor. The idea of reconciliation never made sense to me because there was no time of conciliatory relation to go back to. I am pretty sure my father disliked me from the day I was born.

To my great relief the lawyer was a practical sort, and seemed to appreciate the same quality in me. He said, "You don't need to have a funeral if you don't want to. I'm certain almost everyone is dead."

But I was certain everyone wasn't. And it wasn't only duty that made me schedule a service for the following Wednesday afternoon. I knew my father would live on in any number of ways inside my mind and inside my body. I wanted at least to see his ashes put into the ground.

On Monday I was scheduled to give a reading at Denison University in Granville, Ohio. On Tuesday morning, I would fly to Albany to have dinner with William Kennedy, and give a reading at the State University of New York. The only thing on the books for Wednesday was an AP interview in Albany in the morning, and an afternoon flight to Salt Lake City.

My publicist turned out to be entirely practical, too. "No problem," she said. "We'll change the AP interview to late Tuesday night, we'll fly you to Philadelphia on Wednesday morning. You can rent a car and drive to Bethlehem, do the funeral, then we will get you out to Salt Lake City on the last flight that evening. It's perfect," she said, in her most upbeat, problem-solving voice. "You won't have to give up anything at all."

And that was exactly what I wanted.

I have written elsewhere about the things my father did that wreaked havoc on our small family, and I have now lived long enough to understand that the things he did are not so different from the things a lot of fathers do in a lot of other families, and I don't—have never—wanted or expected any more sympathy than any other person who has made it forty-four years into the world. He drank too much. He cheated extravagantly on my mother. He broke my femur when I was four years old. He threatened violence for anything other than straight As and when I brought home nothing but As for my entire school career he turned violent anyway. He forced himself on me sexually for so many years I am not entirely certain when it began and when it ended. But the worst thing about my father was the way he positioned himself in relation to the world. He believed that any good thing that happened to anyone other than him (me getting straight As, my mother getting a part in a play, Ben Crenshaw winning the Masters, Jimmy Carter getting elected president) was by definition a blow struck him. He would do anything he could to negate, or diminish, or obliterate that stroke of good fortune, no matter to whom it fell.

The last time I had seen my father alive was nine months before, when he had come to California with an eye toward moving into an apartment in Ventura. For the last three days of his trip, he had taken the train to Northern California to see me. Ninety-three himself, he said it depressed him to live with the "old people." He was forgetful, as it turned out, but not demented. Once he started getting three squares a day and regular medication at Country Meadows he snapped straight back to life and spent his time planning his escape route. I took him to see the Giants play the Rockies at Pac Bell Park because sports were always what we did together. I drove him around San Francisco because he had forgotten what it looked like. I took him out to eat at Italian restaurants—his favorite—every single meal for three days.

I changed my schedule around so that I had to leave him alone only one morning. I was running out the door to teach my class when he said, "They let you teach in that?" I closed the door behind me, furious at the extra time I had spent picking the outfit, which was much more formal than my usual teaching attire. When I got to school that day I got two compliments and three disbelieving stares.

On the way back to the train station on the last morning my father said, "Well, I guess this will probably be the last time we see each other." He had been saying something similar to this all my life. If my mother were still alive she would have delivered her line: "You're such a son of a bitch you'll outlive all of us." All of us believed my mother would turn out to be right.

I said, "Well, if you are going to die soon, try not to do it during the Stanley Cup Finals. The Sharks are likely to be in it, and I've got seats." He laughed, and I laughed too. When he boarded the train I thought, Well, if that is the last moment, I'm glad it was a nice one. In my family it never got any more like kindness than that.

*O*n the morning of the funeral I took the curves of the Schuylkill Expressway a little harder than my Rent-a-Taurus should have allowed, but the plane had arrived late, and the lawyer wanted me to stop by the office before I went to the church. The AP interviewer of the night before, Mike Vertanin, had stepped in heroically to fight with US Air when they said it might take days to find my luggage. Without it I would be forced to attend my father's funeral in jeans and a T-shirt, and I imagined him rising up from the coffin, pointing a yellowing finger, and moaning in a Hollywood zombie voice, "You show up at your father's funeral in something like that?" When it occurred to me that there would be no coffin—no body, in fact—I started imagining him whirling up out of his ashes like a Tasmanian devil or *I Dream of Jeannie*. My bag showed up at 3:00 a.m. and I had to leave for the airport at 5:30, but at least I had my good black clothes.

I passed the exit for the King of Prussia Mall. My father was dead. I was waiting for emotion the way a catcher waits for a knuckleball. Sorrow? Regret? Delirium? Joy? There was nothing outside except the bleak Pennsylvania landscape. There was nothing inside except the vibration of the tires on the road. My father was dead. I wouldn't believe it until I saw it, and maybe not even then.

The lawyer plunked about four hundred pieces of paper down in front of me. Underneath every signature a secretary had typed, "Pam Houston, Executrix."

"You're kidding," I said.

"Nope," he said, "That's what it's called, if the executor is a lone female."

"It sounds like a very-high-end dominatrix," I said. "Or one that kills her clients after she beats them up."

The lawyer didn't say anything.

"That's hilarious," I said.

"I'm glad you think so," he said, and then there was just the sound of pages turning and the executrix pen scratching.

"I know it seems like a lot of paper," the lawyer said, "but he's got no property, so this should be pretty once and done."

One day nearly a decade ago, my father had called me to tell me that he had been studying his life insurance policy and realized that there was no scenario in which he would be the recipient of any of the money he was pouring into it, and if I wanted the thirty grand after he was gone, I would have to start making the payments. I declined, and the policy was canceled.

I never wanted what money he had, and I told him so. "Tell you what," I said. "If you can figure out a way to go on a round-the-world cruise that uses up every last dime you have, and then drop dead right as the ship comes back into harbor, I'm all for it. You earned that money and you have the right to do whatever you want with it." In our family it never got any more like generosity than that.

Executrix. My long-lost alter ego. The girl who got straight Cs and always violated curfew and ran away with her tatooed boyfriend to Maui at seventeen. I pictured a black T-shirt with spangly letters. The word itself felt like some kind of a gift.

"Your father," the lawyer said, after a while, "was a sportsman, in every sense of the word."

I begged to differ. He didn't hunt. He didn't fish. He didn't one time in his life sleep on the ground.

All of a sudden I was in Christ Church of the Nativity, the first place I took communion, the place we had mourned the death of my mother fourteen years before. Somewhere in the building there was a container of ashes that used to be my father. At least that was the theory. The minister was a baby-faced stranger; the sickening smell of gardenias hung in the air.

A receiving line formed in front of me. I had been right: There were plenty of people still alive. I did the same thing I had done the night before in Albany, and the night before that at Denison, and all the nights all the way back to the beginning of my book tour in January: I shook people's hands; I thanked them for coming.

I shook the hand of a tiny man who spoke out of a machine that he placed over his larynx. He looked very ill and extremely tan—looked, in fact, as if there might have been a fire inside him, shrinking and charring him from the inside out. He told me that my father always looked out for the union guys down at the plant. He was not the only man who said it, and I was happy to hear this about my father, that for whatever reason, there was this one group of people whose best interests he kept in mind.

The tiny burned man was moving away when another man, taller, louder, was making his way up the aisle with a walker.

"My name is Martin," he said, "and I've got something to say to you," the menace in his voice parting the crowd.

"Your father and I," he said, twining his fingers. "We were like this."

"That's nice," I said.

"And I was the one sitting next to him at dinner when he was turning blue and gasping for breath and falling to the floor. And now I can't get it out of my mind."

"I'm sorry," I said.

"He told me about that last time he went to see you in Colorado," he said.

"California?" I said.

"Colorado," he said.

I said, "Okay."

"He told me you gave him the cold shoulder," he said.

"Really?" I said, "I thought we did pretty well that visit."

"That's not what he told me," he said. The church had gone suddenly silent around us. Even the organ music had stopped. "He told me you wouldn't give him the time of day."

"Well, you know," I said. "My father always did have his own version of things."

"To tell you the truth," Martin said, his voice rising in the silent church, "I'm surprised that you are even here at all."

The hundred or so people gathered in the church drew in their collective breath. The prodigal daughter had returned at last, only to be revealed for what she was: Ungrateful. Neglectful. Selfish. Bad. My father had whirled his ashes together into a rickety old body that called itself Martin. Dead, my left eyebrow. I looked toward the rafters. He probably had the whole place booby-trapped.

"Thank you for coming, Martin," I said. Like a robot. Like my mother. Not like an executrix at all.

The next person in line was a woman named Susie who had been a friend of my mother's. "Pam," she said, "It's amazing. You seem so incredibly strong."

I looked hard into Susie's eyes trying to gauge the ratio of reprimand to compliment. Surely she had been close enough to see what went on in my childhood home.

"They raised me to be strong, Susie," I said, holding her gaze.

She nodded slowly, saying, "I guess they did."

The minister asked us to be seated, and an attractive, much older man scooted into the seat beside me.

"I'm Tom," he said, "I'm friends with Peter Veruki. I knew your mom."

Peter Veruki was my father's longtime tennis partner, who always said my father was like a father to him, but because my father was never like a father to me, I never really knew what he meant. When I had called Peter and told him about my father he cried, and that made me happy too—the fact that there was someone in the world who would cry for my father.

I didn't know Tom, but he was tall and handsome, and because, as an only child, I have had to face every major life event singly, I was happy for his presence by my side. He flirted almost nonstop through the epistle and cracked jokes during the sermon. Toward the end of the Nicene Creed he asked me if I was seeing anyone.

Rain began to pound on the stained-glass windows. We were in the front pew and everybody in church was watching me behave like a bad, bad daughter. My mom's friend Susie, Martin and his walker, even the man with the fire inside.

I looked up into the rain falling on the biggest piece of stained glass and tried again to call up some kind of emotion to attach to my father's death. I wondered if "simply glad" would qualify as a sin, though I'd never paid much attention in my life to what did and didn't qualify as a sin, and I didn't think my father's funeral was a good place to start. My friend Murray said that the year after his own abusive father died was the worst year in his life. That was when he really got mad, he said, about everything he had had to put up with, about all the love he didn't get. I went after rage but couldn't find it. I couldn't even imagine what love might have looked like coming from my father, so I didn't know how to mourn it. It was like an advanced calculus problem, imagining the negative space of something indiscernible, an absence that couldn't ever have been.

When we went downstairs to the tiny chapel for the interment of the ashes, Tom stuck right with me. This will be the story they will tell, I thought, about how that whore Pam Houston got herself picked up at her father's own funeral. And by one of her mother's friends.

The minister pulled me aside and said, "I know his request was to be out in the garden with your mother, but it's raining buckets out there . . . do you mind if we just kind of fake it for now, and I'll make sure the ashes get in the ground after the rain stops?"

"Fake it?" I said. Which the minister evidently took as an affirmative.

I hoped Martin wouldn't make it down the stairs with his walker, but he clomped in just as the ceremony got under way. The minister made his way through the fake interment, and just as he said, "And now we commend Brother Houston's ashes to the earth" and I leaned forward in hopes of actually seeing some of the ashes, my cell phone rang. My ring tone is a little calypso number, one I had chosen long ago for the way it called up thoughts of frozen daiquiris, on a beach, in Maui, with the tattooed boyfriend I never had.

Tom winked at me but I didn't move a muscle. *Let them think it's his phone*, I thought while it rambled through its springy sixteen-measure tune, but of course they wouldn't. This is where the walls begin to fall, I thought. This is where the stained-glass windows explode in from the outside.

The service ended without any of us having even the briefest glimpse of ashes, and the people filed out the door. Tom asked me out to dinner, and I said I was sorry but I had to drive to Philadelphia and fly to Salt Lake City, and he gave me a kiss on the cheek and told me he really envied me my life.

I had almost made it to the door when the undertaker approached me, saying, in a Herman Munster voice, "This is a ring that was on your father's person," and my hand would simply not rise to take it. I had done a lot of things that were difficult that day, but I would not let the ring that had been *on my father's person* touch the skin on the palm of my hand. The undertaker stared at me in confusion while I finally pulled a scarf out of my purse and held it up so he could drop the ring inside.

When it gets close to the end, my friends had told me, *he'll need you to forgive him. You won't even recognize him. He'll be a changed man.* I always knew that at least in this way, my father would be the exception. He built his whole life on a platform of having been the wronged party, and it carried him strong into his nineties. To have investigated that fallacy at any point along the way would have surely cracked him in half.

If I had had time, I would have taken the ring out to the tennis courts south of Bethlehem that were my father's favorite, but I knew I would hit rush-hour traffic around Philly, and I wouldn't have made it to the airport in time for my flight.

I remembered the ring the next afternoon, after my reading in Park City. I stood on the snowy street, digging through my purse and found it—it was already covered with ink stains, like everything else in the bottom of my purse, as if the jury needed any more evidence to convict me of my neglect.

I smelled the snow piled up around me, and the crisp night air. I had made it out of Pennsylvania again, back to the West, the place I had gone to get away from my father, the place where, all those years ago, I learned for the first time to hear my own voice. Even if he had asked for my forgiveness, I wouldn't have had the first idea how to give it to him. Fear takes up so much space in the imagination. There isn't any room for anything else.

If a daughter misbehaves at her father's funeral and the father is not alive to see it, has she really misbehaved? The answer came back as it always did, If at all, not nearly enough.

I looked up and down the street trying to feel my freedom. If the executrix were here, she'd go to a bar, maybe get in a fight, maybe follow the dogs around to all the best Dumpsters. My father was dead, and it was going to take a good long time for me to believe it. All I wanted was a Caesar salad, an email connection to check in with my grad students, an hour to read the book I'd been assigned to review that week, and bed.

I put my father's ring on top of a little snowbank the plow had pushed to the side of the road. When it rolled off the snowbank and into the street, I reached to pick it up, but then stopped myself.

"Be free," I told the ring, out loud, drawing the attention of a Mormon family in the middle of a shopping marathon. "Come to rest anywhere you like." In our family it never got any more like love than that.

The List

TOBIN LEVY

I keep a running list of all the things I'd like to try before I die. Ten years ago, when I was twenty-one, learning how to skateboard, skydive, and play something other than the Eagles' "Lying Eyes" on my guitar ranked high on the list. Also on the list was a sexual subdivision devoted to the yearnings of my inner bad girl. Before I died I wanted to make out with a woman, have a real one-night stand, and endure a bondage session that included a heavy blindfold and a light, romantic beating. I wanted to fly across the country for sex, have car sex, outdoor sex, sex on drugs, and experience a threesome—preferably with two beautiful bisexual men who weighed more than I did and were genetically predisposed to giving compliments.

At the time the tasks before my inner bad girl were as daunting as the prospect of my early demise. I'd had only two serious boyfriends and three sexual partners. With all of them the sex had been kind and forgettable in its unoriginality. I hadn't believed I'd make it to twenty-one, and now that I had, it was only a matter of time before I died without knowing what it was like to have my bony wrists tied to a bedpost by a gloriously naked, relatively hairless man.

I suppose it should be noted that I wasn't born with a terminal illness. However, I was born with a father who has a not-so-subtle propensity toward morbid thoughts. He's a magazine publisher and a news junkie. Before the advent of email, while I was still in junior high and high school, he'd come home from work with packages full of macabre news clippings he'd Xeroxed for each of his three girls. Today my inbox is full of similar articles from my father. They include natural hazards updates alerting me to dust storms over the Red Sea and wildfires in Montana. He forwards me stories about breast cancer, lung cancer, looming pandemics, roller-coaster fatalities, rogue waves, shark attacks, the bleak statistics for surviving an airplane crash, women who've died from pedicure-related staph infections, and the "it's only a matter of time" earthquake that will decimate North America.

Needless to say I'm more than a little preoccupied with expiration dates, particularly my own.

$\mathcal{W}$hile I attribute the premature existence of my "to try before I die" list to my father, I credit Madonna for most of my bad-girl aspirations. I may not have known what a virgin was when her *Like a Virgin* album hit number 1 on the U.S. charts—I was nine—but I knew that I didn't want to be one, only *like* one who was being "touched for the very first time."

Madonna was magic in 1984. Night after night I watched MTV red-faced and diligent, waiting for Ms. Blond Ambition to writhe, wearing gold chains and black tatters, on a gondola through the

Venice canals. A magnificent lion paced the shores in anticipation of her arrival, as did a magnificent man, his face partially hidden by a lion mask. Then it was a feline Madonna, dressed in a white wedding dress, who was doing the pawing—on a bed, at a man. The visual metaphors may have been lost on me, but the realities of the disparate situations, hers versus mine, were not. I was a shy, sensitive child, with a guilt complex about pretty much everything, including calling the operator. She was a grinding, thrusting, crotch-grabbing vixen, who got everything she and I ever wanted, including Sean Penn.

Over the years, while the red-lipped Madonna was morphing into a bad girl of epic proportions, burning crosses and kissing beautiful black men on television, I was transforming into a sexually awkward, disturbingly good suburban teenager, who thought myself lucky, at age twelve, to get my first kiss on the back of a school bus from a stringbean of a boy whose only claim to junior-high fame was putting both of his legs behind his head and then being kicked, by one of the cool kids, in the crotch.

As I was abstinently making my way through high school, Madonna was publicizing her deliciously salacious life. She had gay, straight, and male and female lovers. She dressed up like a dominatrix on stage and then acted out the part of a submissive. Hers was a hypersexuality that seemed devoid of emotional ramifications. To me it was an enviable state of erotic being. Madonna was the kind of woman who would have dirty, experimental, multiorgasmic, unapologetic sex with the lights on. She was a powerfully bad girl. And before I died I wanted to be one too.

*B*y the time I reached my early twenties, I'd yet to realize any of my Madonna-inspired aspirations. (However, between the ages of twenty-one and twenty-two, I did go skydiving . . . twice.)

In fact, embarking on the bad-girl section of my to-do list seemed overwhelmingly impossible. I was living in New York, recently out of a long-term relationship, and still navigating the realities of dating as an adult. It was harsher, less predictable than I'd anticipated. First dates that had ended hopefully with sweet kisses good night were followed by nights spent in tears, clutching a phone that never rang. Like most of my friends, I engaged in casual drunken trysts with men I liked, hoping to match my indifference to theirs. But mine were futile endeavors. Try as I might I still needed the men who had the pleasure of meeting my ornery feline and sleeping in my bed to call. When the phone didn't ring, I still crumpled into a state of self-loathing.

If I was ever going to live out any of my bad-girl fantasies, I would need a man and a much more resilient ego.

Then I met Jim.

*J*im and I had only been together for two months when we bought our plane tickets to Southeast Asia. After the first few weeks on our three-month adventure, it was clear that my boyfriend hated a lot of things about me—my affinity for animals, my small talk, the way I looked—that were never going to change.

Jim ended the relationship after our sojourn through parts of Thailand, Cambodia, Vietnam, and Laos. We were at the Vientiane airport in Laos, heading back to Thailand, when he said the words "It's over." The breakup, although inevitable, felt impetuous and premature. We'd been living together in bungalows one-quarter the size of a New York studio for the past eight weeks. Now we were over, and I couldn't even remember the last time we'd had sex.

This is something I'm obsessive about after being with someone for an extended period of time. Even when I no longer like an ex, it makes me unbearably sad to think I had sex with him, went to bed smelling his skin—a smell I'd most likely been addicted to at one time—for the last time without knowing it was the last time. If only Jim had said, "Just giving you a heads-up, this will most likely not happen again," the last time we were having sex, I'd have made it a point to remember the details. Maybe even written them down.

Two weeks after the breakup, I was in Koh Lanta, a Thai island in the Andaman Sea, living in a bikini, spending my days reading on the beach and my nights drinking Mekong Whiskey with a group of Brits I'd met when I arrived. I assumed Jim was some-where on the Gulf of Thailand. He'd sent me an email saying he was heading in that direction, and I'd replied with my where-abouts. Two days later he showed up at my bungalow. We weren't supposed to see each other until our departure date, which wasn't for another two weeks

"I met the laziest kitty in Koh Chang," he said, trying to make nice with an animal story. We spent the rest of the day walking on the beach, trading tales of our independent adventures. He'd gone scuba diving and bodysurfing. I'd gone camping and had learned how to play cricket. We were tan, relaxed, and happy, hav-ing settled into the tranquil beach life that would be ours together or separately, on one island or another, for the remainder of our trip. We were also going to be sharing my room.

There was a full moon that night. Thailand is known for its full-moon beach parties, the most famous of which takes place on the island of Koh Pha-Ngan. There thousands of travelers convene once a month for a night of drinking, dancing, and mushroom-induced hallucinations. The full-moon party Jim and I went to in Koh Lanta was a smaller version, although Mong, the Thai bar-tender I'd befriended at my bungalow, was already doling out mushroom shakes when we stepped up to the bar. I'd never taken mushrooms, or any other hallucinogenic, before. I'd sworn them off in high school, after hearing about a girl who took a tab of acid, then spent the next ten years believing she was a watermelon. But that night I felt free and adventurous, ready and more than willing to do very bad things, even if it meant that the tile on my bathroom floor would morph into faces and begin speaking to me later in the evening. Jim, who'd always thought me a prude about drugs, drank a mushroom shake, too.

At four in the morning Jim and I decided we'd had enough trance music for a lifetime and made our way up the beach, away from the bonfire and the other travelers. When we could no longer hear *umph-umph-umph* reverberating from speakers or see any stumbling drunks, we stopped. Now the only sound we could hear was the sea hitting rock formations that, during the day, were as pink as a cow's underbelly, but that night, under the full moon's light, were the most beautiful blue-black color I'd ever seen. I looked at Jim, a lithe live G.I. Joe figure with a buzz cut, pale blue eyes, and a mole below his left eye that I'd always loved even if I never loved him. He was standing between the water and me, his face a perfect silhouette against the starry sky. At that moment he was the most handsome man I'd ever seen. I looked down at my shadow on the sand. It, too, was beautiful. This was the first time I'd ever found something about my physical self so enchanting.

Then the harsh realities—of who Jim was, of who we were together—rushed in. They came to me in the form of memories that hadn't yet had time to gestate into comic relief. I remembered the gastrointestinal trauma I'd experienced in Phnom Penh. Granted, I'd handled the food poisoning with the aplomb of a six-year-old, but Jim had scolded me with three days of silence for vocalizing my pain. Then there was our impromptu expedition to Battambong, Cambodia's third largest city and home to the one hotel touted in *Lonely Planet* for its offerings of free porn. I'd never been a big consumer of porn, but Jim was enthusiastic, and I was determined to add spark to our rapidly dwindling sex life, or at least check a little bad-girl behavior off my list. Battambong was a bust. We found the hotel and the porn, but they were both a little too seedy—too much yellow track lighting in the former and too much gruesome bondage in the latter. "Just because the porn sucks doesn't mean we can't have sex," I said. "I'm tired," he replied before turning over and falling asleep. I went to bed feeling rejected and in tears, just as I did a few weeks later when, after having sex, I meekly said, "Jim, um, I'm not . . . I didn't . . . I'm so close." "So what do you want me to do about it?" he said snidely, before locking himself in the bathroom. He'd come, therefore it was over.

There seemed to be an impossible number of memories like these. However, they quickly paled against a backdrop that included a full moon, a dramatic seascape, and a handsome, half-naked man.

Jim was soon pulling down his swim trunks and heading for the sea. I stuffed my miniskirt, tank top, and bikini under his pile of clothes so they wouldn't blow away, and joined him in the warm water. It was so salty that floating was effortless. Jim grabbed me from behind and turned me around so that I could wrap my legs around him. He was standing, holding me up. The kissing was familiar and furious, the culmination of weeks of resentment that the person we'd gone on this trip with wasn't who we'd hoped they'd be. Taking breaks from each other only to marvel at our surroundings and laugh at our fellow travelers staggering by, we stayed in the water until our lips stung and the sun started to rise. When we finally got out, the cool air was exhilarating. We laughed hysterically as we struggled into our clothes so that we could run back to our room and tear them off each other. The lights were dim. We smelled like the Andaman. The pinks and oranges from the sunrise were seeping through our windows. The sex was idyllic yet void of attachment. It was marathon sex, raw sex. The kind where you can try anything you've ever wanted to try because judgment is moot, the kind you can only have with a lover when there is no love. We were free to be selfish, and in being selfish we were both satisfied. It was breakup sex and not by any stretch of the imagination makeup sex. Still, I went to bed happy, having finally checked a couple of things—outdoor sex and sex on drugs—off my list. I'd write the experience down, first in my mind then on the page, and never have sex with him again. Madonna would have been proud.

When Jim and I returned stateside and the relationship was officially over, I was feeling like a zealot in my need to check a few more misbehaviors off my list. The thing about being a bad girl is that it's invigorating, even strangely life-affirming, especially when you've been a poster child for good girls all your life. I was twenty-seven, once again single, and I had no dating prospects. Yet it felt as though I had all the prospects in the world, or at least in Manhattan. It was a powerful place to be, considering I wasn't a supermodel and New York seemed to be filled with supermodels, but lacking in viable single straight men. I came back from Asia a changed woman. The paralyzing static of insecurity that had once filled my head and discouraged my libido had significantly lessened, if only temporarily. I needed to take advantage of the situation. And I did, a few months later with a man whose name I'll never quite know.

He was standing at the bar, wearing a red leather soccer jacket. My friend Andrew and I had gone to our local for a nightcap. We'd never seen this guy before. He was handsome tall, muscular, and he had an accent.

Bad Girls

"He plays for your team," said Andrew, before sidling up to the mystery man and then positioning me between them. Andrew considered himself my gay wingman and an expert in short-term matchmaking. "He's looking at you, so talk to him."

"What's your name?" I said.

"Kraig," he said, in a thick Scottish brogue.

"Huh?" I asked, unable to mask my ineptitude with Scottish brogues.

"Graig."

"Ohhh," I said, even though I still had no idea whether it was Greg or Craig or some name I'd never heard of.

"What's your name?" he asked.

"Tobin."

"Huh?"

"It's a strange name, even in the U.S. What do you do?"

"Football," he said, pointing to his jacket.

"Huh?" I said, making a mental note to excise that word from my vocabulary.

"I plaaay socccer, maaan," he said, patronizing me with his cowboy-meets-surfer version of an American accent.

"I know what European football is," I said, smiling at the very real possibility of finding out what was underneath his jacket. We spent the rest of the night at the bar, talking, flirting, and exchanging banal personal information, like how tall we both were. (Apparently, at five nine, I was a lot taller than most of the women he'd dated.) He was moving to Florida in a week to coach a high school soccer team, meaning that Greg or Craig or whatever his name was was not boyfriend material. Which was fine, since he was also not my boyfriend type. But he was beautiful and beddable, and I'd yet to have a real one-night stand.

"I have to go," said soccer man, at four a.m.

"Huh?" I said. "I mean, whatever." It turned out that he had a soccer game in Queens, where he was staying, early that morning.

"Andrew gave me your number. May I call you?"

"Sure, whatever," I said, looking at a very-pleased-with-himself Andrew.

"He'll call," said Andrew, while we were walking home.

"I know," I said. And he did, the very next day.

That night I had soccer man meet my friends and me at another bar. The reasons for this were threefold: I needed external confirmation that he wasn't a serial killer. I wanted to show him off. And I thought that maybe, with a little help, I'd finally learn his name. My friends were quick with their "He's not a killer and he's beautiful so you have to take him home" commentary. But they, too, couldn't agree on his name. (We argued about it while he was in the bathroom.) So, after an awkward, pronoun-heavy evening of drinking, I took the Scotsman home.

We had a charged make-out session in the back of a cab on the way to my apartment. I unzipped his red soccer jacket before opening the door. He spoke to me in what might as well have been another language while unbuttoning my pants. And then we had sex—dull, formulaic, unintelligible sex. Fortunately he and his soccer jacket left soon after it was over. And I was glad to see them leave. Not because I was disappointed. I'd gotten exactly what I wanted: safe sex in a safe place with a gorgeous man that I chose and then chose to let go. It was intentionally impersonal, something a bad girl would do. And, although the experience didn't technically qualify as a one-night stand—since I didn't meet the man and take him home in one night, but in two—it was close enough. I'd count it as such the following morning, when, in my flushed hangover state, I called Andrew to tell him about the latest thing I'd crossed off my list.

Relatively soon after my one-night-stand, I put my bad-girl to-do list aside in favor of a new relationship. Not that "bad girl" and "relationship" were mutually exclusive. It was the new part that

Bad Girls

didn't mingle well with the dirtier parts of my brain. I spent the following eight months, including my twenty-ninth birthday, desperately in love with a man I'd hoped to marry. And then spent another eight months curled up in the fetal position, after said man broke my heart. During that time I didn't have sex, nor did I *want* to have sex. I was in the middle of an extremely frigid sexual nuclear winter. Even after the blanket of hurt had finally lifted and the bad girl in me began to reawaken, there was frostbite to contend with. The damage felt irreparable until, one sunny Friday, I opened my in-box and found a message from Dave, a former lover, whom I actually loved and still considered a friend.

"Come to my birthday party on Sunday," he wrote.

"That's in two days. You live in LA. And I'm going to Long Island for the weekend, leaving this afternoon."

"Come anyway," he wrote back. "I'll pick you up at the airport, take you to dinner then take advantage of you for thirty-six hours. It will be worth it, trust me." If Dave were the kind of man who used the parenthesis key and a semicolon to make a naughty, winking smily face, there would have been one at the end of that sentence. Of course, if he were that kind of man, I wouldn't have wanted to go.

"I wish I could," I replied, before shutting down my computer and heading to the train station.

Dave was ten years older than me, and one of the first real men I'd dated in New York. The relationship had ended for various reasons: age, timing, distance. But we'd stayed in touch over the years, seeing each other, and occasionally sleeping together, when we both happened to be single and he was in town or when I found myself on the West Coast. It had been years since we'd last been together, and seven years since we'd first had sex. I'd been young and inexperienced then, mortified by even the most innocuous of dirty talk, and by how out of control I felt whenever I was with Dave and in relatively close proximity to a bed.

It would have been an amazing weekend, I thought that night, as the train pulled into my final Long Island destination. Then my phone rang. It was Dave.

"I found you a ticket on Travelocity that has you leaving tomorrow at four and gets you back to New York on Monday afternoon. My credit card information is in there, all you have to do is say yes and I'll hit enter."

"Yes," I said, feeling giddy, alive, and a little nauseated at the prospect of calling into work "sick" from LAX on Monday morning.

Twelve hours later I was on a train heading back to the city. Twelve hours after that, I was on a plane heading west, flying three thousand miles for sex. It was the most spontaneous thing I'd done since Asia. As promised, Dave picked me up at the airport. On the car ride back to his place, we laughed like impetuous children, having temporarily forgotten about all the emotional drama that had, at one point or another, catapulted us both into a disillusioned adulthood.

I'd been to Dave's house at least half a dozen times before, but never under such blissfully illicit circumstances. As planned, we had sex and then went to a nice sushi dinner. He paid. We then came home and had sex again. And again.

That night we laughed about the impossibility of the situation—I was there on twenty-four-hours' notice—and marveled at the ways that sex with each other had changed, gotten so much better, as we'd gotten older. He reminded me about the way I blushed, throwing a pillow over my head, so many years ago, when he whispered something dirty in my ear. I blushed at the memory, then whispered something dirty into his, before embarking on round four.

Dave and I had sex eleven times that weekend—we proudly kept a running tally. As expected, he drove me to the airport on Monday morning. But instead of feeling guilty as I left a message on my boss's voice mail, telling him I'd come down with the flu, I was euphoric in my deception. For thirty-six hours, I'd shirked my responsibility to everything other than my sexual self. As a result I felt high on the plane ride back to New York. The rush was just as strong when I mailed Dave a check, a week later and of my own volition, for half the cost of the plane ticket. In exchange for two hundred dollars, I'd crossed something else off my list. Dave and I weren't in a relationship again; we probably never would be. Still, for the first time in more than a year, I was a truly happy very bad girl.

I am now thirty-one years old, and the content of my to-do-before-I-die list has significantly diminished. Many of the tasks that were before me ten years ago have since been checked off the list. Some, however, were simply deleted in the name of pragmatism (there's no such thing as a light, romantic beating) and self-respect (even if there were compliments involved, at this age, I'd have a hard time looking at myself in the mirror after a threesome). But my bad-girl days are hardly over. In fact, as I get older, and presumably closer either to marriage and children or to my early demise, I feel an even greater urgency to indulge in sexual improprieties, even those I now consider old hat.

"You know, I've never had sex in a car," I said to my boyfriend a few weeks ago. We were on a road trip, driving through West Texas.

"Really." He smiled, taking one hand off the steering wheel and putting it in my lap. Having read *The World According to Garp*, I wasn't going to put anything in his lap while the car was still moving. Then I saw it—a gravelly turnoff leading nowhere. It was the perfect place to pull over, and I was definitely going down that road.

A Good Girl Goes Bad

JOYCE MAYNARD

For the first four and a half decades of my life, I was—with a few minor exceptions—an unusually good girl. For all the seventeen years I lived under the roof of my parents' house, the only memory that comes to mind of an event in which discipline was necessary concerns a time I took a little dirt out of the large ceramic pot where my mother's favorite schefflera grew, for the purpose of starting an avocado plant. Mostly, though, I worked hard at pleasing my parents, and with surprising regularity, I succeeded at that. As for why it mattered so much that I assume the role of a good girl—this is a long and complicated story, no doubt. Short answer being that as the daughter of a beloved alcoholic parent—my father—and another beloved parent who suffered my father's drinking stoically but with profound sorrow, the best thing I knew to do to slow down the drinking and make my mother happy was to be as perfect as I could.

I was a good student. I was skinny, as my mother (a lifelong dieter) had always wanted me to be, and I dressed in outfits she chose for me. I was cheerful and outgoing, while my older sister (never particularly good at being a good girl) holed up in her room reading dark poetry and playing sad songs on her guitar. At the age when some teenage girls rode around in cars with boys and rolled joints, I took nature walks with my father and wrote prim essays in which I expressed my abhorrence of marijuana.

My parents were not the only ones who found my written words pleasing. They met with the approval of magazine editors, first at *Seventeen*, and then at other places as well, where—while still a teenager—I launched my career, a further effort to bring joy to my father and mother. While other young women were engaging in the kinds of activities their parents might have worried about, I sat at my typewriter, clicking away.

One piece published in this period was titled "My Parents Are My Friends." In another I described the experience of lying awake on the top bunk of my dormitory bed (the college was Yale; I'd pleased their admissions team as well) while, below me, my roommate (a bad girl) was having a good time with her boyfriend. I was a virgin (a fact I also announced in print), and though I secretly longed for a boyfriend, the kind of behavior required of a girl to form a relationship with a member of the opposite sex seemed scary to me, as a girl whose measure of nearly everything in her life began with the question: What would my parents think?

When I was eighteen, a famous and powerful man read a piece of my published writing and sent me a letter of praise. The fact that I had won the admiration of J. D. Salinger stood as the greatest accomplishment in a lifelong career of working hard to please people. His words, in that first letter he wrote me, came to be as essential to my existence as air. If J. D. Salinger told me I was talented and perfect, I must be, because he was the wisest and most wonderful man in the world.

So, within a few months of meeting Jerry, I did the first bad thing in my good-girl life, which was to quit my amazing summer job at the *New York Times* to be with him in New Hampshire, and that fall I did an even more bad thing, which was to withdraw from Yale—forfeiting my scholarship, abandoning the books and clothes I'd left there, along with my blue bicycle—to live with him. Forever, I believed.

But though under nearly any other circumstances, my choice to drop out of an Ivy League university to move in with a fifty-three-year-old man would unquestionably have incurred the dismay and vehement opposition of my parents, they remained silent about my choice. No doubt this had to do with the identity of the particular fifty-three-year-old man with whom I now announced I would be spending my life. For a girl like me, the fact of having won Salinger's love seemed like the greatest accomplishment in my still-young-but-driven life.

I spent that year with Salinger writing a book—a 160-page memoir, due to be delivered to my publishers shortly after my nineteenth birthday. And though it might have seemed like a tough problem, telling the story of my life without mentioning either the fact that I had grown up in a family where my father got drunk every night, or that one of the activities I engaged in to remain so pleasingly skinny was a daily regimen of self-denial and bulimia, I steered clear of those topics in the pages of my first book. I confined my musings to safer topics like the Kennedy assassination and the Beatles' first appearance on the *Ed Sullivan Show*.

The other subject I didn't touch in my eighteen-year-old's autobiography was any mention of my relationship with a man known to be as reclusive and protective of his privacy as any writer alive. Not surprisingly it was a source of tension between the two of us, that I was writing this book, and as its publication date approached, the tension between us grew, concerning my desire to go to New York and talk about the book, appear on television, give interviews about my work—and his desire to remain far removed from the stuff of worldly life.

I did not argue with Jerry Salinger about his view that my desire to publish my writing and find readers for it stood as proof of fundamental flaws in my character. I was shallow and vain, he told me—attracted, like a magpie to a piece of glittering aluminum foil, by meaningless worldly success. He went on to say (and this much was surely true) that I was too heavily invested in pleasing my parents. His words were hurtful, but back in those days I didn't argue with anyone I loved and admired. I was a good girl still.

Three weeks before the publication of that first book of mine, Jerry Salinger put a fifty-dollar bill in my hand and told me to go away forever, and I did. He told me how he had come to feel contempt for me, my hollow values, and my hopelessly immature teenage behavior. Where once I had inspired in him the most glorious and extravagant adoration, now what came forth from the man I revered were words that sliced through my heart.

And so—as a girl who had, all her life, measured her worth in the world by her ability to win approval—I was left to view myself as the most unredeemable failure. Thirty years later, if a man I loved were to say to me, of myself, the things Salinger told me that day, I would revise my view of the man. But at nineteen— and believing as I did at the time that these words came from the wisest and most enlightened human being I had ever encountered or ever would—the only person I thought less of as a result was myself.

My book (dedicated to my parents) was published almost twelve months to the day from when I'd received Jerry Salinger's first letter. The book received many glowing reviews. Many copies were sold, though that fact barely registered with me at the time. I was too devastated.

I carried on with my life, for many months and many years after that. I did not return to Yale. Eventually I married. But I carried with me a deep shame at having failed to deserve the abiding love of the person whose love I had most longed to win.

Years passed. Though I continued to write articles and books, I know my parents were disappointed to see me forgoing a career in New York City for a life in New Hampshire, where the most important aspect of my days became the raising of my three children. I was haunted by the sense of having fallen short of my mother and father's hopes for me.

In one way at least, though, I remained a good girl. Though it had been known by many people that once, long ago, I had lived with Salinger, and though not a week of my life went by in which some journalist or curiosity seeker didn't ask me about him, I maintained a fierce and unrelenting loyalty to the requirement Jerry Salinger had laid down back when he had loved me: that I never speak of him or write of him. He was so much more important and valuable than I was, I knew. His voice had spoken on this subject, and so mine must remain mute. The only way I had to prove to him that I was not completely unworthy lay in my silence.

Over the years I published articles and essays about many subjects that would once have seemed unmentionable. I wrote about the experience of growing up in a house where my father got drunk every night. I wrote about being a young girl who stuck her finger down her throat to remain thin. I wrote about the death of my marriage, and the death of my mother. Only one story remained unmentionable, out of the belief that I owed loyalty and protection to the great man it concerned. And I think that for all those years, too, I held on to the picture of myself presented to me by the man I had so revered, who had dismissed me as unworthy.

And then something changed. My daughter—firstborn child, only girl—turned the age that I was when Jerry Salinger wrote me that first letter and all the other ones that followed it. And where, always before, the person I had deemed most deserving of protection and loyalty had been the man who had demanded my silence, suddenly I found myself revisiting that first and most brutal love affair of my life through the eyes of the young girl. Maybe I couldn't see myself as deserving anything more than what I'd gotten from Salinger, but I knew that if it had been my daughter I would have understood that she deserved better.

Twenty-five years had passed since I'd read the letters that had first ignited my unyielding devotion to their author, but I took them out and reread them, now, with the eyes of a forty-three year old woman—the mother of a daughter of her own. Twenty-five years later what I saw was not simply the brilliance and wisdom of their author but manipulation.

When I read the letters as a grown woman, and thought about the events those letters had set in motion in my life, the story looked different, and so did the course my life had taken. I thought about the ways my life and work had been shaped by the events of that sad and confusing year so long ago, when Jerry Salinger plucked me out of the pages of the *New York Times*. I thought about the book I'd written when I was very young—a memoir in which I had kept hidden the truest parts of my experience, at a cost of my own voice. Not as an act of vengeance, I think—only a desire to locate my authentic voice—I decided to tell the story again. Only the real one, this time. Not the one constructed to please anyone, or to spare me the wrath of a powerful man's displeasure.

Twenty-five years after the last time I'd set foot in the home of the first man I ever loved—the man who had remained, for me, like a religion—I paid him a visit then, one more time. Once, long ago, it had been he who'd instructed me to give up my good-girl ways as a writer—my well-established habit of attempting to ingratiate myself with those I loved—in favor of simply telling the truth. He had criticized that first book of mine for its inauthenticity concerning the real story of my parents, my father's drinking, my family. "Write in your strong voice," he told me then. No thought, as he spoke those words, that the day might ever come when the need to tell an authentic story, in my own voice, might find me writing about him.

Never before in my life, and never since, have I encountered greater rage or greater contempt than what Jerry Salinger expressed to me the afternoon I paid him that visit on the eve of my forty-fourth birthday. But in a strange and profound way, looking into the eyes of a man I once loved, as he shook his fist at me and pronounced me a person beneath his contempt—a woman he now witheringly dismissed for having "loved the world"—freed me from a quarter century of silent deference. Perhaps some part of me knew that an avalanche of criticism awaited me when I ceased to comply with the code of silence, but having survived the wrath of Salinger himself, I gave little thought to what anyone else would say about me now.

The book I went on to write, my second memoir, was published two years later—the most authentic work I'd ever produced, I believed. A full twenty-five years after the events it described had taken place, I had told my real story, and having done so, I believed I had finally laid to rest an experience I'd carried with me more than half my life, like a heavy stone pressed against my heart. Now I could go on with the rest of my life, tell other stories.

After the publication of that book, an outcry occurred in the literary world, in which a kind of venom was expressed—not so much against my memoir, even, as against me—unlike anything I'd encountered. Review after review I read (before I gave up reading them) spoke of me as the shameless exploiter of a great man, a "predator," a woman who had violated every code of decency and acceptable behavior by invading the privacy of a man whose whole life bore testimony to his wish to be left alone. There were hideous caricatures accompanying these reviews, vicious hate mail, and Web sites full of angry postings from lovers of *Catcher in the Rye*. The only good thing about my book, one critic wrote in *Time* magazine, was the fact that at least now that I'd told this story, nobody would ever have to hear from me again.

Once, visiting New York, an old friend who'd invited me to a dinner party called back to suggest, gently, that I'd do better not to attend. "There will be Salinger fans present," he told me. "It wouldn't be a good idea for you to be at the table."

And so, for the first time in my life, perhaps, I was a bad girl. I hadn't done what I was told this time. I spoke when I was supposed to keep my mouth shut. One of my critics made reference to a scene in my book in which I hazily described an episode of forced oral sex. "There she goes," the woman wrote. "Joyce Maynard and her big mouth." Nearing the age of fifty now, having raised three children and worked as a writer for close to three decades, I remained—at least to my critics, and there were legions of them—the aging former sex partner of an icon, cashing in on her one claim to fame.

I have lived through a number of hard times: the end of my marriage, the deaths of my parents. Struggles with my children, struggles to support my family. Challenges in my work. And of course, that first terrible loss of love, when I was young, that marked me in all kinds of lasting ways.

But it is possible that no experience I have lived through has been more painful, in certain ways, than the fall of that year when I published that second memoir. The true one.

*W*hen I was eighteen I'd lost my voice, and when I was forty-five, I reclaimed it—finding as I did so that a substantial portion of the literary world believed that in presuming to tell my story I had committed an unforgivable moral offense.

Now came a moment when—as a woman with a lifelong hunger for approval—I had to confront, full on, the condemnation of a crowd of critics, aligned in the view that I was a reprehensible person. (Salinger himself remained silent and removed, as I had known he would. No need to wonder anymore what he might think of me now. I knew.)

And so, as a woman who had spent a significant portion of her lifetime assessing her value based on what those in authority said about her, I might simply have retreated to the darkest corner I could locate.

The experience did not silence me this time, or fill me with self-hatred and shame. That critic who wrote that he'd never have to read another book of mine was wrong. So were those who suggested that the only event of meaning or significance that ever happened in my life—the only story I had to tell—had been that once, when I was young, I'd shared the bed of a famous and important man.

Once, when I was young, a famous and important man chose to become a part of my story, and I dared to acknowledge that it happened. It was not my only story, not even my first story, but it was one of them. Telling it laid it to rest. Telling it, and surviving all of what that telling brought upon me, freed me from what I had feared more than anything else, which was the picture of myself, displeasing those whose good favor I sought.

All my life I'd been afraid that if I were ever to be a bad girl, no one would love me anymore. But what does it mean, anyway, if what it takes to be loved is the denial of one's own story?

And what is a bad girl, really, but a girl who doesn't always do the things other people tell her she's supposed to? Sometimes, it's true, a bad girl may be someone who cheats or steals or hurts people or lies. And sometimes a bad girl is just someone who tells the truth.

Laura the Pest

LAURA LIPPMAN

On a dull, overcast day in October 2000 I spit my teeth out at work. Well, pieces of my teeth, two back molars, cracked by weeks of literal grinding. The broken teeth would require repair, of course—temporary crowns, then permanent ones. That fix would lead, eighteen months later, to a white dot on my gum, the signal that an infection had begun to fester beneath the crowns. Root canal would fail to fix the infection, so an oral surgeon would open up my gum along the left side of my mouth, insert what felt like a fist-size object, putter around in there for the better part of an hour, then close me up and send me on my way with a bottle of Percocet. But all this was to come. At that moment the only thing I knew was that I held the yellow, cracked pieces in my hand. They looked more like dislodged kernels of popcorn than actual teeth.

"Look," I said, cupping the pieces in my palm and holding them up with a kind of awed brio, the way a child displays something particularly disgusting. "It's my teeth!"

My direct supervisor, H, backed away from me. "Please," he said. "I don't want to see that."

*I*t was a time in my life when a lot of people, coworkers and even friends, were backing away from me. I was radioactive. You could smell failure on me, the gamy, acrid sweat of a persona non grata. My newspaper career of nineteen years was in free fall, derailed by an editor who felt—well, to be honest, I can't know what he felt because he never deigned to tell me. I know only what I was told, via various intermediaries. Minions, I guess you could call them. After six years in the *Baltimore Sun*'s feature department, where I had been one of the most productive and lauded employees, I was essentially demoted and sent to a suburban bureau. My pay wasn't cut, but the bureaus were considered lesser postings, reeducation camps for the terminally unruly. There were two kinds of reporters in the suburban bureaus at that time: young ones on their way up, and old ones on their way out. At forty-one, I was one of the old ones.

"*I*s it because of the books?" I asked the features editor, P, entrusted with the thankless task of telling me to clean out my desk downtown. For six years I had been writing crime novels at the rate of one a year, garnering generally nice reviews and even winning awards. Still, I had never taken a leave of absence to work on the books, and I produced more copy for my section than most of my colleagues, so I didn't think my extracurricular work could be held against me. I was fast, too, and versatile, so versatile that I had twice been reassigned to the city desk for big elections, much in the way that actresses were "loaned" between studios in Hollywood's heyday. True, I had complained bitterly about being sent back to the city desk, but I had done what I was asked to do. In fact, based on how much animosity I had engendered in both Maryland's governor and Baltimore's mayor, it would seem that I had done my part pretty well.

"You just haven't been producing enough," P said.

"I have a very high byline count, one of the highest in the department."

"But you don't do the right type of stories," P said. "Stories with nuance. Unexpected stories."

"What about the story of the woman who was selling her wedding dress through the classifieds, or the man who bought an engagement ring the day before Christmas? Everyone loved those."

"Well, then you should have done more of them."

"But I couldn't do more of them because I was always being tapped to do the stupid thumbsuckers that the editors wanted. Quick riffs on *Survivor* and politics."

*L*et me be clear. The conversation above is re-created from memory, and I stand only by the gist of it, not the specific words. But I can be quite definitive about what my boss said next—words that I would repeat minutes later, in a conversation with my union shop steward, words that would be repeated again and again over the next year. The feeling was, P said, that "you no longer do your best work."

Your. Best. Work. My mind flashed back to elementary school, when we were graded not only on achievement—the standard A, B, C—but also effort—1, 2, 3. One grading period, I had received a B and a 2, and my parents had told me solemnly that they didn't care about the letter grade, as long as I had a 1 for effort. And here I was, downgraded to a 2 again. It was one of the most shameful moments of my life.

But with those words—"You no longer do your best work"—P had, unwittingly I believe, opened the door for a grievance. The *Sun*'s contract at the time prohibited punitive transfers. If one was transferred for not doing one's best work, it was arguably punitive. That would be up to arbitrators to decide, a long and arduous process. The trick was that filing a grievance, in the *Sun* culture, was a kamikaze mission. Even if you won the battle, they would then find a legal way to screw you. The top boss, the one who was behind the decision to move me, disliked being challenged. As it happens, I had just had a little clash with him two months earlier, when I complained about another reporter's unethical and unprofessional conduct. Coincidence? Again, I'll never know.

My father was a recently retired editorial writer for the *Sun*, and he told me what I already knew to be true: If I took my medicine, went to the suburbs, and did a great job, they would bring me back downtown. To survive in newspapers for more than a few years—and my father had put in almost forty, thirty at the *Sun* alone—one had to be adept at this kind of reinvention. The *Sun*'s Catherine wheel turned slowly, but they always let you down eventually, if only out of inattention or boredom. A feud requires energy, focus, discipline. Newer, tastier victims would offer themselves up.

And I had strong economic incentives to endure my punishment in silence. Estranged from my husband and in the middle of a divorce, I had no idea what my financial future would be, how much I would be obligated to pay under the divorce settlement. I also wasn't sure that novel writing could ever pay my bills. The rule of thumb for going freelance is current salary plus one-third. My next publishing contract would have to show a big jump to hit that milestone, and it wouldn't even be negotiated for another year. My father's advice was solid and commonsensical, perfect for a longtime good girl who wanted to get only 1s for effort, no matter the grade.

The thing is, I didn't want to be a good girl anymore. I had pretty much chucked goodness out the window about seven months earlier, when I had allowed my then-husband to take me to the airport, kissed him good-bye, and told him I would see him later. After a weekend with my parents at their winter digs in Georgia, I returned to Baltimore and called my husband, announcing that I had left him and was now living in my parents' vacant apartment. Later I would say to friends: "If the bosses at the *Baltimore Sun* wanted to fuck with me, they should have gotten to me before I was a veteran of marriage counseling."

My first day in the suburban office, I learned that my bosses downtown were ready to play hardball, too. I was told to go sit in my car outside an apartment complex forty minutes away *just in case* the downtown reporters failed to get an interview with a woman whose underage son had caused a fatal accident. She was at an all-day court hearing, and my colleagues would have to be stupendously incompetent to miss her. Still, I was to sit there all day, no matter what happened. Nineteen years as a prizewinning reporter and I was back to the kind of job given the greenest of rookies. I managed to talk my way into the house at one point, getting past the woman's boyfriend on my bladder's behalf, but he wouldn't let me stay inside, and he wouldn't talk to me. I spent most of the day in the front seat of my car, reading a delightful mystery novel about a constable in Wales.

About four o'clock, I blandly called my direct supervisor. "I came to work at nine-thirty," I said, "and I haven't been allowed to go to lunch. I'm almost an hour from the office, and the drive back counts as part of my working day. So if you don't release me at four-thirty, I'll be on overtime. I'm calling in advance for approval, as you now require."

Overtime, like grievances, was another contractual right that ambitious reporters declined lest they anger the bosses. They would work five, ten extra hours a week, never asking for time-and-a-half to which they were legally entitled. Instead they would be rewarded with gift certificates from American Express. One of my friends once worked an astonishing amount of overtime, perhaps a hundred hours in a single month, and was offered a fifty-dollar AmEx gift certificate in lieu of the money she was owed. "What do you think they'll think if I take the gift certificate instead of the overtime I'm owed?" she asked me. "I think," I said, "they will think you can't do arithmetic for shit."

Given the choice between paying me even an hour of overtime and releasing me, they released me, but they were angry about it. The game was afoot. I had embraced my new identity as a pain-in-the-ass, and the top bosses, the ones who didn't see me day to day, were more determined than ever to quash me.

I knew the contract pretty well—my shop steward was also one of my best friends—and I never hesitated to invoke it. Try to send me to a 3 a.m. assignment on my birthday, with no advance notice? Sorry, but the schedule cannot be changed, except by mutual consent, after it has been posted. Make me write a story that I consider idiotic? Under the contract I could pull my byline. "I'll file a grievance!" I sang into the phone time and time again, making life hell for the middle managers charged with telling the big boss about my obdurate ways.

So my hazing became more subtle. Given difficult assignments, I was not allowed to fail. One day, for example, I arrived at
work and was informed that a fire had killed a large number of
purebred Pomeranians. The top boss, B, was very keen on a
human-interest feature about the owner. But the owner, of
course, had been displaced by the fire, and no one knew where he
was. I no longer remember how I did it, but I found the man and
learned the name of every single dog killed in the fire. The story
that the boss was allegedly so keen to have? It was buried on
page 3B.

Then there was the attack on the USS *Cole*, which killed a local
man. I was sent to his family's home, charged with getting an
interview and then returning to the office to take feeds from various reporters and braid all the information into a sidebar. The
young man's parents were, understandably, desolate, and wanted
nothing to do with the press. There were reporters clomping all
over their pretty front yard, television trucks lined up on their
quiet street. "We really don't want to talk," the mother said to me
over and over again. I gave her my best smile and said that I understood, that I was so sorry for her loss. And then—I just didn't
leave. I stood there and stood there and stood there, knowing that
such persistence often paid off. Eventually they surrendered and
gave me the quotes I needed. Driving back to the office, I experienced none of the adrenaline rush of getting a story on deadline.
I felt ashamed.

I remember that evening so well. It was a Friday and I had
planned to leave at quitting time for a mystery writers' conference in Philadelphia. Instead I was in Baltimore, working late
and—of course—putting in for overtime. When an editor balked,
I reminded her that I had sacrificed my trip and possibly forfeited
my conference fee. "I have a little advice for you," she shrilled.

"You won't ever speak of your books if you know what's good for you." Hmmm. So maybe there was something to the theory that I had been sent to suburbia for the crime of writing crime novels.

Instead of going to Philadelphia when my workday was over, I went to my new apartment, still largely empty, and assembled the bed that had arrived that day. I then sat in my new bed, one of the few pieces of furniture in the apartment, and ate take-out Indian food while listening to the New York Yankees beat up on the Seattle Mariners. It's been six years now since the night I'm describing, and I moved out of the neighborhood four years ago, but the Indian place still knows my order to this day—vegetarian samosa, nan, lamb saag. That's how many take-out meals I ordered and ate by myself that year.

It was lonely, being bad. I felt like Ramona Quimby in the children's classic *Ramona the Pest*, exiled to the playground benches for pulling another girl's hair. Ramona didn't mean to be bad, not really. She just wanted to see if the other girl's perfect curls would bounce back like a spring. But once she was forbidden to touch the other girl's hair, Ramona couldn't help herself; she had to do it again. And, in Ramona's defense, the other girl was pretty insufferable. Ramona's crime wasn't hair pulling. Her real infraction was refusing to bow to the kindergarten teacher's authority.

As Ramona sits on the bench, two young children stare at her through the fence, in awe of her badness. In being exiled from the downtown newsroom to the playground bench of the suburban office, I had inspired the same kind of distant regard. I also had learned how few true friends I had in an office where I had worked more than a decade. The best ones, the true ones, stood by me, and I am grateful to them to this day. But some coworkers abandoned me, as if my problems were cooties they might catch.

———

$\mathcal{I}$t was two or three weeks after the USS *Cole* bombing that I spit out my teeth.

And the scary part is that I still had a year to go. A year of being bullied and called to account for the oddest things, although never directly. Instead the downtown bosses always telephoned my poor supervisor, H, and harangued him. "Why was Laura in the downtown office? She's not supposed to be there." "Why does Laura have a piece in the feature section? She's not allowed to write for features even on her own time." One day I filed a page 1 story on the last day of school, a story that was praised by almost every editor and reporter on the staff. Only the top boss withheld his approval, instead calling H to interrogate him on how I managed such a feat on deadline. I could hear H's mournful answers to B's questions, and thereby infer what was being asked. B clearly was keen to catch me in some sort of ethical breach. He wanted to know how I had found the boy who was central to the story, how I had learned so much about him, yet still managed to write the piece in less than three hours. Later H—a sweet man, who had no stomach for being in the middle of this fight—would say to me: "That was one of the finest stories I have ever read in all my years in journalism. Of course we didn't submit it to any of the contests because . . ." He shrugged. He didn't have to finish the sentence. I knew the story had been left out of contests because it carried my byline.

The thing is, I had decided to take half of my father's advice. I was doing the best work of my career out in that suburban bureau, finding offbeat stories where—to quote a favorite line from Yeats—executives would never want to tamper. A profile of a nursery owner preparing for spring. The quixotic tale of a mild-mannered teacher who had built his own speed bumps in defiance of the local authorities. My stories were frequently on page 1. The local city magazine, fully aware of its cheek, anointed me the *Sun's* best reporter. And I actually loved my colleagues. The managers may have tried to pit us against one another, create dynamic tension between young and old, but a small office is innately collegial. We had names and rituals for almost every day of the week: Picnic Tuesday, Wild Shirt Wednesday, Italian Sausage Thursday, Popcorn Friday. When big news broke, we were a formidable team, working together without ego or conflict.

Still, the grievance process ground on and ground me down, taking its toll on far more than my teeth. I developed hives and inexplicable ear infections. I had a frighteningly short fuse in all aspects of my life, not just at work. I was, in short, a mess.

Almost a year to the day after I spat out those pieces of my teeth, my bosses did something to me that I can compare only to *Gaslight*, the old film in which Charles Boyer tries to drive Ingrid Bergman mad in sneaky and sinister ways. They asked me to stop working on a project that they had already approved, on the grounds that there were other stories that required more urgent attention. But when I asked what they needed done, they didn't actually have anything for me. I had to go out and find work to replace the work that I was doing because—Lord, I don't know. By that point I had given up trying to understand their motives and intentions.

Coincidentally, I had once written an article about someone in the same situation in which I now found myself. A manager at a state agency couldn't be fired, so he had simply been stripped of all responsibility. He sued to get his job back. This was at least fifteen years ago, but I can see him in my mind's eye still, a soft-spoken man with a neatly trimmed beard explaining to me how he filled eight hours a day. He sat at his desk, reading. "Anything you want?" I asked, thinking that wouldn't be such a bad gig. "Oh no," he said. "I read texts about personnel, my field. If I don't do things related to my job, they could fire me. So I have to fill my days the best I can." It was like some bizarre update on Dumas— *The Man in the Iron Mask and a Gray Flannel Suit.*

I don't remember what happened to that middle manager and his lawsuit. But I could see that I was being set up to fail in a similar fashion, and that was something I wasn't going to allow. I called a psychiatrist who had been helpful to me during the end of my marriage, and told him that I thought my bosses were trying to drive me crazy. The psychiatrist wrote me an open-ended excuse, saying I shouldn't return to work until my grievance was resolved.

It didn't end there. There were times when it seemed it would never end. In fact, arbitration for my case was originally scheduled for September 14, 2001—three days after 9/11, when no planes were flying, grounding the corporate lawyers in Chicago. That fall, while my colleagues were covering the biggest story in my lifetime as a journalist, I was being sent to a company psychologist and administered various tests, to see if I was goldbricking. Ultimately even the company's own hired gun agreed that I was in genuine distress, and he didn't think I should come to work either. It's still not clear to me if he thought the company was at risk from me, or I was at risk from the company.

Two weeks after that consultation, with the rescheduled arbitration only a few days away, my employer and I reached what I am still obligated to call a confidential agreement. I am, however, allowed to note that I bought a new car the next week, and a new house three months after that. I'm not saying these things are related, mind you, just that this was the timeline. Signed agreement on November 21. Bought a car November 26. Bought a house February 14.

*M*y year of living cantankerously is long behind me. I am a good girl again, with excellent relationships with everyone in my working life. Frankly, being bad was exhausting. And debilitating. Whenever I look back on that time, I see those little shards of teeth in my hand, remember how H backed away from me in revulsion. And whenever I try to tell the story, I find that few objective listeners believe me. "How could they be mad at you?" they ask. "Why wouldn't they be thrilled to have a novelist on the staff?" Again, I'll never know, but I can say this much: When another colleague, one in better favor, sought to take a book leave, the top editor told him that he knew that no one could work at a newspaper full-time and write a book because—oh, Rosebud moment!—he had tried it and failed.

At the *Sun* it was traditional for departing employees to have a celebratory cake. Knowing that no one would give me a cake, I bought my own and brought it to my coworkers on my penultimate day of work. It was a simple white cake with strawberry icing, not one with a good-bye slogan and elaborate roses.

H came over and took my hands in his. "Laura," he said, in his lovely deep voice, "I have to ask you to leave the premises. According to the lawyers."

"You'll have to remove me physically," I said. "I haven't signed the agreement yet and, in my opinion, I'm entitled to be here and take my possessions." He backed away, and I packed up my desk, then had a slice of cake with my friends.

Plan D

KIM ADDONIZIO

*I*t was the last frenetic night of the big conference, and a few hundred people who weren't too old or too hungover had gathered to party down one last time in the hotel ballroom. Under the requisite mirror ball, most of the attendees stood around while a few wild souls gyrated to oldies from the sixties. The DJ kept exhorting the crowd with comments like, "You cats know how to rock and roll, don't you?" It could have been a conference of urologists or ghost hunters or nanoscientists, but it happened to be a conference of writers, many of whom were overmedicated professors released from their small-town colleges for a few days of intensified drinking, schmoozing, and airing of professional resentments.

I was wandering the ballroom, stoned out of my mind, bothered by a left eye that was watering profusely from an accidental squirt of champagne earlier—apparently, the yeast in champagne is the irritant—and I'd had too much Scotch besides. The pot and alcohol were courtesy of my friend Jeff, whom I was now looking for. I was at that pleasant, slightly hysterical stage of being moderately fucked up, where the most appealing course of action is to get quickly to the next stage, that of near-obliteration.

Jeff had been an aspiring professor but was now the personal assistant to a famous woman writer; he mostly interacted with the assistants of other famous writers. When Oprah called, her people talked to Jeff. It was a lucrative gig, so Jeff could afford the best when it came to intoxicants. I thought of Jeff as my supplier; every time I walked out of a panel (Strategies for Reaching Underserved Communities in the Creative Writing Classroom) or reading (Tribute to a Newly Dead Writer We Didn't Pay Much Attention to Until Now) or hospitality-suite party (Free Booze for Important People and Attractive Female Grad Students), he would be there to catch my eye and say, grinning, "Wanna go to my room and get high?" No doubt he hoped to get lucky, but all that happened was that we'd smoke his hallucinatory pot from his blue metal pipe and drink copiously from the several bottles lined up on his hotel dresser-cum-wet-bar, and gossip about other writers' love lives and who was publishing where, and then we would fall awkwardly silent until I staggered up from one of the matching orange chairs and reeled back out to the next scheduled event.

But now I'd lost Jeff, so it was time for Plan B: Find someone in the ballroom I recognized who could buy me a watered-down drink at the cash bar near the dancers. I caught sight of an associate professor named Lori, resplendent in a one-piece skintight tiger suit—she was one of the few women here with any real style—but she was busy grinding her pelvis to "Louie Louie" in the direction of a much younger man. Good for Lori. I took another survey of the dance floor, dropped plan B, and headed for the hotel bar upstairs, hoping Jeff was there. On to Plan C: Find

Jeff and get more pot and alcohol. Plan D was to hit up a stranger
at the bar. I was counting on Plan C or D to work. I find it's important to have a plan, to keep some sense of control, some belief
that even if there's no order to the universe, even if it's all chaos
and darkness, you can navigate your way through it with some
existential dignity. At this time of night I figured there would
be plenty of drunk men to choose from, and I had on my tight
black jeans, high-heeled combat boots, and tight Betty Boop
T-shirt. In other words, they were fish in a barrel. I was pretty
sure I wouldn't need Plan E. Plan E was to go back to my room,
throw myself on my orange bedspread, and weep uncontrollably
for my own sorrows.

The hotel bar turned out to be jammed; there were so many
conversations filling up the room I couldn't even hear the light
rock station that was usually playing. This was where all the hungover writers had sensibly repaired to after the evening's reading
and reception. I spotted the back of Jeff's head. Oddly, he had on
a different shirt, and he seemed to have let his hair grow out a bit
in the hour or so since I'd seen him last. Still, I strode right up and
punched him on the shoulder.

Okay, so he wasn't Jeff. The man who turned around had
bright green eyes, or maybe they were blue. The main thing, the
important thing, was that he was dreamily attractive, and clearly
as happily surprised to see me as I was to see him. Neither of us
could believe our luck. I explained about Jeff as I glanced around
the room, making sure he really wasn't there to bother me, while
my new friend ordered me a vodka cranberry. In about ten minutes we had progressed from flirtatious conversation to kissing,
while the men to our right muttered drunkenly to each other
about the luck of other guys. "How come this never happens to
Cookie?" one of them said. His friend had been calling him John,
so maybe Cookie was what he had named his dick. I could have

told him why it never happened to Cookie—he was holding forth on safe sex, dropping witticisms like "rubbers are for tires"—but I was busy exploring the inside of my new friend's mouth with my tongue. His name was Ken; it was stitched in red on his jumpsuit. He'd just gotten off work, which involved installing refrigeration units or something equally, blessedly foreign to literary life, and he had come to visit his sister, who tended bar here. Seeing how wasted I was, she began serving me straight cranberry juice—not that I noticed. Ken mentioned it after I came back from a fourth trip to the bathroom off the lobby.

When the bar closed I led Ken up to the eleventh floor, where I was sharing a room with my friend Diane, another writer. She'd known me long enough to have forgiven me for more than one similar transgression. I hoped she was in a forgiving mood again. I cracked open the door; the room was dark.

"Diane," I whispered. "I brought a man home. Do you hate me for it?"

From out of the darkness came her benediction: "No, Kim," she said. "I love you for it."

It didn't occur to me until later that this comment might be ironic.

We tried to be quiet. But gradually, as things got under way, Ken and I got louder. We laughed while he tried to get my boots unlaced in the dark and unpeel my jeans. We laughed when I knocked over a glass on the night table—the drink I'd brought with me from the bar. When his roving hands discovered my pierced navel he said, "I've never met anybody with an earring in her belly button." More laughter.

In the next bed Diane turned over and sighed. Another turn, another sigh. Each was a long exhalation that might mean she was turned on, or that she had had enough of my slutty ways and would never speak to me, let alone room with me, again. It was impossible to tell, and it wasn't the time to do a check-in with our feelings. I was too busy feeling Ken's tongue move to where his hands had been.

We stayed up until almost dawn, and then he left without either of us exchanging cards—something I'd been doing with complete strangers for the past three days. Not that Ken would have *had* a card, but I could have given him mine, and maybe asked for his phone number. I could have called him up and asked whether he thought the universe was essentially random, or possibly invisibly organized according to some divine plan, and he could have responded with an appropriately hopeful metaphor from the world of refrigeration; I was casting him in the role that Robert De Niro played in the movie *Brazil*. But it was more like the movie *Last Tango in Paris*, or the beginning of it anyway, before the Marlon Brando character falls in love with the young French girl and becomes needy and pathetic and wants to know all about her. Ken and I had an understanding. We came, we stripped, we conquered loneliness for a few hours. That was it. He put his tongue down my throat one last time, and then we parted.

The alarm woke me a couple of hours later. I had to catch the hotel shuttle to the airport. My friend Diane—possibly now my former friend—had already left for her flight. She probably hated me for keeping her up all night, and for whatever other horrible crime I had committed and forgotten; there seemed to be a few gaps in my memory. My head hurt so much I could barely move. I couldn't remember, for example, whether Ken and I had actually fucked, or if we'd just fooled around. I looked for a shriveled condom or a torn-open foil square: nothing. I had to pack and get on a plane, and I was going to puke any minute. I hate that feeling. I stuffed everything into my suitcase and duffel and made it downstairs in time for the airport shuttle. I kept my sunglasses on and hoped I wouldn't throw up on my fellow writers, who appeared not to notice that I could barely sit up. They were talking about their programs. Their programs, their students, their teaching loads, their hoped-for sabbaticals, their publications, their grant and fellowship applications, their literary journals, their lives that apparently, at least at this moment, did not involve wild nights with refrigeration installers.

On the plane at last, I kept my sunglasses on and found a free row of seats where I could lie down. I vowed never to drink again, if I could only make it home without throwing up. I have a horror of throwing up, even when it is the thing that will probably make me feel better; keeping down whatever is making me queasy means that I'm in control. I vowed never to pick up another man in a bar, ever, even if I didn't keep my first vow and found myself in a bar, stoned and drunk with one eye watering from champagne. And if I did end up with somebody, I was going to carry a concealed tape recorder, and play everything back later so I would know for sure whether I had actually compromised myself.

I do remember a few things. Ken told me he'd been left by a woman a couple of weeks before. He had come to the bar depressed, thinking about her; the idea of ever being with another woman was inconceivable. He was suffused with her, her, her. Her name was Kristi, with an *i*—he spelled it twice to make sure I got it, while he was fumbling in the dark with the hooks on my leopard bra. In the plane I could still feel his hands sliding down my back and smell the sweat I'd licked from his armpits. I was traveling away from him, Ken Somebody, at hundreds of miles an hour. I was sick and sour breathed, and in the white of my left eye a red blotch had appeared and was spreading like some miniature crimson star being violently born. I was a writer who would never be a tenured professor—a throwback writer, the kind who came to conferences and drank too much and committed inappropriate acts with inappropriate people instead of chatting up somebody who might help my career. What career? I couldn't really connect that word to what I wanted.

I curled under a couple of thin airline blankets, taking deep, shuddering breaths. I thought about how stupid writers' conferences were and how I never wanted to go to another one. I thought about poems I wanted to write, and about Ken and his girlfriend, Kristi, and about how long it had been since I'd been with a certain man who had drained the shot glass of my heart, slammed it on the bar, and walked away. Hurtling over towns and cities and bedrooms far below, I remembered that just before Ken had left me, he had called me an angel, and I realized then that for him, at least, I was.

Skipping Christmas

Postcards from the Underworld

SUSAN CASEY

*G*od, I hate Christmas.

I don't mean that in a Grinch-like way. Bring on the happy people, joy to the world, larger meaning of the day, all that. And there's nothing wrong with a few presents. But that's not the way things go. It's a mess, this holiday. It's a nation of overextended, overwrought people working on a fast five pounds and a credit card hangover. It's a forced march to the mall to find the perfect gift for all twenty-six people on your shopping list. (In return you'll get twenty-six things you don't want.) It's price gouging and Eastern Bloc lineups and the annual high point on the suicide bell curve. Relaxing break from the rest of the year? Spirit of love and peace? As if. Take stress, guilt, depression, social awkwardness, and bankruptcy, toss in prolonged exposure to relatives, and the pressure will crush your lungs.

If you think about it, so many yuletide conventions are ill advised: Let's everybody hit the airport at exactly the same time. Drink heavily with the boss. Kill twenty million trees. Over time I've come to dread the entire month of December. Especially last year—the holidays that loomed ahead had promised to be extra-unbearable. There were family dustups and excess stress, tight deadlines and a misbehaving boyfriend. Plus, since I live in Manhattan, the land of many outstretched hands, I am required to purchase small envelopes, stuff them with cash, and distribute them to everyone from the substitute night doorman at my apartment building, to the woman who shapes my eyebrows. I did the math and realized that I had fifty-seven people to pay off. Christmas was making me very, very cranky.

And then the idea occurred to me: Why not just skip it?

"There's a machete under the driver's seat," Kevin said, gesturing toward the floor of his Toyota 4-Runner. "And I've got an extra spear for you." We were in his driveway in Monterey, California, loading gear and preparing to drive clear down the spine of Baja. Kevin was a marine biologist and a close friend; when he'd mentioned that he and another biologist, Will, planned to take a three-week trip over Mexican back roads, camping, surfing, and spearfishing on the way, I'd immediately invited myself along. Not that I had ever speared anything, but going with them meant I'd be out of the country for the entire holiday season, and then some. There would be good tequila down there, and more of my favorite things: ocean, desert, wild animals, roadside tacos, a distinct lack of rules.

Once I got past my mother's frosty silence, no one else had really seemed to care that I was skipping Christmas. In fact most people were jealous and wished they, too, were running out on the madhouse that has sprung, mutant-like, out of what was probably once a significant spiritual event. This year I would be looking for personal meaning in a place that actually might deliver it. I had sent the presents early, rsvp'd "Sorry!" to all festivities, packed my bags, and flown to the West Coast in mid-December, a good week before the airports began to resemble mosh pits. By December 20, when the serious holiday panic began, we'd be safely across the Mexican border.

I was crashing a trip designed for men by men, and I was very pleased about that. Being female is a fine thing (for three weeks of the month, anyway), but that Y chromosome is a big advantage when it comes to travel. Let's face it, a small blond camping on her own does not exactly have an all-access pass to rural Latin America. And I knew that these two would be ideal companions as they were laid back and funny but seriously competent at the same time. Will spoke fluent Spanish; Kevin could fix anything. Both skills were likely to be required where we were going. Travel guidebooks had warned of danger, urging extra insurance and emergency medications. By their accounts Baja would be filled with extreme conditions; with spiny, thorny, poisonous things; with ruthless *banditos* and corrupt *federales* and nights like bottomless pits, with the likelihood of breakdowns in places so remote that if you were not prepared you might get stuck there permanently, your bones bleaching slowly to dust.

I explained this to friends, most of whom responded by saying: "You're going camping with two guys? For a *month*?" And then, in a lower voice: "Where will you sleep? Will you all, like, be sharing a tent?"

"I wish."

But no, I told them, I'd be sleeping in the back of the truck. (If my boyfriend, who had recently become my ex-boyfriend for the third or fourth time, got another impression from my travel plans, that was fine.)

Certainly life in the 4-Runner would be cozy. Kevin had packed a vast array of spare parts and repair gear. He'd built a rack that would hold three extra ten-gallon gas cans to go along with the fan belts, toolboxes, drill bits, bungee cords, air compressor, and duct tape. We loaded all of it into the back, arranging and rearranging the space to cram in even more emergency supplies. I didn't see what could possibly be missing, but Kevin fretted about the absence of a spare CV joint, whatever that was. As I had never heard of the thing, it was hard to imagine an urgent need for one, and I talked him out of a fifth trip to the auto supply store. By the time we finally hit the road, the truck looked decidedly Joad-like.

We stopped to provision in San Diego. As the three of us hit the grocery store, Will mentioned that we needed to stock up on cheese, to use as graft for bribe-seeking Mexican policemen. They tended to target people driving with surfboards, he said, pulling them over and demanding a "donation." Donations were expected to be about sixty dollars, but friends had passed this tip along: There were other things they'd go for.

"Cheese?" I said. "They want *cheese?*"

"Yeah," Will replied. "Apparently they really love Monterey Jack." He tossed about ten pounds of it into the cart.

Though we had a cooler, most of our supplies were dry goods. The real plan was to hunt for food. We would live off the ocean. Thus the spears. Kevin's was the most impressive: it was a Palau gun, handmade from a single piece of teak, and it even had a trigger. "Yep, it's pretty lethal," he said cheerfully when I asked whether the speargun worked as beautifully as it looked. Will's spear was imported from Australia and had a fancy six-pronged barb on the end. I had been given a Hawaiian sling, a long pole with a loop of surgical tubing on one end and a sharp tip on the other. It was the spear equivalent of training wheels. Nonetheless I was proud of my weapon. Running around the desert with spears and machetes beat the hell out of sitting in my parents' living room in Toronto, watching the cats pull ornaments off the Christmas tree.

Tijuana passed in a blur of color; signs touting cut-rate prescription drugs, street vendors hawking sombreros, garish piñatas, cheap guitars, all manner of trinkety junk. We continued south. *No Maltrate Los Señales* (Don't Mistreat Signs) read a highway sign that was riddled with bullet holes. It was widely reported in the guidebooks that Highway 1, Baja's main (and more or less *only*) artery, was a highlight reel of potential automotive trouble, a puncture carpet of tire-jabbing rocks with large sections of pavement simply missing. Happily it turned out to be in decent shape, with asphalt pretty much where you'd expect it and only the occasional gaping pothole. Highway 1 wasn't the widest road in the world, however, and there was no shoulder. Two vehicles could barely fit side by side, so if an eighteen-wheeler came up against an extrawide pickup jammed full of chickens and donkeys, things got interesting.

Will was itching to reach a place about halfway down the peninsula that I (having been sworn to secrecy as to its actual name) will refer to as Las X. He'd camped there years before and had been dreaming about it ever since, describing it as a kind of "feral Shangri-La." Getting to Las X would require some dicey four-wheeling, but once we were there, Will said, we would never want to leave. It sounded alluring: The Sea of Cortez inches from the tent, pristine wildlife, deluxe fishing, and, on our arrival, a local population of three.

Puerto San Isidro consisted of a single dusty road, and we drove down it at dusk, past a lavender trailer twinkling with

Christmas lights and a rickety house sporting a sign that said "Donations Accepted." A thin dog lay out front, looking hopeful. Despite the guidebooks' warnings, it was clear that this was a safe place. Out here, one hundred miles south of Ensenada, there was nothing but scrub desert, sand dunes, and the endless Pacific. We set up camp on a bluff.

Now we were truly off the grid, it seemed, and so I was surprised to see a strong signal pop up on my cell phone. I decided to call my family. My parents would be home, I thought as the phone rang, and maybe even a brother or two. My mother answered.

"Mom, hi! It's me!" And I was off and running, pouring out descriptions of the trip, the wonders of Baja, the people—I loved the people—the tamale lady at the side of the road, carefully pouring hot sauce into a baggie; the gap-toothed smile of the man who sold dates; the general friendliness that seemed to run like bedrock through this place. Even the stray dogs were nice, I told her.

"Good for you, Susan." Her voice had a clipped tone that I recognized: She was pissed off.

"What's wrong?"

There was a pause, and then it all came out: "You've always run and hidden from this family," she said. "And to me family is sacred. We're our own little tribe and you have to be loyal to that no matter what. You can't pick and choose when you're going to be a part of it."

This was a bit of a sucker punch, but it wasn't the first time I'd heard the complaint. December 25 mattered to my mother in a way that I didn't understand. She did not share my delight at having cut out on the whole deal, turning my allegiance to the tribe of Kevin, Will, and me. The thing about family obligations, she was saying, is that you're, well, *obligated*. Be a conscientious objector to Christmas materialism, fine, but only if the form of your protest does not involve nonparticipation. Good daughters did not bolt for rural Mexico at the height of obligation season. There wasn't much I could say to this, so I said good-bye and then stood for a time, looking up at the dizzying beauty of the stars. They were packed into every square inch of the sky.

In the morning we looked down and saw a sparkling bay wrapped by a wide span of beach, capped by a rocky point that the guys liked for its spearfishing potential. We headed there, four-wheeling over the dunes. Our intentions were simple: Hang out for part of the day, then make a push for Las X. But fate had other plans.

"I knew I should have brought an extra CV joint," Kevin said, sliding out from under the truck, wiping engine oil from his hands onto his pants. For two hours we'd been trying to make it up a steep dune, but the four-wheel drive had seized up and we kept sliding backward, miring ourselves deeper into the sand. (As it happens, a CV joint is what powers the four-wheel drive, and yes, having a spare one on hand would've been swell. Oops.) We would have to turn around and drive back to Ensenada for repairs, or we could kiss Las X good-bye.

Luckily Baja is a kind of fix-it mecca. It has to be. In a place this desolate, largely devoid of services, AAA, working gas pumps, or pretty much anything but the school of hard knocks, a function-ing vehicle is a lifeline. Everywhere we'd see the sketchiest con-veyances doing advanced things: a rusted-out Datsun beetling up a sixty-degree incline of scree, for instance, or a decrepit school bus plowing through thick sand. Given a coat hanger and a piece of duct tape, these folks could make anything run. That was the good news. The bad news was that our CV joint was a foreign model, and tomorrow was Christmas Eve, not a day traditionally devoted to major truck surgery. We wondered if anything would be open.

 nsenada is Baja's third-largest city, with a population of about 250,000 and a high per capita ratio of auto repair stores. And yes, they were open. But no, they didn't have the part we needed. Things were looking bleak until Will began speaking Spanish with a group of men gathered at a taco stand. If we were game for driving into one of the city's more dangerous neighborhoods, they told him, there was a guy who maybe knew a guy who had an uncle who might have the CV joint we were looking for. They gave us directions.

The repair shop was a vivid turquoise adobe, its front wall devoted to a painting of a great white shark (*tiburón*, in Spanish) holding a CV joint in its jaws. It sat on a dusty cul-de-sac in a bustling barrio of ramshackle houses and colorful bodegas with Tecate signs hanging above their doorways and steel bars lacing their windows. Señor Tiburón himself was not the least bit predatory; he was a rotund, grandfatherly man with a white mustache, and as he came out to greet us, he struck me as a fine substitute for Santa Claus. Will described our situation, and he began to nod his head vigorously, pointing to a garage filled with sparkling auto parts. He set to work on the truck; Kevin and Will assisted.

Behind the repair dock lived an odd assortment of animals. There was an enormous white hen, two huge rabbits with calico spots, an anvil-headed German shepherd, and several miswired roosters crowing at random intervals. A pair of fighting cocks with twitchy faces and rattlesnake eyes looked out of wire cages. They were disconcerting, those killer chickens and giant bunnies, so I went around to the front of the shop and sat on the curb.

Almost instantly a posse of children appeared. The tallest boy, who appeared to be the group's leader, was holding a puppy that was the exact dirt color of the street. The dog was wrinkled and somewhat hairless, and it resembled a tiny old man, albeit one with very pointy ears. The boy crouched down beside me, a look of confused curiosity on his face. "Are you spending Christmas here in Ensenada?" he asked in Spanish. By now most of the neighbors had come out of their homes and they stood in the road, staring.

Lo siento, no, I said, and this turned out to be true. Three hours later, with fresh hopes and all four wheels at our disposal, we drove south again to a spot called Punta Baja, where we camped in a wind-blasted patch of dirt and weeds. It was a cold gem of a night, with the ocean thundering softly in the distance. Will fired up the stove to make tequila toddies, and we toasted not spending Christmas Eve in any kind of domesticated way. Kevin raised his glass to an enormous full moon: "Look," he said. "Maybe Jesus was a Druid!"

Perhaps it seems disrespectful to be hoisting a tumbler of tequila to Jesus, but how can anybody really be sure that a church is more sacred than a Mexican cowfield? How can any religious artifact be more miraculous than the emerald-colored hummingbirds we'd seen that morning, zipping around a flowering cactus? Joy doesn't come in one-size-fits-all (even if it's presented in a Bergdorf's box). It comes from whatever flips the switch in a person's heart. I can't think of a better Christmas present than this: Everyone gets to decide for themselves what is holy.

The truck's shock absorber fell out just south of Punta Baja. We'd been scouting for surf breaks, driving slowly along a dirt path by the ocean, when a rattling noise began. And so we spent Christmas morning parked in a deserted seaside town while Will sorted through tools and Kevin snapped on surgical gloves and slid under the truck once again, improvising a repair from a rubber flip-flop and a piece of radiator hose he found lying on the ground. I stood off to the side, looking around. The village had a tattered, ghostly air, and the wind blew through it as though it wasn't even there. It consisted of more than a dozen rough-built houses, some trailers, numerous fishing boats on blocks, and even an outboard motor or two, but it was completely abandoned, not a soul in the joint.

It's unsettling to come across the dwellings of others but find them vanished, and I walked to the edge of a bluff as though I expected to see the town's residents gathered on the beach below for holiday pancakes. Instead I ended up finding a shrine. It was a lonely little thing: breadbox-size, casket-shaped, and made of cement. Someone had gone to quite a bit of trouble to put it there. Inside sat a cracked statue of the Virgin of Guadalupe, Mexico's most beloved saint. I've always had a soft spot for this icon, and she must have taken a liking to me as well, because I looked past her and saw the perfect surf break, long rolling overheads in the jade green Pacific.

Though it wasn't the first time we'd found waves, these were the most appealing ones I'd seen. Other breaks had looked scary, with ripping undertows, sudden closeouts, or shallow rocks nearby. They smelled of facial lacerations. These Christmas waves were long and round, and they broke over a sandy bottom. We stayed in the water for three hours.

Afterward, we drank holiday Tecates while our wet suits hung drying on the side of the truck. Opening the tailgate, Kevin pulled out his duffel bag. "For Christmas I'm going to break out a new pair of pants," he said. I looked down at my own pants. They were filthy with fish blood, red wine, chocolate, sand, dirt, dead animals, charcoal, toothpaste, and campfire smoke—and far more interesting that way.

I called my family to say Merry Christmas, but no one answered the phone.

At the rate we were going, it seemed as though we'd never reach Las X. Meanwhile we'd passed several checkpoints manned by weapon-toting *federales*, but there had been no shakedowns, no sly handoffs of Monterey Jack. The ice in the cooler had long since melted, and the bricks of cheese had begun to fill the truck with the stench of sour milk and moldy gym socks. Neither Kevin nor Will would agree to throw it out, though, arguing that "smelly" cheese was the most expensive type at fine food stores.

Two days and one flat tire later, we made it—and Las X did not disappoint. The last twenty miles to our campsite wound through a landscape unlike any other. Here the Sea of Cortez met the Sonoran Desert, two worlds hard against each other with their edges exposed. The palette was complex: sienna earth and baked-sage ocotillo, granite boulders casting steely purple shadows, clouds the color of mercury, and rugged foothills that went from violet to rust with the light. The water unfurled before us, a flat slate of navy.

There was something about Las X that you noticed immediately: The place was littered with dead things. Coyote skeletons lay next to dolphin and pelican skulls; femurs shared the sand with rib cages and vertebrates and the brittle filigree of wings.

"What's with all the bones?" I asked.

"It's harsh here," Will said. "That's what makes it so beautiful."

Baja has never been easy. Sixty million years ago, give or take a few eons, the peninsula was sheared from the Mexican mainland by volcanic eruptions and the violent collisions of tectonic plates. (The San Andreas fault bisects the Sea of Cortez.) Its first human

inhabitants were primitive tribes that enjoyed polygamy, hallucinogenic plants, and the odd human sacrifice. The Spanish colo-
nialists and Jesuit missionaries who arrived in the seventeenth
century considered wild Baja to be desperately in need of a taming, and they built a string of missions for the task. They came to
save souls but ended up taking them instead, introducing small-
pox, plague, typhus, and other diseases that wiped out most of
the native population. Hurricanes, fierce rains, earthquakes, and
other weather extremes erased the rest. Any living thing that had
managed to live here now had thrived against the odds.

All around us there were plants I'd never heard of; boojums, for
one, towering green stilts twisted into Seussian shapes; and the
giant cardon, a cactus on steroids. There were animals with
charmingly odd names like the Baja pocket gopher, the spotted
skunk, and the white-tailed antelope ground squirrel. In a single
day we'd seen ospreys building stick fortresses and egrets mating
in the mangroves, dive-bombing pelicans, and ibises stabbing the
sand with their long beaks, various herons looking statuesque,
and black gulls hunting with a gimlet eye. Coyotes tiptoed around
the camp. As he crawled into his sleeping bag that first night, Will
had encountered a golden scorpion with an angry, jabbing tail.
And that was before you looked into the water, into the parallel
universe that lived beneath the surface of the Sea of Cortez.

Spearfishing 101A had consisted of a few terse instructions:
"Just sit on the bottom. Fish are curious; they'll come up to you,"
Kevin said. "And then you plug them." I stood knee deep in the
ocean holding my spear, as he and Will adjusted their snorkels
and prepared to swim off.

The bay was ideal—a reasonably shallow reef next to a rocky
point full of the kinds of ledges and crevices that fish love. We

had hiked three miles to get here, and if we didn't want to eat granola bars for dinner that night, someone was going to have to catch something.

Taking a deep breath, I pulled down my mask and dove into a rainbow of creatures: sea anemones with willowy arms, amber and black angelfish with elegant fins. Fleets of striped coronet fish darted above scarlet starfish and leopard rays. Larger shapes moved in the shadows below.

I knew that the ornamental fish, the beauties that make any reef seem like a giant aquarium, weren't for eating. And they seemed to know it, too, not even flinching from the spear. The eating fish were bigger, cagier, and far less flashy. They lived in deeper waters, zipping away at the slightest movement. I shot my spear in their direction a few times, but it was clearly a mismatch. Shifting strategy, I swam to the point. Snappers darted in and out of nooks and crannies; anxious faces peered up from holes. As usual the larger contestants were lurking near the bottom. My Hawaiian sling bounced off the rocks, got stuck in the sand. The sport was a lot harder than it looked.

I was becoming frustrated when suddenly, a good-size balloon-shaped fish swam up and hovered in front of me, oblivious to the weapon. I pulled the rubber tubing back like a slingshot and let go. The spear made a satisfying *whunking* sound as it hit, and the fish's face registered a distinct look of surprise and irritation. It wriggled on the end of the spear as I swam toward Will, who was treading water nearby. It occurred to me that the catch had been a little too easy.

I pushed my fish forward. "Is this bad?"

He laughed but looked distressed. "That's a *boxfish*." A slow, friendly reef dweller. Not an ornamental, exactly, but hardly a candidate for the grill. He grabbed the fish and pulled it off the spear. Amazingly it shot away, quite alive.

"Don't worry," he said. "I couldn't eat my first fish either."

Kevin swam by with a triggerfish in his dive bag. Triggers are gray, plate-size animals with miniature buckteeth, leathery skin, and what looks like a horn sticking out of their heads. Though you'd never know it by looking at them, they taste delicious. Will had a bagful of clams, and the two of them headed farther out on the reef to search for lobsters. Not wanting to be the only one who failed to provide, I swam back to shore. I had an idea.

Pulling off my mask and fins, I made my way across the rocks to Kevin's pack. Lunch was in there, and it included several slabs of very smelly cheese. I popped one into my dive bag and swam back out.

Okay, maybe it wasn't the most sporting thing in the world, baiting the reef with tainted Monterey Jack. But I wanted to see what would happen. And I didn't expect to catch anything, anyway. If the bigger fish sidled in for the score, at least I'd get a better look at them.

Suddenly, every creature wanted to hang out with me. There were snappers and damsels and jacks and even a curmudgeonly scorpionfish, all newly friendly. Hooking the spear to my weight belt, I crumbled the cheese between my fingers and sprinkled it around. I was very popular now. Even the flounders came closer.

"It is tempting to try to live without an underworld, without soul, and without concern for the mysterious elements that touch on the spiritual and the religious," wrote the famed biologist E. O. Wilson. Las X, it seemed, was the antidote to what Wilson was warning about—the danger of life becoming ordinary. This was an underworld, all right. If the point of Christmas was to encounter those "mysterious elements," I felt I had a far better chance of doing it here. Back home, America was wrapped up in the postholiday sales: DVD players for $49.99! Half-price tinsel!

(Buy now to get a jump on next year's festivities.) Here in the desert there was nothing to shop for and no preconceptions about what "good" girls did or didn't do. Quite simply, Las X defied me to take my wild side—a big chunk of my soul—for granted. Yes, my family mattered. But so did this.

$\mathcal{A}$head in Baja were sublime things I didn't know about yet: a very personal encounter with an octopus, for instance, and a haunted city with a turquoise river running through its center. A hitchhiker. Cave paintings. A French bakery in an ancient colonial square. Severed shark heads strewn across the sand, hundreds of them. But even before I came upon these things, there was this moment. I cruised around with my cheese while the snappers glimmered and a spotted pufferfish appeared like a visitation, fins fluttering as sunlight filtered down through gathering thunderheads and illuminated the reef. Everything was peaceful. Everything was moving. And if you'd asked me what would have made me happier than this, I couldn't have told you.

Independence Day

KATE MOSES

*S*hould I wear the elephant belt buckle, or the donkey?" my mother asked me. She was standing in front of the mirrored doors to her closet, holding first one and then the other red-white-and-blue belt to her waist.

"Suit yourself," I said from where I sat on her bed, turning the pages of my book.

"You are just no fun anymore." She pouted. I glanced up, shooting her an incredulous look. But she didn't see me: She was studying her own face in the mirror, scraping a smear of lipstick off one tooth.

It was 1976, the year of America's Bicentennial, and liberty, that summer, was thick in the air and in the stores of the single shopping mall in Anchorage, Alaska. My parents had moved us to Alaska a couple of years before, the last teeth-gritted upheaval in a death march of domestic relocations, all hopeless attempts to save their disastrous marriage. Anchorage—it even sounded solid, a place where a family at sea could reach safe harbor, then go straight into dry dock and have all their barnacled misery scraped off before the leaky vessel broke up on the shoals and sank under its own splintered weight.

But like I said, it was 1976, and it was the Fourth of July, and it wasn't safety but liberty that smelled like the bright red polish my mother used to paint her toenails before she put on her strappy new sandals. She was thirty-six, she had been married for nearly seventeen grim, disappointed years, and she was giddy with the thought of having not just two weeks free of the open animosity between herself and my father, but also an invitation to the German Club picnic: a weekend party with people who felt no shame for their appreciation of imported beer. She was getting dolled up, ripping off sales tags, deciding between politicocommercialized belt buckles to wear with her new denim miniskirt, lacing the gathers of her dirndl blouse to show off her delicate collarbones and her small breasts. "All you need is enough to fill a champagne glass," she said, cupping her boobs through the white eyelet; she had repeated this bit of maternal wisdom so often you'd think I'd have become immune to the embarrassment it caused me, but I had not.

I did not want to go to the German Club picnic. I did not want to watch drunken, red-faced fathers hand lit sparklers to their small children. I was fourteen, and I wanted to stay home reading in my bedroom with the door closed, if not locked. I was not even sure I wanted to be with my mom.

Where was my father? He was (conveniently, my mother would have said) thousands of miles away, with my two brothers. Though it often seemed that my mother kept me briefed on every detail of my parents' life—however miserable, sordid, or private—

apparently there were still occasional negotiations between my mom and dad that she conducted without my intervention as her confidante and coconspirator, and the decision that my father would take my brothers on vacation to Hawaii, leaving me at home alone with her, was one of them.

For much of my life I would have relished having my glamorous, free-spirited mother to myself, and come to think of it, for most of my life I *had* had my mother mostly to myself, thanks to her truly unhappy conventional marriage, which had turned out nothing like the bohemian adventure she'd fantasized. I was called "Sis," and I became her "little mommy" and her "best friend"—the maternal toddler who would cover her with blankets and dab her brow with a cool cloth when she was sobbing, wretched, and pregnant yet again; the loyal nine-year-old companion who wouldn't tell Daddy that she'd kept me home from school to watch old musicals all afternoon with her; the twelve-year-old who listened and consoled and tried to come up with a plan of escape when she gasped, "I hate him. I hate him! You've got to get me out of this."

Throughout my childhood she mesmerized me with the mementos and stories of her naughty, irrepressible past. She told me she used cuticle scissors to cut hundreds of minute, perfect holes in her mother's favorite slip to make herself a "lace dress" when she was four; in high school she regularly balanced on top of toilet tanks in her saddle shoes so the nuns wouldn't catch her smoking in the lavatory. She and her boy cousins once broke a watermelon—so they could eat it—over an old lady's head on their way to church. Out of her bureau drawers and jewelry boxes she produced black-and-white prom photos and fragile, dessicated corsages and individually wrapped sugar cubes, on which were written—in her perfect, spidery, Catholic-schoolgirl hand—the indelible, capricious details of parties and dances where she had pocketed her discolored treasures and been thrown into pools in her organza formals.

My brothers were not invited into our rituals of female bonding, and they resented me for it; my father, needless to say, rarely figured in my mom's breathless stories, or in the photographs of lanky young men easing their hands about her waist. The one story about my dad that I could picture most vividly was not really about him at all: Panicked at the realization that she was marrying a quiet, serious, immigrant law student she hardly knew, my nineteen-year-old mother begged her mother to call off the wedding, to buy her a plane ticket to Paris, to do *anything* but let her get married the next day. She was standing on a chair while my grandmother, curlers in her hair and pins in her mouth, measured the hem of my mother's going-away dress. "Don't be ridiculous," my grandmother said through clenched teeth. "The caterers are on their way."

A gregarious, seductive renegade—the total opposite of my introverted, frightened, conservative dad—my mother sought out some existing social structure wherever we moved over the years, and in each of my parents' failed, cross-country rearrangements, stuck in the same life she didn't want, she found chameleonlike ways to enlist allies, and to rebel. "Pretend I'm the babysitter," she would instruct my brothers and me after we'd dropped off my dad at an airport or a train station for one of his many business trips; we were small, and we thought it was a game. Her San Francisco–style cocktail parties were notorious in the buttoned-up suburbs of Philadelphia and Washington, DC, in the early seventies—my father, however, couldn't finish a single martini without throwing up. And when we ended up on Alaska's last, traumatic frontier, my mother somehow turned herself into a card-carrying affiliate of the Anchorage German Club, wearing dirndl skirts and sitting on committees planning the next Oktoberfest and trading recipes for moosemeat sauerbraten.

"But we're Irish," my older brother complained.

Only my mother liked the German Club. My dad's opinion hardly mattered—even my brothers and I believed our dad had no friends, and apparently no desire for any: All he did was work. Perhaps the three of us children would have found the German Club more appealing if we had been younger, but we had endured being the new kids at six different schools in four states, and we were now the chronically unhappy teenagers of chronically unhappy parents. There were no other children in the German Club near our age, and we were appalled when our unsuspecting, socially anonymous father was drafted into playing Saint Nicholas at a Christmas party. ("Have Bill do it," I heard my mother urge, "nobody will ever recognize *him*.") We sat, bored almost to the point of stupor, through slide shows of other families' vacations in the Tyrol. In an increasingly rare case of sibling solidarity, together my brothers and I made fun of the anachronistic, oom-pah-pah names of the club members—the Hansels and Gretels and Friedrichs and Liselottes, the children named Wolfie and Brunhilde and Magda and even Adolf (*always* called "Dolfie").

Our mother didn't care: The jovial, fun-loving German Club had taken her in. They called her *Liebchen* or Katarina, not Kathleen. They drank and they smoked and they told bawdy jokes, even when children—narrow-eyed, frowning, teenage children— were in the room. They—well, one of them—slapped her on the bottom when she was passing a bowl of schnitzel around the table, then they—all of them—laughed heartily. Their tears fell into their beer steins as they listened to her play a brutalized rendition of "Edelweiss" on her guitar. After putting up with our whining for a while—we didn't want to sit around in someone's basement rumpus room singing folk songs, or eating caribou bratwurst, or babysitting any more blond children whose favorite storybooks were written in a language we didn't speak—she mostly stopped dragging us to the German Club's events.

Nonetheless I felt a profound discomfort with my mother's adaptation to this Arctic-Teutonic subculture. At twelve, thirteen, fourteen, however, I didn't know why, beyond my petty, specific-to-the-occasion complaints: No, I didn't want to spend a Saturday making strudel; no, I didn't want to see my brothers wearing lederhosen, *ever*. It wasn't even so simple a matter as jealousy over my mother's attention: Yes, the German Club had my mother in its thrall, but that didn't mean her eye was any less fixed on me. In fact, in some ways I was relieved for the distractions of the German Club. My mother was deep into her Bavarian phase when I started my period at thirteen, and that girlhood milestone is most memorable to me because it marks the first time I kept a secret from her. I didn't want to tell her; I knew what she would do. She was, I already knew too well, incapable of discretion. So I kept the news to myself for two years, and she didn't have a clue.

(I might never have told her—I had no intention of telling her—except that in my sophomore year of high school, a mental-case gym instructor began tracking all of our menstrual cycles on a chart in the girls' locker room; she insisted that we bring notes from our mothers to verify when we had our periods. Faced with the humiliating prospect of failing gym, I finally told my mother I'd gotten my period. Her reaction was just as I expected: lots of boo-hooing, hugging, my-baby-is-a-woman, cartoon tears foun-taining. I begged her not to tell my father or my brothers, to keep it "just between us"—a calculated gambit that had its intended appeal, though it engendered more hugs and tears. Then she raced me to the grocery store for "supplies," mascara trails dripping over her money bones from under her sunglasses. To avoid the mortifying public scene, I persuaded her to let me sit in the car while she went inside the store alone. Even so, she outfoxed me: As I sat in the car listening to the Bay City Rollers, she walked out of the market blubbering delicately, blowing her nose—a beatific madonna behind huge Jackie-O shades—and behind her, pushing a shopping cart overflowing with the largest boxes of Kotex known to mankind, was a teenage bag boy. A boy from my high school. A senior.)

No, it wasn't jealousy or a child's sense of exclusive, rivalrous proprietorship that made me feel so threatened by the German Club. Perhaps it was the opposite impulse. It took many years—long after the divorce, long after I and all the rest of my family, one by one, left Alaska for good—that I recognized the perfect storm that had hit us when we got to Anchorage: The rough seas of puberty surged, my parents' marriage rocked in its final, creaking paroxysms, and my mom became a St. Pauli girl. The German Club had appeared just as my young and beautiful mother was lashing for survival, and independence. And so was I.

So. I did not want to go to the German Club picnic. At all. It was a weekend-long affair with the German Club families and couples and hangers-on camping along a stream somewhere in the mosquito-ridden greenery "just outside of Anchorage." I did not want to go, but the idea was never broached that my mother might leave me behind. I *had* to go, or she could not. She pleaded; I resisted. There would be no one my age there, only little kids. There would be nothing, by virtue of her own rules of etiquette, for me to do: "You can't bring a book," she told me. "It would be rude." Finally we struck a deal: We would go, but only for the afternoon. We drove off in our station wagon with nothing but the clothes on our backs—my mother had decided on the donkey belt because it was cuter, not out of any party loyalty—a spray can of Cutter insect repellent, and a German potato salad (lots of vinegar, soggy bacon) in a bowl covered with plastic wrap.

Three hours later (Alaska is a *big* state, my mother flexible with facts when it served her), we parked in a painfully green, grassy meadow at the end of a dirt road. Winnebagos and Airstreams and colorful tents were set up all around the periphery of the meadow, at the edge of the birch forest that surrounded us. You could hear the trickling rush of water from somewhere under the trees. Picnic tables were set with embroidered linen cloths, and there was a beer keg sunk into a garbage can filled with ice, the top of the keg draped with a beach towel to keep it extra cool. My mother was greeted by her lederhosened and dirndled friends, and they immediately herded her away to play cards or accordion or yodel or whatever. I stood by the car.

"Can I set up your tent for you?" Helmut or Hans or Arne asked me.

"No!" I answered over my shoulder, yelling to get my mother's attention. There she was, sliding through the long, neon grass in her slick new sandals, held by the manicured hand, like an enchanted, red-toenailed princess being led into the forest by the green-clad woods folk. "We didn't bring anything," I continued. *"We are only staying for the day!"* I bellowed. My mom nodded weakly, mouthing "Killjoy" at me, and I wandered off.

Sullen and instantaneously bored, I walked toward the trees and over to the stream, bookless, to watch with mild interest what the little children were doing at the water's edge. They had been catching tree frogs and tadpoles, dozens of them, and dumping them into buckets with water and silt. The tadpoles looked like tadpoles anywhere, smoky gray and gelid, and they squirmed away from your fingers when you tried to touch them, burying their blunt heads in the mud while their tails continued to twitch: children hiding their faces in their mothers' skirts. The tree frogs were incredibly tiny, deep dark green and speckled, with sticky rounded toes. The kids were all shoeless and businesslike. They paid no attention to me, deep in the fantasy they were creating around their captives. There was nowhere else to go, so I stood around farther up the stream bank, listening to the seconds pass and picking at birchbark, which came away from the tree trunks in long flexible strips, like paper.

After a while, who knows how long, a huge man staggered over to watch the little kids. He was enormous, broad-shouldered and tall like a giant, like a stereotypical Aryan giant but with long-ish seventies hair and Tom Jones sideburns. My father still had a crew cut. The German giant wavered slightly in place as he contemplated the children and their frogs, his big fist curled around the handle of a pewter beer stein. Even without it I would have known he was drunk. He lurched to the edge of the stream and asked the children if he could see their frogs. One little boy lifted up a plastic measuring cup full to the brim with tadpoles and murky water. The giant took it, looked into it for a moment, then turned his back. Only I could see that he was pouring the contents of the measuring cup back into the stream. From where the children stood, behind him, it looked as if he was pouring the measuring cup into his beer.

The kids were too stunned to cry or shout, all of them imagining the tadpoles tumbling through the foam, flagellating upward through the amber liquid. Then the giant turned back around, facing the kids. He tossed the empty cup, then lifted the stein to his mouth and drank. Two or three of the kids broke into sobs. They all ran to find their mothers, yelling. I watched the giant from where I stood near the trees. He drank down the beer in his stein, then he lumbered away.

I stalked off to find my mother. It was starting to get misty— not rain or fog exactly, just drippy and moist, and cold Alaskan air. My mom was sitting at a table under the awning of one of the Winnebagos playing poker with the men, someone else's sweater draped over her shoulders. A couple of the kids had already beaten me there; they were talking to one of the mothers through the Winnebago's screen door, their tan faces (how was it that they were always tan in summer? this was Alaska!) streaked with tears. My mother was studying her cards. She held a cigarette lightly between her thin, elegant fingers, tapping ashes into a tartan plaid ashtray weighted with sand.

I hissed into her ear, loudly so everyone at the table could hear. "Your drunken friends are drinking live tadpoles in their beer," I lied. "I saw it. There's a giant man torturing the little kids."

The mother at the screen door was talking over my head in German to one of the men at the poker table—Hansel, the president of the club. Hansel responded in German, then turned to my mother next to him. "Andreas," he said, raising his eyebrows meaningfully. "It was just a joke, don't worry," Hansel said, now to me, launching his bleary face into a big smile. "He's a bachelor. He doesn't understand kids. Go back and play now; he won't bother you." He picked up his gaudy ceramic beer stein and poured some of it into my mother's plastic cup. "*Prost!*" he said to her, touching his beer to hers. "*Prost!*" all the poker players responded, raising their dorky ceramic steins and taking swigs of beer.

"Let's *go,*" I breathed to my mother, now more quietly; getting everyone's attention had backfired. She kept playing her hand and smoking. She took sips of her beer, leaving lipstick on the rim of the cup. I kept mumbling and standing ominously behind her camp chair. Finally she whispered back. We would stay through dinner, then leave.

I didn't want their disgusting sausages. I didn't want the potato salad. There was nothing to drink but beer or Hi-C. I was absolutely unaccommodated. I paced in the drizzle, slapping mosquitoes. The barbecue had to be moved indoors, their caribou short ribs and mooseburgers cooked in the kitchen of a recreational vehicle.

Time and the evening dragged on—Alaska, remember, land of the midnight sun. The card game, interrupted while the little kids were fed, had been moved inside Hansel's Winnebago. I sat, furious, my arms crossed, in our station wagon. I watched the other mothers' valiant attempts to light sparklers for their children, and I watched the damp sparklers sizzle out. I read the Ford Torino handbook I found in the glove compartment. The kids had all been put to bed in the tents—despite the fact that it was still daylight—when I gave up twirling the car's radio dial, hunting for a viable station, out of fear that I'd wear down the battery and we would never leave. I waited until the trees started to blacken and the sky turned a bruised shade of blue (was it nine o'clock? ten? eleven?), then I trudged in my soggy shirtsleeves to bang on Hansel's door.

Where were all the other mothers now? My mother sat like a queen among courtiers, the only woman surrounded by bearded men in leather suspenders, the air thick and acrid with cigarette smoke. I couldn't get anywhere near her. They were crowded around the RV's built-in dining nook. Andreas the giant was there, nodding semi-consciously over the poker chips, slamming his stein on the linoleum dinette table with every swig.

"Every party needs a pooper," my mother singsonged when she saw my accusatory face at the door. "That's why we invited you. Party-pooper!"

"*Prost!*" said Hansel, raising his stein.

Hours after I'd figured it out—but was still trying to forestall the truth with a poisonous look from my perch on the shag-carpeted steps of the Winnebago—my mother admitted the bad news: We were staying. She cited the long drive in the dark, that she'd left plenty of food and water for our pets, etcetera, etcetera. We would sleep in the car. We would leave first thing in the morning.

There was nothing for me to do. Even if I made a scene, no one was on my side. Someone offered me a jacket, which I refused. Eventually I got tired of staring my mother down as she played poker, and I went to bed in the back of the station wagon. It adjusted to a nearly flat position, though the surface was hard, corrugated plastic, and all I had to cushion or cover myself was a threadbare chenille bedspread that had been demoted to car blanket after our dog had puppies on it ten years before. It was impossible to get comfortable, and I was explosively angry at my mother.

Somehow I fell asleep. I only knew this to be true because I woke to darkness, and to the ripe scent of soured beer on skin, and to my mother's shrill whisper: "Sssh! Wait a minute—you'll—"

Andreas the drunken giant was in our station wagon with us, my mother in the middle. I pretended to be asleep. My mother kept whispering to him to stop, and he was slurring and cajoling. The blanket kept pulling around, and the voices quieted, replaced with the rhythm of breath and the textured sound of bodies and clothing. It went on endlessly, longer than the entire endless day. I couldn't stand it. It had to end. I grabbed the edge of the blanket and yanked it violently over myself, rolling as far as I could to the edge of the car. There was a sudden drawn-out silence. Then there was the click of the door opening, and the grass-cushioned thump of Andreas's expulsion from the car.

"Sis," my mother whispered to me. "Sis . . ."

I refused to answer.

The next day when I awoke, my mother was already up and out of the station wagon. I was hungry. The German Club mothers were serving breakfast at the picnic tables; I could smell eggs and bacon and pancakes when I opened the car door.

Paper plates were tumbling over the wet grass as I walked across the meadow to breakfast. Hansel's wife served me at the kids' table. All the women were wearing kerchiefs over their hair, even my mother, who was sitting with the men at another table. She was smoking, not eating. She had her sunglasses on. She didn't look in my direction. Hansel, who had been sitting next to her, got up and shambled over to me.

The little kids were fighting over syrup as Hansel made his awkward speech, muttering to me under his breath from the other side of the table. My mother must have asked him to talk to me—Hansel, the president of the German Club, the patriarch, the figure of authority, *oom-pah-pah*. I wanted to roll my eyes, but I kept them fixed on my plate. Hansel muttered something about my parents, about something breaking, something else about the stupid behavior of drunken men. Already my appetite was gone. But whatever happened, Hansel assured me, the one thing I could count on was my mother.

My heart sank. Anything, I thought, staring at my cold eggs, but that. "I'm not hungry," I called over my shoulder at the assembled Anchorage German Club, and even if I had been I wouldn't have admitted it. I stomped back down to the edge of the stream. I was hoping my mother would be sufficiently shamefaced that she'd want to leave soon. Until then I didn't want to talk to anyone, and I especially didn't want to talk to her. I planted myself on the gritty bank, its moist cold seeping up through the seat of my jeans, but I didn't care.

The wreckage of the kids' water games from the day before was still there. There were pie pans filled with silt, wet socks, the spoons they'd used to dig. I saw that after the Sturm und Drang of the tadpole-swallowing giant, they'd gotten back to business: There were more tadpoles and tree frogs in the buckets and pots, arrested overnight in an inch of muddy water. Andreas's pewter stein was there, full of stale beer.

It occurred to me that I, too, was a captive, trapped, at least for the three hours I'd be stuck in the radio-compromised car with my mom, and another week alone in the house until my father and brothers got back to provide their own particularized versions of confused, resentful static. Hansel had been wrong about one thing—in this instance I couldn't count on my mom. I didn't know what she would say to me, how she could possibly explain herself. Whatever it was, I didn't want to hear it. I didn't care about her excuses or her reasons. That in itself—I didn't care, I didn't want to hear *any more*—chilled me far more than the wet stream bank.

There was rustling in the bushes downstream. I looked over, and there was Andreas's colossal back. He was hugging a tree on the bank with one arm. He was pissing in the stream. His beer stein was beside me—he would have to walk right by where I sat to get back to the campsite.

I did it quickly, unthinking—as if I'd been primed for such an action. I knocked the lid back on the stein, and tadpoles poured over my wet hand.

Andreas came crunching through the brush. For a moment I held his bloodshot gaze. There was not so much as a flash of recognition, let alone embarrassment or apology. I picked up his beer stein and held it out to him. "Here," I said.

He took the few steps toward me and reached out for the stein, leaning far down from his giant's height. He jerked his head, I guess in some sort of gesture of appreciation. He cocked the lid with his thumb and drank, still looking at me. I saw them through the glass bottom of the stein: swimming small and unfinished, vulnerable, trapped, as he drank them down.

"*Prost!*" I said.

Everything I Know about Being Bad
I Learned in Hebrew School

ELIZABETH ROSNER

Once upon a time, I believed that a quintessential feature of being Jewish meant that I would be rewarded for asking questions. But somehow things didn't quite work out that way. Instead, I learned that by daring to challenge the modern Orthodox rules of my upbringing, I would be considered a rebel and a troublemaker. Maybe I was born into the wrong tribe, or at least the wrong family, but the 613 commandments that form the foundation of Judaism just about brought me to my knees. And I was supposed to be grateful.

My father's determination to provide me with a full-scale Jewish education alongside my secular one filled me to the point of bursting with regulations and prohibitions. Having outgrown the first few years of Sunday school, I was forced to attend Hebrew school several afternoons a week, in addition to my public school attendance. No amount of protesting, regular and vociferous, could persuade my parents not to send me. I developed weekly stomachaches that occasionally convinced my mother that I was too sick to go, but usually the carpool showed up on time and I was driven off to my doom.

I hated the content of my Jewish education even more than I resented the hours spent in dusty, stifling classrooms among children as bored and restless as I was. I was both perplexed and outraged by the seemingly infinite prescriptions involving my most basic habits. Forbidden food combinations focused with specificity on keeping milk away from meat. In other words no cheeseburgers, no glass of vitamin D with my steak, no butter or white bread for the chicken sandwich. Eventually I appreciated the humane philosophy behind this, the idea of not "drowning a calf in its mother's milk." However, attempting to explain it all to my friends as they headed to McDonald's was no small feat. You've never ever had a cheeseburger? they wanted to know. And what do you drink with your dinner?

This bizarre diet paled in comparison with the list of what not to eat at all: anything deriving from a pig, any type of seafood with a shell, and any animals that had only one stomach and no cloven hooves. There were supposedly rational determinations behind all of this. Often I marveled at the elaborate details of the rules. Grown men sat around and debated these questions? For centuries? Even today?

Although as a girl I had been spared the ordeal of circumcision, it soon became evident that there were numerous *female* body parts to keep covered up. Shoulders, for example, were dangerous, and thighs off limits. For some reason it was my job to ensure that men weren't tempted by my flesh. This was especially critical when it came to being distracted from their devotion to prayer by my provocative displays. No upper arms. No knees. Some ultra-

Orthodox codes even prohibit any glimpses of elbows and ankles. Not to mention hair. The neckline? Forget about it. Cleavage? Are you kidding? These were the days of miniskirts and halter tops, but not in synagogue, God forbid. Not on your life.

Indeed, in synagogue, the situation was dire. Girls and women were seated off to the side, separated from the men by a chest-high wooden barrier, and we were never allowed to read from the Torah scrolls or even to touch them. We were unclean, I was told. Blood. This news came to me just as I was learning about my body, my given female body, and the onset of the monthly event we would sometimes call the Curse. I thought I might go crazy with indignation—to think that I had no choice about my bodily functions, my body parts, and yet according to Jewish custom, I was a walking set of problems? There were ways for me to purify myself after having my period, I was told, by immersing myself in a ritual bath. This was intended as some holy form of consolation.

As for what was not allowed on the Sabbath—the twenty-five hours from sundown Friday night to an hour past sundown on Saturday—the territory was vast beyond belief. No turning things on or off (television, lights, cars, appliances; my sister learned to unscrew the lightbulb inside the refrigerator so that opening and closing its door didn't break the rules). No touching money, no writing, no cutting or tearing. No cooking of any kind. Sentences beginning with "Thou shalt not" went on and on. The lists of exclusions exhausted and mortified me. I kept envisioning my life stretching ahead with huge signs reading NO along every corridor.

My increasingly desperate desire to know *why* did not go over big in Hebrew school, or at home for that matter. Told I ought to defer to the greater wisdom of my elders, and to respect the teachings of the Torah, I began to suspect a giant conspiracy. No matter how kind seeming my teacher (Benjamin Friend, his real name!) or how jolly and warm the smiles and voice of the rabbi, the messages were unmistakable and always the same: Obey the rules. If you study hard and follow the instructions, you will be a Good Jew.

And by the way, boys have one set of rules and girls have another. *Stop asking why.*

I became furious, a raging feminist at the age of nine, long before I ever heard of such a thing as women's rights. *Was* there a women's movement in 1969? I wouldn't have known. The point was that nothing seemed *fair.* Instructions in prayer dealt one of the most painful blows of them all. Boys in my Hebrew school class were instructed to recite the following among their daily morning prayers: "Blessed are you God, ruler of the universe, to whom I give thanks for not making me a woman." I remember sitting at my tight little desk, the kind where the chair was permanently attached, and wanting to scream. *What did they mean?* Girls were instructed to insert the following substitution: "Blessed are you, God, ruler of the universe, to whom I give thanks for making me as I am."

I can recall the shock and damage of those teachings to this very day. To see the smug faces of my male classmates, in contrast to the embarrassment and humiliation of the girls! I could not begin to understand why countless generations of females before me had not only endured this situation but had apparently embraced it. I wanted to cry, to scream, to break things. I wanted to break all the rules I had ever been taught, just to show them how much it *hurt* to be so dismissed, so blatantly relegated to second-class citizenship in the Jewish world. But when I opened my mouth to protest about inequality and injustice, I was told that such "differences" between men and women were part of the Divine Plan. That this was a contract between me and God, that this was how it was all designed, infuriated and depressed me. I did not want to make this kind of deal, but my objections were dismissed everywhere, including in my own house.

I tried denouncing these indignities to my father, desperate to feel heard, at the very least. I threw my Hebrew school notebooks on the ground, swearing I would no longer attend class. My father thundered right back, reminding me that my education was not optional. Girls have their own special roles in Judaism, he insisted, toeing the party line. He went on to lecture me about the other religions, and the ways he considered their treatment of women to be degrading. Not in Judaism, he asserted with pride. Jewish women are honored, treated with such respect and value that they are practically sacred. Think of it as a privilege! my teacher, Mr. Friend, offered. Girls aren't even obligated to recite the daily prayers because they have other things to do, like clothe and feed and care for the family.

Where was my mother in all this? Essentially she remained on the sidelines, practicing her own form of nonviolent resistance. She said she was Jewish "on the inside," and that feelings mattered just as much as behaviors. Your father has his way of being Jewish and I have mine, she said. We don't all have to be the same. Translated into my language, this meant that she got to avoid synagogue, except on the High Holidays. Somehow she had managed to let herself off the hook.

Every Saturday morning, when my father dragged me out of bed to join him and my sister and brother on our walk to synagogue (no driving the car, remember?), my mother went shopping. Through snowdrifts in the endless winters of upstate New York, I trudged along like an indentured servant. My father made us walk through the parking lot of the notoriously anti-Semitic country club, claiming it was a shortcut, the hypotenuse of the triangle. He told us to hold our heads up and stick out our chests. When we got to the synagogue, I had to be sure to remove the pants I'd been allowed to wear for the snow. Pants were not for women, after all. And while my brother sat beside my father and murmured prayers with the men, my sister and I took our places on the side. In the unclean section.

My mother kept a kosher home, complying with my father's preferences. I imagine they must have agreed on this a long time ago, maybe even before they married. But when we ate out at restaurants, she ordered shrimp cocktail and ate it in what looked like a pleased silence. My father looked away in disappointment. I felt myself waiting for my turn to grow up and break rules whenever I was in the mood. A couple of times, feeling defiant and caught by divided loyalties, I told my father I was going to accompany my mother on a shopping trip instead of heading off to pray. It seemed that the walls might collapse or the roof explode. I remember my father shouting not at me but at my mother, for "setting a bad example."

Meanwhile my older sister began what felt to me like a series of personal betrayals. Instead of fighting by my side against the system, she seemed to be falling in love with it. When it came time for her bas-Torah, the Orthodox version of a bat mitzvah, which took place on a Sunday and was awkwardly shared with the other girls of her age group, my sister acted as though she was proud. I watched while her male peers celebrated their individual rite of passage with elaborate glamour, but my sister didn't seem to mind the contrast. That summer she went away to a religious camp and returned a changed person. She began praying a few times each day, rocking back and forth just like the men in synagogue. She told my mother that our current practice of keeping kosher was inadequate, and suggested that the kitchen needed any number of improvements. I was horrified.

The following summer my parents decided that my sister's overnight-camp adventure was so successful it should be repeated, and that it would be a doubly good idea for me to join her. There was no end to my screaming, but once again I was powerless to refuse. Thus my twelfth summer was the worst of my life. Summer camp among Orthodox Jews. Need I explain?

I spent my vacation enduring the equivalent of an eternity in hell. For starters sleeveless shirts and shorts above the knee were forbidden, despite the fact that the temperatures ranged in the high nineties at all times. Prayer services occurred three times daily, not including grace after meals. Boys and girls were not permitted to swim at the same time. And it just kept getting worse.

The body taboos baffled me all over again. What, I wanted to know, was so terribly worrisome about shoulders? What unspeakable acts might be inspired by the inches of skin above my knees? Pennsylvania was too far away from New York for me to consider running away, and I was too scared to try hitchhiking. We were in the middle of nowhere, that was all I knew, and I was trapped. My bunkmates, all of whom attended Jewish day schools in New York City, had absolutely no idea what I was so upset about. This was simple and ordinary life for them. Just the summer version.

It turned out that there was a fast day in mid-July, surrounded by more than a week of days in which we were not allowed to swim, for religious reasons I didn't fully comprehend. And the praying? My God, the praying! All these kids had memorized the extensive litany of prayers to the point where they could close their eyes and chant for hours, at top speeds that took my breath away. I learned to move my lips and pretend, because my own slow reading took way too long. The fakery was my only means of blending in. But the bile in my throat was rising, and about to choke me.

After the disenchanting ritual of my bas-Torah, in which I was supposedly initiated as an adult into the congregation, my father and I had a world-class argument about Hebrew school. When he insisted that I still had to continue my studies as long as I was living in his house, I told him I would no longer attend classes at the Orthodox synagogue. In the Conservative synagogue, where men and women got to sit beside one another during services, a slightly more broad-minded curriculum was available. I stood my ground about going there instead. If I was being forced to learn something, I was going to choose the conversational Hebrew-language class. Prayers were over. And as for Jewish activities, the only one I could stand to participate in was Israeli folk dancing. I had noticed there were boys involved.

When boys began showing up with increasing frequency on my radar screen, I realized that keeping secrets could become a new form of resistance. My father forbade me to date non-Jews, and naturally they were all I wanted. I sneaked out of the house to meet boys named Charlie and Matthew and Chris, kissed their Catholic lips, and tried my first tastes of beer. I wanted to taste everything. I wanted to choose according to my very own desires: my dates, my food, my clothing, my praying. I wanted not to be a good girl or a bad girl but simply to be myself, a follower of my own sense of right and wrong. I wanted to be free.

Once my father followed me to the ice cream parlor and caught me with a boy. Not a Jewish one, of course. I had lied about meeting a girlfriend, and my father saw right through me. (He always claimed that a spot appeared on my forehead when I wasn't telling the truth.) But even getting caught and then grounded for the crime of my deceit couldn't make me righteous. I argued with my father about everything, including God, but he silenced me with his certainties: I will always be older and smarter than you, he said.

My rage got so fierce I knew there was really no cure except to get out of the house. At the ripe age of sixteen I figured out how to graduate early from high school and a way to engineer my formal escape. Although my initial brilliant plan was to hit the road and wander Europe with a backpack, I found a more legitimate approach that my parents couldn't deny me. Sponsored by Rotary International as an exchange student to the Philippines, I flew to the other side of the globe, as far from home as I could get without leaving the planet. And for the first time I saw what it might really feel like to leave my Orthodox Jewish world behind.

Here was my big chance to break rules with no one looking over my shoulder. Pork? Prawns? My hosts were offering me every forbidden food, calling them delicacies and insisting I try them all.

I hesitated, thinking of the struggles that had defined my life. The good bad daughter. My public school and my religious school. The Jewish boys and the non-Jewish boys. Surrounded by a sea of Catholics, thousands of miles from home, I had every reason to forget about *us* and join up with *them*. No father's threats admonishing me to obey, no older sister setting her obedient example. Plates heaped with roast pig and shellfish were arrayed before me. All I had to do was open my mouth and lift a fork to my lips.

At the dining room table of my Rotary family, I felt utterly alone with my language, my beliefs, and my history. What was I doing there? And who was I? What came to me was both a thought and a feeling, a vivid sensation that I was not just another "messenger of goodwill," as I'd been instructed by Rotary. I was carrying my parents' stories under my skin. I was their blood, their very bones. Their miraculous survival during the Holocaust had led all the way here, to me, sitting among a group of brown faces, all waiting for me to take a bite of their most generous, most welcoming meal.

I astonished myself. I shook my head no. In this strangest of strange lands, the only familiarity and individuality I could retain was what belonged to me on the inside, in my body. Given the freedom to choose my own rules, for once I wanted to stay loyal to my tribal code.

"I'm Jewish," I said.

All around me puzzled expressions deepened. Prepared now to explain that I was simply practicing my religion every time I sat down to a meal, I tried to remember what I'd been taught about the reasons for keeping kosher. I would have to learn a few things, I thought. I might even have to study some books on Judaism! But before I could begin to tell them about the unclean animals and the numerous restrictions, I was stopped in my tracks.

"What," my new family asked, "is a Jewish?"

As for the rest of my rebellion, it's a longer story. Even when I returned (a vegetarian) from the Philippines at age seventeen, I never did live at home with my parents again. I spent a year at Brown University, but couldn't quite find my equilibrium there. My sister was at Harvard, happily involved in the Jewish community of students at Hillel. She got engaged to a Bible scholar, and followed her increasingly strict adherence to Orthodox codes. I needed more distance from everyone. I needed a coast to call my own.

My permanent home is now in California. But my so-called bad behavior has sent me along a meandering path without any clear destination. To this day I wrestle with the unresolved question of my membership in the Tribe, what it means to be a Jew, and more specifically, a Jewish woman. I eat shellfish now. I do not observe the holidays or practice the rituals. I married (and divorced) a non-Jewish man, and I have continued to be drawn toward men from the "other" world, though I swear it's not by design. I just like them better, that's all.

Am I still just saying no after all these years? It seems to me I am mostly determined to say yes, to make my choices without the demanding loud voices of prohibition and tribalism in my ear. But does that make me bad by anyone else's standards? Ask my father. Ask the rabbi. They are likely to shrug and say that maybe I'm finally old enough to make up my own mind. Suddenly I wonder if that ancient prayer can be my new mantra for self-acceptance: "Blessed be God, ruler of the universe, to whom I give thanks for making me as I am."

Author Questionnaire

KAUI HART HEMMINGS

AUTHOR QUESTIONNAIRE

The purpose of this questionnaire is to supply accurate information about you and your work. Please indicate if there is any information that you wish to keep confidential.

Proposed title of your book: How to Party with an Infant

Fields of interest or study, avocations, hobbies: I used to like snowboarding, surfing, and skateboarding, but now I have a baby. I used to like cheap gin and skinny boys with big ears, but now I have a husband. My husband used to like jumping through campfires and off mounds of red dirt on his loud, growling dirt bike, but now he has me. We watch a lot of TV, and not in an ironic way. LC is so much cooler than Kristin. Janelle should win *Big*

Brother. Whenever I watch *The Office* and see Pam and Jim I think, That's what happens to English majors. That could have been me. I hope Jackie finds love in *Work Out*. I think Dog the Bounty Hunter's wife needs a breast reduction, for the sake of her career. Those things must weigh more than all the bags of heroin they found in Eugene's squalid apartment.

Are you a full-time writer? I'm pretty much a full-time writer with the occasional teaching job at Stanford or the University of San Francisco. I had to cancel my class at Stanford because I couldn't find day care, so now I'm permanently blackballed for being "unreliable." Whatever. Finding good day care is like searching for *kine* bud in Oklahoma. At first I found a babysitter who'd come over, and I'd shut myself in my room to write, after first hiding all of my rap CDs so she'd think I was a normal mother. It wasn't the ideal situation. She said "Hecka" instead of "Hella." She wore orthopedic shoes, and I kept thinking that this good girl was a bad influence on my child. I didn't want my daughter to grow up all whispery and giggly like Jenny, who, by the way, had Hilary Duff on her playlist. One month Jenny was real busy studying for finals, and I tinkered with the idea of finding a new situation. Then she found out I was a writer and asked if I wrote children's books, and that sealed the deal. Good-bye, Jenny. Everyone asks me if I write children's books. It's so retarded. Actually children's books can be dirty sometimes. In *The Runaway Bunny* the mother says to the boy, "I'll make like the wind and blow you," and in *Spot Goes to School* the teacher asks Spot what he has brought to show-and-tell, and Spot says, "My bone." I mean, come on.

But anyway, I finally found the perfect day care that my daughter loves. She goes just two days a week while I go to the office I rent with other writers. Now, of course, anything she does, my playdate friends say, "Oh, she must have learned that in day care." If she sings, it's because of day care. Talks, day care. Talks in sentences, day care. I want to tell them, "Put your kids in day care. Let's see what happens. I'll bet a million G's they come out not even able to say 'Ga.'"

Please list any other books you have published. Please note any awards the book may have won: I published a collection of stories. The *San Francisco Chronicle* named it one of the best books of 2005, and I sort of hold on to that like it's a leash attached to a rabid pit bull. The book hasn't won any awards. No reprints or rights, no pictures of myself in magazines crouched on my knees and looking up into the lens like it's a hand offering kibble. I wanted the book to be nominated for a Young Lions award so I could fly to New York and live it up with Ethan Hawke and Terrance Howard, a change of pace from the writer's parties around here with the cheap wine and SUV-size blocks of cheese, all the standing around and listening to the boys talk about their latest accomplishments like being published in the *Chugachoochoo Review* or some shit. My book probably sold, like, two copies. It got good reviews though, from pretty much everyone except from a woman who said it was too "workshopped," a criticism I loathe. I mean my job is to polish the stories. If I didn't she'd call them sloppy. It's like critics see an MFA and immediately say, "These stories appear to be workshopped." No kidding. It's like reading a science article and saying, "It seems he has done research."

Please write a brief description of your proposed book: This is a book of stories (God knows why I'm writing more stories—the adopted Namibians of literature, cute but not flesh and blood) set in San Francisco about parents and their children. It's about kids and parenting, essentially. Two years ago, when I was twenty-eight, I got knocked up by my boyfriend (now husband) in a cabin in Squaw Valley (snowed in with Syrians—think hookahs, liqueur, unlimited incomes), and now I'm the parenting expert.

What inspired you to write this book? All the stupid shit affluent mothers do and say. I feel mean because in the title story, "How to Party with an Infant," I essentially use direct quotes from emails and conversations I've had with other mothers for the purpose of making them appear ridiculous. I feel like a high school student, a mean girl, soaking in the gossip, then turning around and enlarging it for the sake of entertainment and enhanced self-worth. But at the same time I have read the story aloud and have received great encouragement from mothers and fathers who say, "I fuckin' relate." One mom shoved me and said, "Thank God someone's talking about babies sucking the life right out of you." "Um," I said. "That wasn't really my intention. . . ." "Your life is gone. Just gone," she said, looking off into the distance. Another mother, who looked just like the kind of mother I was making fun of, rubbed her hands together and said, "You are so bad!" People like when other people behave badly. It lets them off the hook. And so I guess what motivated me to write this book was the desire to behave badly while hiding behind the plush curtain of fiction.

How did the idea originate? Remember that often the most incidental stories make interesting publicity. We were at the playground, my daughter and I. She went to the sand pit to play with another baby around her age. I couldn't tell if it was a boy or a girl, which was intentional, I assumed. It was one of those organic San Francisco babies dressed to look like a migrant worker or a lesbian. The mother was driving me nuts. She repeated every action the babies made. Hers picked up a shovel.

"You've picked up a shovel," she cooed.

My daughter picked up a plastic pail. "You've got a pail."

Hers tries to stand up. "You've stood up. You're walking. Oop, you've decided to come back and play. No, no. She's playing with the bucket. Can you share? Are we learning to share?"

"I'm still learning that," I said. I tried every day to blend with my new species.

She looked at me in that condescending, green-party kind of way.

"I mean, we all are. As a civilization," I said.

"That's true," she said. Christ.

Fortunately my daughter grew bored of the It's Pat baby and tottered away, and I thought I should, like, write about this, not this exact incident, but something about . . . I don't know, I'll think of it later.

In another incident I was part of a chat where mothers were offering advice to a mom whose baby is so cute everyone wants to touch it and she needs ways to politely say no.

Now I feel incredibly guilty for doing this because I'm taking things that people told me in privacy and am using them for my own personal fulfillment as a writer. Even though I've made the mothers smarter than they really are, this sort of behavior is frightful, yet I can't help it. I want to share with the world:

> "First of all," one mother said. "People who touch babies are creepy. Everyone wants to touch Janey, especially when she was neutropenic (no white cells)—people just pawed at her like she was Nicole Kidman."
>
> Second mother: "It's because there are no children in San Francisco. They're like Birkin bags. I'd just avoid crowded public places and neighborhoods like the Mission with high immigrant populations, which have a high risk of multi-drug-resistant TB."
>
> Third mother: "It's disgusting. And my daughter is drop

dead so she gets touched all the time. She has these piercing blue eyes and rosy cheeks that just scream, Fondle me! The other day this bumlike person kept trying to remove her socks and smell her. She's a bum magnet. I keep antibacterial wipes ready and wipe her hands immediately after contact."

Fourth mother: "Try saying, 'She bites!' or just explain that she has stranger anxiety and if anyone touches her she twitches. They may test this and try to touch her anyway. Just go ahead and lie. Say she has an awful rash the doctor hasn't identified yet, or just run away, pretending to chase a butterfly."

See. Aren't you glad I behaved badly and let you in on this exchange? I guess the idea to write the stories originated in being a part of conversations such as these, being an outsider, an infiltrator. I want to capture the way we parent. I want to judge and be judged right back. I want to be a tattletale. Perhaps I want to bring my old, bad self into my new good-girl life, what with the playdates and casseroles and antibacterial wipes. Writing these stories is a way of keeping in touch with the person I once was. (Are you there, bad self? It's me, watered down and fattened up.) Because I have that list of naughty antics: drugs, drinking, window smashing, jail (just one night), promiscuous yucky sex, stealing, flashing, having keg parties in your nice suburban home while your Dad's trying to run for governor, you know the drill, but all these things are now as distant as the Bering Strait and I'm glad for that, but still, you don't want to turn your back on the people you've outgrown.

Which scholarly journals do you recommend we target to promote your book? What are scholarly journals?

If you could construct an interview for yourself, what questions would you want to be asked?

How do you keep in such great shape?

Where did you get that fabulous outfit?

Your writing is fantastic. Why don't you get five hundred thousand for your first book like other young writers whose work put me in a coma that received an eight on the Glasgow Coma Score?

This isn't a question, but I just wanted to say how slamming you are. You don't look like a writer. I mean you could be in Maxim's Hot 100.

Proudest moment? Re-creating Julia Stiles's drunken dance scene in the movie *10 Things I Hate about You* to the song "Hypnotize" by Biggie Smalls at a stranger's birthday party on a wobbly picnic table.

Future goals? I want to let you off the hook. I want to do the dirty work and let you relax and enjoy yourself. I want to somehow wield the bad and the ugly into something captivating and true. Writing, to me, is going on with your bad self, it's sassing back, acting out. It's flipping off, turning conventions inside out. It's also an act of love, really. It's giving and sharing, communicating, listening, answering questions, but creating more. It's warming yourself up as you stand outside looking in at all the people smiling by the fire.

Dinner

JENNIFER GILMORE

There was no doubt that I had been bad. Little bad things first: I confess it was I who drank most of the fifth of vodka that Zach Sorenson, dark, weird, dangerous Zach, snuck in to the first junior-high-school party. That was me making out with him in the half light, right there in front of everyone—the next day my head thrown over the toilet in what would begin an inordinate amount of time spent in this undignified pose.

And then years later sleeping out with Elaine Lannan, the two of us dragging our sleeping bags into her backyard beneath the mottled suburban stars, the first times just us, so happy to escape our homes! Then more vodka, then the pot, then leaving the sleeping bags to sneak out to the bars all night long. But back then those were only small girl things, part of growing up, at the very least a casualty of adolescence. Some bad girls have fun: They lay claim to a sexy youth of rebellion, too many boys shagged, rainbows of pills and powders that lead them out of small worlds and toward alternate-universes, and into an adulthood of every kind of defiance. For me, sadly, being bad, turned in on itself; it was never fun and carefree, it always went alone, did damage. Being a "bad girl" remains an individual experience, and how I've come to define the term starts well before anyone placed two hands on my hips and brought them close, before I'd ever marched on Washington for women's rights or slipped a tab imprinted with any unicorn or pot of gold beneath my tongue.

It had started innocently enough, though already the girl I had gravitated to was damaged. When Elaine—whose father barely knew she existed since her stepmother had killed herself and whose older sister, the one who had found their mother dead in her bed, was already dabbling in cocaine—and I got together, we downed Almost Home cookies and bowls of Cocoa Puffs, the milk loaded down with extra sugar, eating until our stomachs looked celiac, round and hard as beach balls. This is what so many girls did after school in eighth grade. But when Elaine said, *You know I heard a way*, we were the ones who did it. Or was it I who told her? I was in the throes of that terrible time when my body was changing: from boy straight and skinny to moon curved. Over and over again Elaine and I performed our ritual, until we worked at it separately and differently and were driven to it for different reasons. In the end we both ended up in fairly bad shape.

Maybe Elaine Lannan started it, or maybe it was just dinner hour in my home. The dinner table was where all things stopped and started. My parents worked, and dinner was the time we would meet up at the end of each day, Mom, Dad, my little sister, and me. I had to tell my friends not to call from six to eight, my father insisted, a throwback to his own dinner hours where he had to dress for the meal and name the symphony on the Victrola before sitting down to dine. While my tests were different and more subtle, my dress far less formal, in this hour or two we were expected to discuss the day's events, global and domestic, and listen to the trials and tribulations of our parents' workdays, my mother in overseas development, my father with his own business in international consulting. My sister is five and a half years my junior, so the current events fell largely on me: A woman vice-presidential nominee! Ghadhafi nearly started a war! Can you believe Chernobyl? And then my mother usually talked about Africa or one of her male bosses, and my father discussed the prospect of his next business trip.

My parents, who went at each other with a rage I would only recognize much later when I saw it in myself, were calmed at dinner, lulled by the day apart, perhaps, by food and the focus on what their children would bring to the table. I ate and ate and ate, and so did my sister, led by our mother, who always picked from a small bread plate in order to help her eat smaller amounts. We had seen old film of my mother—black-and-white footage taken by her father of a plump little girl roller-skating, her dark curls frenzied as she fell into the grass, the footage of her saddle shoes taking each shaking stair until her sweet round face took up the whole screen. To my mother there was no disputing that she had been fat—though she really just looks like a pudgy little girl in those reels—and having since gotten thin eating apples and avoiding the Wellesley afternoon teas, there was not a chance in hell she was ever going back.

My mother would have liked her children to have escaped her obsession with food, but of course, it is what she passed down to us, a gift wrapped so sweetly we couldn't help but grab for it as she slid it under the dinner table to both her daughters. And so began my life as a person who lied and cheated and stole to maintain a habit I don't even now completely understand. It's something that the grown woman I am looks back on, still that girl who was driven to this, but unable to wrap her head around the degradation of that disease. The way I took laxatives from the corner store, stole candy bars and biscuits from Roy Rogers, charged up hundreds of dollars a month of Stouffer's Macaroni & Cheese and frozen quiches and buckets of ice cream at the corner grocery, and then rid myself of all of it before it stuck to me in all my growing places: thighs, breasts, hips. My days became filled up with this, me cutting school just to eat and rid myself, eat and rid myself, an unstoppable cycle that made me look my parents in the eyes at dinner, smile, and then throw up everything they had served me.

*T*hen, for six months to a year I was good. I resisted food and survived on Alba 77s and ice cubes. My body began to diminish, quickly and beautifully to my eyes. I bought a dress from the twenties at a vintage shop in Georgetown and it was the equivalent to a size 0. I remember it shimmered gold and slipped on easily, skimming my body's worst parts, and I thought how finally I was lovely and good and done with eating. My father thought I looked terrific, until my thinness began to terrify. Boys who'd once flirted with me coughed when I entered a room. *Gain some weight*, they'd choke under their breath. I was thrilled, but alas, that terrible excess called me back, and my brief stint in what I thought to be the pure state of anorexia was short-lived. It was unsustainable, and when I turned back to food, *food!* my savior, *food!* my nemesis, food, food, food, this time, I had lost all semblance of control.

*I*t was August, just before senior year was to start, and I was heading for field hockey tryouts. Yes, I played Varsity field hockey, starting defense. Or at least I had the previous summer; this summer I had been unable to do anything but succumb to my addiction. So my system was, let's just say, *down*.

August in suburban DC, a swampy mess, and I had binged that morning. I feared I didn't get the boatload of food I'd ingested out, and so I downed a bottle of syrup of ipecac a few hours before tryouts. Ipecac is what they give to children who've ingested rat poison or cleaning solution, something that needs to get out immediately. It's what they give to the bad girls who have had it up to here and take a bottle of pills to end it all. I don't know how it does this but that stuff goes down into your body and brings everything up—yes, the ice cream and quiches and muffins and cereal—but also the bile and sometimes the stomach lining. And it spends you. Your body is so relieved when the mutiny is over that it celebrates by letting you—letting me—for one moment be free of wanting.

You get where this is going. The humidity, the running, the sun bearing down, the ball hitting shins, the awful mouth guard, that wooden stick sliding out of my hand. I remember thinking of my bad timing, as I leaned over to vomit green bile on the goal line. I still remember the shock of the goalie's face and the steam of late August, the pound of the track team circling the field, and the scream of the cicadas as Mr. Harrison, our coach, ran over from the bench, bent down, and dragged me away.

*M*y parents drove me to the hospital from our suburban Maryland home the next day. I remember the dream state of rising from the window seat in my attic bedroom where I had watched the street as a girl and where last night I blew smoke out the window. It was as if I'd been plucked from that seat by some great hand and driven off our tree-lined block, where once I rode my blue Schwinn in springtime, and into the big bad District, the large houses framed by wooden fences and lilacs and fox dragons turning quickly to liquor stores and gun shops, fried chicken stands and run-down churches, to reach the hospital.

When my parents dropped me off—their elder, sixteen-year-old daughter who could no longer function—I could tell they were saddened, though I couldn't say if it was by their failings or by mine. I think they were more relieved than anything. Who could blame them? I was relieved, too.

When they left, the nurse—Indian from India—took me to my room and began to rifle through my stuff.

"Sorry," she said, holding up a pink disposable razor. She set it on the bureau—smooth, blond veneer—beneath a Monet lily print, framed in plastic and covered in fingerprints, as if the person there before me had been feeling for a trapdoor there. The print hung where a mirror might have been.

The nurse found all the secret pockets in my luggage, and removed the sheet of laxatives, also pink, that sweet color that belies the potential for damage. I had taped the blisters flush against the bag, and she removed them along with the package of Almost Home cookies I had thrown in in a last-minute panic before they took me.

Najeem smiled and replaced the offending objects with a stack of books: a blank diary, a twelve-step guide, and *The Best Little Girl in the World*, a novel that told of an anorexic's undoing. While intended to provide an empathetic story and a cautionary tale, it also provided many techniques and tactics, a handbook to anorexia, and I had long ago read it for new ideas.

"For your progress," she said, her dark tapered fingers touching the spine of the journal. "This might be helpful too," she said. Her fingers lighted on the twelve step guide.

"Not for me," I said. Already Elaine's sister had been in Narcotics Anonymous, and I knew then what you had to do to get through it. "I don't believe in God," I said. "Any kind of higher power."

Her beatific smile made me want to smack her. Hard. "You are so young," she said. "Sixteen. My goodness, you don't know what you believe yet."

"I do," I said. I had belief: Buried somewhere beneath the layers of my memories was a synagogue, a place filled with light and bowed heads, a shofar blowing in the new year, an ark opening, but for me, this was not then high enough.

"Here are the rules," she said. She ran over them, tapping them out on her fingers, smiling. One, no exercise; tap tap, two, no locked doors; tap, three, bathroom doors locked for one hour after every meal, no exceptions, tap tap tap tap. No mirrors. "I will be your nurse," she said. She smiled broadly. "If you have troubles, you come to me, okay?"

I nodded. Already I sensed what I would come to know well: the generic feeling of being a patient. Everyone the same girl in a paper robe, waiting in line for something.

I knew then I would never seek Najeem out. And, as I predicted that morning when my parents waved good-bye and she brought me to the nurses' station and checked me in, I would not write one word in that blank white book, only because she asked me to.

The hospital was a vessel for damaged, rotten girls, and there was a hierarchy to their badness. The anorexics—Jane and Betty and Susan—were all trying very hard to be good. But the bulimics, the camp I was tied to despite my efforts, were bad. We were bad to the bone because everything about us was dirty, even our secrets and lies.

I was one of the youngest ones. I had never seen girls or women with stories like these. In the daily circle of group therapy I learned things a Jewish girl from Chevy Chase, Maryland, doesn't know too much about at sixteen. Around the circle: this one with her twelve abortions, this one also a Wellesley girl, I noted, who carved deep ravines in the insides of her arms, this one who had set herself on fire, this one who lived in the projects and had been a heroin addict, this one who had been raped by her foster grandfather.

And they were there because of food?

"We all have to eat," the therapist would say. "And we all deserve to."

From my place in the room, these women were total badasses, and yet we all suffered from the same thing. Their teeth were rotting, their nails were bitten to the quick, their hair was falling out, they were dying. Was I?

I switched from Marlboros to Kools, a hospital staple, readily available for trade. I felt like an immigrant, learning the rules and regulations of this new world I had entered with hope, then to be faced with the ghetto's stark reality. I remembered all my grandmother's stories of how her parents came to this country, to give us everything they didn't have, she'd tell me. Everything.

I thought the anorexics were pure, beautiful ballerinas. I was ugly and base, bad, but not as bad as the enormous Thelma Lee, who ate and ate, all alone, but never had the wherewithal to get it out of her. Nights I watched so many of them in the communal room writing away in their hospital-issued journals, the sound of pen so hard on unsuspecting paper. Was that the sound of getting well, of being good? Fuck it all, I thought. I was supposed to be studying—every week I had scheduled phone calls with my English teacher. College, my parents warned, was not to be put off. Not in our household. Everyone in my family had gone to college. My grandmothers knew each other at Wellesley, for god's sake.

Each night we all waited in line to take our vitals. Najeem, some kind of Indian saint, smiled as we all shifted in those horrible robes we had to wear so the anorexics couldn't put rocks in their pockets, so the cutters' wounds would be exposed, so those nurses could see our veins and arteries, to be sure they still pumped blood to our (broken?) hearts. Step on the cold scale, thermometer in the mouth, the nod of the head, the *zip* of the blood pressure cuff, the rainbow of pills in white cups. The nurses did not look up—133 pounds, 120 over 60, 94.6, no meds. This was me.

Every evening *Hamlet* stayed on my bedside table, and I blew smoke at the TV.

In addition to therapy the hospital trained us in more concrete ways. We ate three meals a day. Each evening I spent an inordinate amount of time deciding on my meals for the next day, which had to be a certain amount of calories, but not too many. (Once I got two bran muffins—the yummy, sticky buttery kind, instead of one, and word spread quickly around the ward how I'd gobbled them both down quickly and hadn't told the nurse on duty to please take one away.) All the food groups had to be represented. Afterward the bathrooms were always locked. There were no exceptions, and once I had to ask a male nurse to come to the bathroom with me so I could pee.

There were programs to ease us back into the world as well. After the first week, for example, certain girls were allowed to go downstairs to the hospital cafeteria, as opposed to eating on our own ward. This was dubbed "cafeteria night," and the anorexics fretted, hanging to the back of the line, as the bulimics, relieved finally to be able to eat, *as we'd become accustomed*, fought to get immense scoops of tuna salad and cottage cheese on their plates.

Then there were grades of getting out of the ward, earned by points on the road to goodness. At first we could walk in the hallways, which the anorexics always took as an opportunity for exercise. Eventually we could go out of the hospital onto the grounds, with a nurse. When Najeem offered herself up to me, I declined, dreading the mere thought of walking beside her and her beatific, almost holy presence. Every time I saw her bent over a patient, or unwinding the blood pressure cuff—*ziiip*—I would shake off the memory of sitting next to my mother in synagogue, the hard wood of the pew, the dust of the prayerbooks, light filtering in, the peace of those moments when nothing else could pull me.

Walking with Najeem would mean she would want to discuss my progress. She would want to know how my reading was going, my studies for school, my journaling. Was that progress? I had been rendered unable to be bad, taken away from it, and so I was being good. Does that mean I was fighting to be well? It's a question I still ask myself from the perspective of someone who is no longer gripped by this disease: How did that happen? I don't remember a battle, only succumbing and succumbing, hating and hating, and succumbing again.

After I'd been there for four weeks, I had the opportunity to walk on the hospital grounds with another patient from the ward. She was a librarian, a compact woman with red hair and freckles—so many of the women were redheads—and she was not high on the bad list as she was only in because she didn't feel in control of herself. We didn't talk much, other than about books (she had not read *Hamlet* in years) and vegetarianism (meat, we agreed, was bad both for us and for animals). For the first time I watched people outside the ward. The world had turned from steaming summer to fall, the leaves were already changing. Field hockey games were being played without me. We passed the very famous children's hospital, and I thought of all those young people from all over the world inside, bald from chemo, missing limbs, all victims of such a range of diseases and injustices I couldn't then name. And I, not much older than some of them, was in the next building in the eating-disorder ward, two floors down from the psych ward. The privilege of what I was going through horrified and embarrassed me, and walking by I wished I had been a true victim, a good girl who needed to be wheeled around the shining ward, nurses and doctors looking at their charts and clicking their pens at how well I was doing, handing me stuffed bears and telling me approvingly how I was a survivor and not to worry, they would not let this disease take me.

The world was still going. Jessica McClure fell down that well, but most of the girls laughed at the way this captivated the nation's attention. The stock market had dropped by more than 20 percent, and Wall Streeters were putting their mouths over the exhaust pipes of their Ferraris in the parking garage of the Dakota in Manhattan. Some of my friends were in college, and I imagined their lives there, an expanse of openness and city rooftops, beer, political activism, and the sexy youth I had meant to be having. I was a child all over again, but my body was too tall to fit into that house of childhood.

And yet, and yet. There were things to learn, if not from twelve steps or a novel that became a movie of the week starring Jennifer Jason Leigh. There was the memory of my mother, starving herself, getting perms, and boarding a plane to the developing world. There was my father and the terrible disappointments his business had wrought. His failures. My sister who grew larger and larger. It's all part of the psychic burdens we carry in our youth if we can't find a way to rid ourselves of them. Do good girls carry them with ease?

Still those women wrote and wrote, their noses so close to the page. Today today, today *what*? We got our vitals taken? We ate macaroni and cheese and didn't die from it? We couldn't find our bodies. I shared a bathroom with a nuclear physicist who weighed sixty-five pounds and who wandered the halls crying that she was a pork chop. Her brain was so fucked, wires snapped and broken, exposed, that she couldn't remember anything her notes told her about being a nuclear physicist. We couldn't see ourselves either—sometimes I'd try to get a glance in the glass of some swinging door just to remind myself: You are here.

Another rite of passage was buffet night. The young girls—Jane and Betty and Susan and me, the sole bulimic of the young group—all of whom might in a parallel life have been class president or PTA treasurer or captain of the cheerleading squad—planned it.

This was one of the true tests of how we would survive in the world.

"Life is a smorgasbord, can you manage it?" asked Delia, the hard-assed nurse with the heart of gold who, in the afterschool special, would be played by Dustin Hoffman.

We talked for days about what we'd have for dinner.

"A potato bar!" Jane said. She had started losing her weight by chewing potatoes and spitting them out in her parents' kitchen sink.

"Mexican fiesta!" Betty said. She knew she would be able to refrain from even one bite of it.

The endless possibilities thrilled us, and we had many meetings before the big evening finally came. I don't remember what we had, but we had a tub—a massive vat—of fudge ribbon ice cream for dessert.

It is a blur to me even now the way I descended on that ice cream, as if it and it alone would give me respite from this place, these pleading nurses, these sick, bad women whom I could hear making love to each other, hard, all night long, and then who fought without discretion over breakfast, who each night covered their burns with salve, who showed up for therapy covered in Band-Aids. The ice cream would block out the memory of the dinner table, the pleading of my father who begged me over and over, no, demanded it, that I never be mediocre, never, never. My great-grandparents who had come here with nothing.

Poor Jane. She had learned to question quietly: "Do you really think you need that third bowl of ice cream?"

"Shut the fuck up, Jane!" I told her, shoving massive spoonfuls in and around my mouth, wanting to strip down and jump into the stuff.

I remember her stunned face that told me no one had ever spoken to her this way. No, it told me, people don't speak to one another this way.

I tried to race to the bathroom, to erase all the damage, head backward toward before dinner, but also before *this*. Perhaps I thought I would get there before the bathrooms were locked, or perhaps I thought I could break in, break into that disgusting place where the sixty-five pound pork chop either did sit ups or tried to throw her insides up every morning. Delia stopped me.

Delia, of all people. Najeem would have been nicer.

"Nope," she said.

"Nope?"

I tried to get past her.

"No," she said. "You need to sit with this. You need to sit with this *feeling*."

In the afterschool special I slide down, my back to the bathroom door, in despair, tears streaming down my face as Delia, dressed in parachute pants and a Members Only jacket, leans in, takes my hand and sits with me until the feeling of wanting to jump out of my skin and erase myself goes away.

In my story it happened this way, too.

*O*ne of the final tests of how you will fare in the real world, away from the Disneyland version where everything is monitored—every breath and pound and calorie and emotion—is the infamous Day Pass. This is when the patient leaves the hospital grounds for the duration of one day. Rumors ran rampant about Day Pass. Those who had been in for months told stories of girls getting as far as the parking lot, and then running back to the safe comfort of our little ward. Others, it was said, left and never returned. It was rumored that one girl came back an entire week later, stumbling through security completely naked, carrying only a Diet Coke.

I, of course, went home for dinner. What else could I do? After all, I was still sixteen, though I was not the same girl as when I'd left. It was *supposed* to be a test. My father and I drove that journey in reverse, past the pawnshops and run-down gas stations, into the smooth asphalt roads that winked with the mica chips I used to think were diamonds stuck in the road. We drove past roundabout driveways and oak trees, past the country club, where, until a few years previously, Jews weren't even allowed to be members. I'd been to bonfires there, all the preppy boys in their khakis and light blue oxford shirts, the Catholic schoolgirls with their deep tans, drinking Milwaukee's Best.

"Why are we here?" I'd said to my friend.

"Because this is fun!" she'd said, and I'd nodded in agreement.

My father and I pulled into our driveway, and my mother came to the door, wiping her hands on her pants.

At dinner we talked about current events. The stock market was a disaster. Thatcher had been rerereelected. And Cicciolina had won a seat in the Italian parliament.

"The porn star!" My father nearly screamed with excitement when I'd asked, Who?

We talked about some of the other girls in the hospital, some of whom my parents and sister had met when they came in for family therapy.

"So terrible," my mother said of a new girl who was drastically underweight, as if it was only this girl who was seriously ill.

My father joked about Tootsie, the black lady with the fun husband who shared can-you-believe-we're-here stories with my father before and after meetings. "That's some lady," he said.

No one looked at anyone. My parents did not fight that night; there was a willful stillness that teemed with everyone's private fear, his or her own hostilities. My sister shoveled food into her mouth, and I took to the wine. I was going to contain myself, and I did, clenching my teeth and eating just enough of the rice, a good helping of fish, some salad. I didn't refrain, and I didn't overdo it, but still everyone fidgeted when the meal was over, not sure if I would hit the bathrooms or how they'd stop me. I didn't even try, and could not have said then or now if I felt the urge.

But being in that house, everything from before came swooping back and caught me breathless, a slap or a kiss from the past set in images: my mother brushing my hair into pigtails, my father hanging stars from the ceiling for a birthday, my grandfather's hat on the couch, a menorah lit for all eight nights, my father's terrible pointing finger, my mother sitting quietly at her little plate, my silent sister with her head turned down.

And then the most recent memory, of the night before I left for the hospital. Though I'm sure nobody knew where I was going, a group of boys I knew from school came to toilet-paper our house. It was late when they showed, and I saw them stomp onto our lawn as I sat at the window smoking. I could hear them laughing, their large white arms set against the blue-black of the night, pitching roll upon roll over my father's prized dogwood, the massive oak, even the bending hydrangea. I did not know their meaning as I watched the arc of one roll travel by my window, followed by a stream of paper, a comet, a shooting star, which then caught and broke on a single branch.

The next morning was like snow in August, and my father was furious.

"What is this?" he said when he opened the door for the morning paper. "What on earth?"

I don't think it's possible that he turned to me and asked me, What have you *done?* but that is exactly what I was thinking when he came back in, shaking his feet as if to brush off snow before coming inside.

*O*n the way home from Day Pass, my father took me to a 7-Eleven for a carton of Kools and to the movie store to pick up a video for the ward, which some visitor would then return. The anorexics were so annoying: *Arsenic and Old Lace! His Girl Friday!* The bad bulimics didn't care; the older ones wanted nothing to do with me, so caught up were they in a triangulation of love I could then only guess at.

The lights were blinding in the movie store, and I scanned over boxes, until I settled happily on *Harold and Maude.* I had rented it with my friend James one night before all this had happened, and the impossible story of this young mod guy, in love with an old hippie woman, drove us to fits of laughter.

I kissed my father on the cheek when he pulled up in front of the hospital building. It was one of those times when what I had done had such clarity—I had been so bad, I had disappointed him, and look where I was headed.

Down down down to the basement of the hospital where there was a floor of vending machines. I knew this from the time some woman's need for food was so base and clear she had fantasized aloud about going there with a fistful of quarters.

The feeling—the guilt, the terror, the need to obliterate every memory and emotion—was fierce in me that night as I scraped together my change and started at the machines. I got two Twix, a Reese's, and a packet of Cheetos. I ripped the packages open and devoured the contents, *like an animal,* and that was it, the change was out, I couldn't get any more food. The fluorescent lights flickered above my head, and I could hear someone sweeping the floor above. It reminded me of an empty high school gymnasium, and I felt like that girl in the movie as I stared into the warped glass of the machine, wanting and wanting and wanting, but seeing only my sad face juxtaposed over every kind of snack food a girl could ever want.

After about ten minutes I made my way up to the ward. Why not? Where else would I go?

"How was it?" Najeem chirped, checking my bag for contraband. I wished for Delia, strong, dykey, singular Delia who barely tolerated me and my impossible innocence, not this nurse who would do backflips to have me make it to step 3: Turn your will and your life over. I'm a goddamn Jew, I wanted to tell her, but she would tell me that Jews can also humbly ask to remove shortcomings, which, of course, would be step 7.

"I got a movie," I said. Could she see the bits of chocolate on my teeth, the cheese dust on my fingers, along the corners of my mouth?

Slowly the newest patients who couldn't leave gathered around. I felt like I was in a zombie movie.

Najeem looked at it, cocking her head. "I don't know this one," she said.

"It's hilarious," I said. "With Ruth Gordon." Watching with James on the couch I had been so comfortable. It dawned on me I might never feel that again.

Jane said, "I thought you were going to get an old black-and-white movie."

I shrugged. I wanted to say: *Fuck you and Cary Grant, Jane,* but I didn't.

"A comedy! Wonderful." Najeem led us into the main room.

I felt ill from the home-cooked dinner, so unlike the measured, deliberate hospital food I had grown accustomed to, and then all that chocolate stuck in me, sitting there, waiting to come up. I could hear the Twix bar begging to be given new life, feel the Reese's scratching to be set free.

The movie began. I'm not sure if I remembered that Harold is obsessed with suicide and funerals and that this is what drives the comedy. And I'm not sure if I meant to bring this movie that makes fun of suicide and funerals into a place where this was not a laughing matter, but Najeem's face went stone cold as she watched the opening scene where young Harold tries to hang himself.

She marched up to the VCR and snapped it out of the machine. "Did you do this on purpose?" she said.

"No," I said. A new patient stood behind me and I hadn't even thought about how her arms were still bandaged from her last try. I tried not to think of Ming, who had set herself on fire, *To* break free, she'd said, weeping.

"You need to think about this seriously," Najeem said.

"Okay," I reached for the movie.

"In your room," she said. "You need to think about what this means now."

I was stunned. I was being sent to my room. To my room where there was no television, no smoking, no mirrors, no people. To my room where I would be alone next to a locked bathroom, alone with that stack of awful books, a blank journal, and bloody *Hamlet*.

My room was just off the communal one and I dragged myself to it and threw myself on the bed. I could hear Najeem saying to the girls that this was making light of suicide, but that suicide was not a laughing matter.

"It's a serious thing to do and not everyone is lucky enough to make it through to watch silly movies like the one we just saw."

I rolled my eyes and turned face down into my pillow. When the movie went off, the television had stayed on, and now it pounded through the wall. I am not lying when I tell you, it was the *Miss America Pageant*. This was what was on television, and I believe it was Miss Tennessee who was up for her brief interview.

"What do you wish for, what do you wish for?" Gary Collins asked.

"First of all," she said, "I'd like to thank God." She paused. "For giving me so many gifts."

I tried to cover my ears with my pillow but I couldn't escape the visual image of this woman, a long thin drink of water in a sparkling evening gown. She was tall and lovely and she glowed, I was sure of it. She could sing, too, or dance, or walk a tightrope, and I realized then that she was perfect and smiling and good. What made her that, and me, well, *me*?

The winner of the pageant would actually turn out to be an oncology nurse from Michigan who devoted her tenure to hospice care. Who knew she was perfect on the inside too? After another six weeks I would leave the hospital, though Najeem would warn my parents and therapist against it. She didn't think I had read her books or written in my journal, and she was convinced I brought that movie in with the worst intentions.

"She has not done much to participate in her recovery," she said of me. "She never came to see me of her own accord."

It was agreed—by whom I still don't know—that I had things to do. The world was spinning so quickly, soon it would be winter.

People were starting to hear about their early-decision applications. The holidays would soon be upon us. If I stayed much longer it would become impossible for me to nudge my way back. Into the world.

I would apply to college and go, as planned, as if there had been a question, and then to graduate school and so on. I would do all the right things set out for me to do.

It was not over when I left. I took Najeem's books with me, and, two decades later, they are still stored beneath that window seat in my childhood room of my parent's house, unknown to them, I'm sure. I never did read them, or write in that journal. I believe the body—and it *is* the body—gets better when it *can*. Last I'd heard Elaine Lannan had become a real estate agent in northern Virginia. Did she ever have to stare her illness down, did she conquer it? Who she is now, on the inside, I'll never know.

I would struggle with this issue for years, and then, slowly, I chewed myself out of the net of it. Many other bad things would replace it, a long line of bad-girl clichés that have settled in to too much wine and a penchant for dramatic arguments, before I got well, or before I became myself. It's still there though, in the pit of my stomach, the past, dinner, my damaged youth, a tight fist, a ball of hair and bones, something contained but always always waiting.

Alma Mater

SUSAN CHEEVER

*H*oused in a gray stone turreted castle on sweeping lawns above the Hudson River, the Masters School was run by a headmistress with gray hair in a severe bun who wore white gloves for all occasions; she had the support of generations of similar headmistresses whose portraits glared down from the paneled walls. In those days students read Hawthorne and Housman, but they also learned to curtsy. Success was a talent at field hockey, a direct but respectful way of speaking with adults, and the ability to flirt with Exeter and Hotchkiss boys without giving anything away. The school is different now than it was in 1959 when I was there as a student, and different than it was in 1980 when I returned for a fateful visit. Still, it is the ramparts of this bastion in the woods of Westchester that spring to mind when I hear the phrase "bad girl."

Bad girls are born, not made. My earliest memory is of throwing a red metal toy truck at a boy who had somehow annoyed me in the Sutton Place Park sandbox. As it happened, he was the son of a wealthy scion of the neighborhood. At the age of three I was banned from my local playground. Neither was I good at home. One night around that time, when bedtime seemed particularly unjust, I made so much noise banging my head against the wall that the neighbors called for help and the police came.

I invited trouble, and trouble seemed to like me, too. My mother sketched me as a toddler arguing with raised fists. My parents didn't say I was bad; they told me I was "difficult." My father read me O. Henry's story called "The Ransom of Red Chief," about a child so difficult that his kidnappers begged his parents to take him back. His parents didn't want him either.

At school my difficulty became a more serious issue. By the eighth grade I was regularly failing classes. My parents began to get the first of hundreds of concerned notes written by school administrators that would punctuate my educational career. So to straighten me out they sent me to the school which had just changed its name to Masters from the more formidable Miss Masters School. Sometimes the school was even called "Dobbs" after the town of Dobbs Ferry, where it was located, not that a Dobbs girl had anything to do with the bustling river town between the lacrosse fields and the river. At Dobbs the rule against smiling in the halls had recently been rescinded. Everyone seemed to miss it.

From the beginning my blue serge uniform with its white, wide-collared middy blouse and pastel knotted tie was always twisted or spotted. I trailed scraps of paper with assignments scrawled on them and wrappers from the candy I ate on the train to school. Physical education classes featured me flunking the fitness test and fumbling the ball. I couldn't manage to sit still for the required hour of study hall; I found myself outside on the grass almost before I knew what was happening. Classmates called me the wanderer of Masters Hall.

Teachers called me disobedient. I began to hear the word "attitude" all the time. My mailbox was stuffed with demerits. I was rejected by the school literary magazine in a public ceremony that imitated the club initiation rituals at the Ivy League schools for which we were supposedly headed—unless of course we were lucky enough to get a marriage proposal. Marriage was the rosy future for the good, good girls to whom a nice young man would want to propose. This future seemed unlikely for an overweight fireball with a bowl haircut by Gino of Ossining and a bad girl's compulsion to break the rules.

I often spent lunchtime weeping in the little jewel box of a chapel in one of the building's turrets. Sometimes I spent the whole day there, kneeling at the tiny altar and praying for some kind of deliverance and eating Triscuits from a box smuggled into school. I would spread my books out on the narrow pews and gaze out at the trees. Life was a misery, and the poets I read seemed to echo my feelings. The poet George Meredith wrote that man was nothing but a "longing handful of dust." That was me. Books became a secret refuge—a tiny jeweled chapel of the mind.

At night I stayed up late talking with my distinguished writer father about those books. My parents wouldn't contemplate a change of school. Instead my father tried to cheer me up by telling me about *his* awful high school experiences. He proudly recalled how he had been expelled from preparatory school, and how he had written a story about it which was his first published work. The story, titled "Expelled," was well known (you can read it in the Library of America edition of John Cheever), and my father never seemed to regret losing his education to gain the beginnings of a career.

One night the poet E. E. Cummings came to read at the school;

he was an old friend of my father's and we swept triumphantly into the school to greet him. He and my father embraced wildly. They thumped each other on the back and roared out unladylike obscenities to express their delight in seeing each other. The faculty in their shirtwaist dresses and pumps looked on with bemused disapproval. After the reading my father and I drove Cummings home to his apartment on Patchen Place in Greenwich Village in our family Dodge, and his acid, hilarious commentary on the school and its soullessness felt like water in the desert to a parched, lonely-sixteen-year old. Cummings was a bad boy who hated rules, despised women with white gloves who lived in "furnished souls," and even taunted death in his poems, but his elegant handsomeness, his Harvard background, and his extravagant talent seemed to make that all right.

Sometime in the autumn of my junior year, my famous "attitude" went from remorse to defiance. I might not be good at school, but I was good at being bad. I was *very* good at being bad! I cut classes and blew off homework. I helped stuff a school election ballot box, and I cheated wherever I could. I decided that I would never marry and said so at every opportunity.

At the same time a shift in my parents' lives changed everything. My father wanted to move upstate; my mother did not. In their disagreements there was talk of sending me away to school. The door had been opened, and I was not too demoralized to bound through it to freedom. I was enrolled in the Woodstock Country School in Woodstock, Vermont. I was told that this was my last chance. That was fine with me. Woodstock was heaven— a wonderful coeducational boarding school run by a charismatic educator who understood exactly what I was going through. His name was David Bailey, and I loved him. I never wanted to see a flash of disappointment in his amused, intelligent eyes. At Woodstock no one cared where you did the work as long as you did it. "Physical education" at Woodstock was a loose term: I took long walks during the gorgeous New England autumn and learned to ski when it snowed. I made the honor roll. A boy kissed me. I was thrilled by the intimacy and passion of the teachers. With their help, I even got into a good college.

But the Masters School wasn't through with me, nor I with it. Twenty years after I left the school I was living in New York and enjoying some success. I had become a teacher and a writer. My husband was a handsome and respected man who seemed thrilled to share a life with me. One day I got a call from—of all people—the new headmaster of the Masters School, a man named Mr. Wright, asking if I would speak at the school's commencement in a month's time. I laughed and explained that I hadn't even graduated from the school. I recounted the story of my abrupt departure at the end of my junior year. But the new headmaster seemed to find my history absolutely charming. At first I resisted him. I tried to describe in detail my difficulties with the school, but Mr. Wright assured me the school was different and that the old repressive rules were relaxed. He wanted me to give a reading in a week and then speak at commencement. He had, he said, already ordered my robes.

I was convinced. My appearance at the school where I had met with all those humiliations would be a fabulous reconciliation, I thought. I could finally become the obedient WASP princess my parents had so desperately wanted. At last I would fit in. I would be a good girl for all the world to see.

I bought an expensive gabardine suit and matching pumps and invested in an expensive haircut. I would belong; I would belong! I thought long and hard about what to read from one of my three novels. I didn't want to bore the girls. I wanted to let the ones who might be suffering in on the secret that the world was a wide, wild place. Like a prisoner tapping the wall of a cell and hoping for an answer, I wanted to telegraph a private message of freedom to those bad girls who might be—as I had been—miserable and in despair. I wanted to surprise the complacent and give heart to the lonely.

With my bad-girl instincts, I chose a powerful, sexually explicit scene from my second novel, *A Handsome Man*, about a woman being molested by her stepson under cover of a restaurant table-cloth. "They had finished the soup and were waiting for the lamb chops. She felt (his) free right hand slipping under the edge of her skirt and onto her knee beneath the level of the table. She tried to move her leg but the table leg was in the way. His hand inched up her thigh." As the young man violates her, he carries on a conversation with his father about the possibilities of fishing the next day. "'Had you thought about fishing for salmon, Dad?' He began to manipulate his fingers around the edge of her underpants. She was terrified. Trapped like an animal caught in the lights of an oncoming car." It is a scene about the insidious way power can work; a scene which is full of surprises. Perfect, I thought. As I stood in the school's assembly hall I opened the book to read and looked out over the girls' faces with love in my heart. Their faces seemed to be tilted up toward me asking for help. There I was, standing at the same podium where Cummings had stood, reading my own work. What a homecoming. When I finished reading the chapter, there was a moment of silence and then some moderate clapping.

After the reading I went back to the teachers' lounge but no one seemed eager to speak with me or congratulate me. Still, I was amazed and hurt when the formerly friendly headmaster called me the next day to say in a very unfriendly tone of voice that I wouldn't be speaking at the school's commencement. I was no longer invited. I was surprised and devastated. I should have known. The Masters School would never want me. How could I have thought otherwise? When I asked why I was no longer welcome, the headmaster sounded so angry that he could hardly speak through his rage. "You read a sex scene to ninth grade girls!"

he sputtered. "What did you think you were doing?" Months later and after hours with my therapist talking about what had happened, I came to understand that although my head was eager for reconciliation with the school, my heart was still furious.

It would be nice to report that, standing up at the podium in front of the school I had decided to be bad, to shock the girls and their teachers in the spirit of E. E. Cummings and my expelled father. That's not what happened. I wanted to be good—I would have given all the literary credits in the world to fit in with that audience. In spite of that, in a completely unconscious way, the bad girl took over.

A few years ago I heard the story of my reading at Dobbs in a different form from a parent whose child was at the school. The school had done me wrong, the story went, and I had had my revenge by reading something inappropriate and shocking. I had done it on purpose in order to show up the uptightness of the school I despised. That's what they thought.

These days I am teaching again, and I often think of the teachers at Woodstock and the way they made learning exciting. I even appreciate the one great teacher I had at Dobbs—an English teacher whose intelligence couldn't save me. I'm still writing books, but teaching is my first love. I look back at the girl I was in the 1950s in high school and she breaks my heart. I remember the woman in the 1980s who unwittingly destroyed the reconciliation she so desired and that also makes me sad. In fact, perhaps bad girls aren't bad at all, maybe they are just sad girls, girls adrift among the shoals of others' expectations and society's weird reefs; girls who haven't found the lives they were meant to lead. I did find my own life, and so my story has a happy ending. I pray for all those who are still out there, dreading school in the morning, hoping that lightning will strike, tangled in the webs of the past. I wish them all the luck in the world—I wish them all the luck I had, bad girl that I am.

Lisa the Drunken Slut

MAGGIE ESTEP

*I*n Granville, Georgia, I met a girl named Lisa who was a self-proclaimed drunken slut. Lisa would prove to be the prototype for all my close female friends to follow.

The Sex Pistols were famous, Jimmy Carter was president, and I was fifteen when my father, a nomadic horse trainer, was offered a job in Georgia. We moved from our perfectly pleasant situation in upstate New York to Granville, a tiny dusty town miles from anything I could conceivably call civilization.

We arrived in Granville in a caravan, like Gypsies, replete with a van full of horses, bedrolls, my father's current girlfriend, Kitty, and his ex-girlfriend Debbie, who was helping out with the driving. I was riding in Kitty's car as she chain-smoked and sang Allman Brothers songs at the top of her lungs. Kitty had never set foot below the Mason-Dixon line but seemed to think the South would be some benevolent place where southern rock wafted from speakers strung to town lampposts and whiskey flowed from public water fountains. I was more guarded in my optimism. Particularly once I went to enroll in the local high school. It was in a dreary one-story concrete building and looked more like an overgrown ranch house than a school. The creepiest thing was that all 157 students attending this school had the same thin, reddish hair that I'd only ever seen on dolls. Amazingly, they stared at me like *I* was the freak. I had very dark hair and wore skimpy T-shirts that revealed my sudden attempt to grow armpit hair in homage to Patti Smith on the cover of her album *Easter*. I was cool. I knew that. But they didn't. And they stared. They weren't overtly hostile, but I immediately sensed they would one day reach a level of doll-haired mass hysteria and do something like put me to death on a softball field, a place where I had suffered past humiliations, as I had a huge fear of things being thrown toward me.

I scowled at all the doll-haired people and, at lunch, instead of going to the cafeteria, I stood outside, chain-smoking cigarettes and dwelling on the fact that this whole Georgia thing really wasn't going well. I was on my third consecutive cigarette when a blond-bombshell-type girl swaggered out of the cafeteria and made a beeline for me. She had big, feathered blond hair, huge breasts, a tiny waist, and ample hips. Her lips were painted vivid red, her jeans were two sizes too small, and she walked mincingly atop five-inch-heeled open-toed sandals.

"Where the hell did you come from?" she asked when she got within a few feet of me.

"Uh, New York."

"Jesus. You're far from home."

"Yes," I agreed.

"They're gonna lynch you," she said.

"Who's gonna lynch me?"

"Just *they*. Everyone except me. This is a nasty little place, in case you haven't noticed. Drink?" she asked, producing a pint of bourbon from her big red purse.

I accepted a swig.

"I'm Lisa," she said after she'd recapped the bourbon and returned it to her giant purse.

"Maggie," I said.

Lisa motioned at my armpits. "Whadya got hippie parents make you have hairy pits like that?"

"It's natural," I said, sticking my chin in the air. "And no, my dad is a horse trainer, he's totally not a hippie." This was true enough. My father, although in possession of a very wild side, had always dressed conservatively in button-down shirts and nice trousers. His hair was always carefully coiffed, and he accessorized well with expensive cowboy boots and beautiful belts. Even when doing barn work.

"And I don't live with my mom, " I added, "but she's no hippie either. She's very fashionable." This part wasn't entirely true. My mother, also a horse trainer, had always been gorgeous and had in fact had a brief fashion phase when we'd lived in France with her second husband, but the moment we returned to the States, she packed away the tailored skirt suits and returned to her Wrangler jeans. She didn't have hairy armpits, though, that much I was sure of.

"Huh," said Lisa, pulling a long drag from her Marlboro 100. "Your father's a horse trainer, huh? What, like at the racetrack?"

"No. Jumpers."

"Oh," said Lisa. I could see she had no idea what that meant but she clearly wasn't the kind of girl who admitted to any gaps in her knowledge.

"So who you gonna fuck around here?" Lisa asked then.

I was shocked and tried very hard not to show it. For one, I hadn't done any fucking; for two, I hadn't hung around anyone who casually talked about fucking, mostly because I hung around with my father's girlfriends, who probably did a fair amount of fucking but had the good sense not to discuss it with me since, presumably, the bulk of the fucking was with my father.

"Um, I don't know," I said, looking down toward my feet.

"No one at this goddamn school, I hope. These guys are disgusting creeps."

"Oh," I said. I knew I should brazenly ask her "So, who do you fuck?" But I didn't. Not that it mattered since she promptly sated any curiosity I might have had.

"I'm fucking my kid sister's school-bus driver," Lisa said. "He's forty. But he's hot."

"Oh," I said.

"Is that all you ever say?"

"What?"

"All you ever say is 'Oh.' What are you, shy or something?"

"No," I said, then looked down at my feet.

"Come on, you need to loosen up," she said, taking the bourbon from her purse once more and making me take a swig.

I was a little tipsy for that afternoon's classes, but I was considerably happier. Lisa wasn't like anyone I'd met before, but she didn't have doll hair and she had spoken to me and therefore I adored her.

One weekend two weeks into life in the South, I was in my room, avoiding the bickering going on in the living room, where Kitty and Debbie, my father's ex who still hadn't left, were fighting about something. The phone started ringing. The girls were too busy fighting, so I emerged from my room and answered.

"Hello?"

"Darlin'?"

"What?"

"Is that Maggie?"

"Yeah," I said guardedly.

"This is Zack Maxwell," the guy said.

"Oh," I said.

My father and Kitty and Debbie and all the crazy horse people I knew talked about Zack Maxwell in semireverential tones. He was a disreputable horse dealer, but in a nice way. He robbed people, offering them five thousand for a horse worth twenty-five, charming them into thinking they were getting a good deal, then turning around and selling the horse up north or out west for fifty grand. He was infamous. And as shady as he was, no one really seemed to dislike him. But why Zack Maxwell was calling me, I didn't know.

"I want to welcome you to Granville," Zack said.

"Thank you," I said tentatively.

"Can I take you to lunch?"

"Lunch?"

"Yes, Darlin', lunch," said Zack Maxwell.

"Now?"

"I'll pick you up in half an hour," he said.

"Uh," I stammered. But Zack Maxwell had already hung up.

"What was that?" Kitty asked, looking at me suspiciously, like maybe I'd been speaking with one of my father's ex-girlfriends.

"Zack Maxwell," I said.

"Zack Maxwell!" Kitty and Debbie shrieked as one.

"What's he want with you?" Debbie scrunched up her brow.

"I dunno," I shrugged.

"Well what did he say?" Kitty asked.

"He's taking me to lunch."

"Lunch?" they barked like seals.

"Uh-huh," I shrugged.

"Why?" Debbie asked.

"I have no idea."

"Well I know why," said Kitty.

"Why?" asked Debbie.

"He heard she's cute," Kitty said.

"She's *fifteen*," said Debbie, aghast.

"Exactly," Kitty said smugly. "This is the South. People marry their cousins, and fifteen is practically middle-aged."

Both women looked at me and frowned.

"You're meeting him right now?" Kitty asked.

"Yeah. He's coming to get me."

"Does your father know about this?" Debbie asked.

"I dunno," I shrugged.

"Well, I'm going to the barn to tell him," said Debbie, slamming the screen door as she left.

"I have to get something in my room," I said. I didn't want to tell Kitty I was changing my clothes, that I was intensely attracted to the idea of Zack Maxwell. Plus, it'd give me something to report to Lisa, who thought me mentally defective for having failed to find a love interest in the two weeks I'd been living in Granville.

"It's okay, Maggie," I heard Debbie call out, coming back into the house.

'What's okay?" I asked, emerging from my bedroom.

"Your father says Zack's allowed to take you to lunch."

"Oh." The lunch date's preapproval seemed to indicate that Zack's intentions were pure.

"Here he is now," said Kitty, who was still standing at the kitchen window, staring out. "He sure came quick."

I walked over to the window to get my first look at the guy. He sauntered out of his pickup truck, pushed a cowboy hat back on his head, and squinted up at the sky like Clint Eastwood. He wasn't tall but he wasn't short. He was on the slight side. He was wearing a button-down shirt tucked into clean-looking jeans. After staring toward the barn for a minute, he gazed over at the house, right at the kitchen window. He saw me. I stared, he stared, and then he grinned. He had a gap between his front teeth. He was handsome. Maybe he'd take me away somewhere to be his child bride. I would chain-smoke, drink whiskey, and bake cookies for my beloved.

"Nice to meet you, Darlin'," he said after Kitty had grudgingly opened the front door and let him in. He kissed me on each cheek, then tried to do the same to Kitty, but she only let him have one cheek.

"Zack," Debbie said, nodding at him with her chin.

"Debbie, nice to see you," said Zack Maxwell.

If Zack felt scrutinized by this tribunal of women, he didn't show it. He took my elbow.

"Ready, Darlin'?" he asked.

"Yes," I said.

Zack held the door open for me. "After you, Darlin'."

We didn't do much talking. Not on the way to the restaurant, not in the restaurant, not on the drive home. Now and then, he'd ask me things about how I was adjusting at the new school or what I liked to do with my spare time. I mentioned my collection of Patti Smith records, and he looked at me blankly and asked if I knew how to rope a calf on horseback. When I admitted that I did not, he said he'd teach me. I liked the sound of that. I didn't ask him if he had plans to leave his wife and three kids, but I had a vague idea that after the calf-roping lesson, he would get rid of his existing family and take me away. It wasn't so much that I was an immoral slut, more that my brief life had been strange enough that the whole situation seemed fairly normal.

Before dropping me off at home, Zack asked if I'd like to go to lunch again some other time.

"I guess," I shrugged. I was a fifteen-year-old punk rocker; he was a thirty-four-year old married horse thief. But that made it exciting. Plus I was sure Lisa would be pleased.

About a week after my lunch with Zack, my father announced we were going to a horse show where he was showing Olias, a cranky gelding he'd been trying to sell for several years, to a potential buyer.

"Olias will ride up with Zack's horses. Zack's gonna be up there trying to sell those two mares he got last week."

"Oh." I said. I was going to see Zack again

A few days before the horse show, Lisa gave me a ride home from school in her little white Camaro. She wanted to give me counsel.

"Let him fuck you in the ass," was the first bit of advice out of her mouth.

"But he hasn't even kissed me yet."

"And maybe he never will. But you gotta take it up the ass if you want to keep him around."

Lisa's credentials for keeping men around didn't seem to be that great, since she was experimenting in lesbianism, not out of a healthy same-sex curiosity, but more because some older woman was willing to buy her booze if Lisa went down on her.

"She's a redhead. I don't know if it's a redhead thing or what, but she got the biggest bush I ever seen. That thing is like a golf course," Lisa said, swigging down some Jack Daniel's.

"Drink up, little girl," Lisa said passing me the bottle. I swigged though I couldn't help but think of Lisa's mouth in a golf course of red pussy hair. Still, who was I to turn down free booze?

"And another thing you gotta do is put stuff up his ass. All men are homos basically. They want to fuck us up the ass, but they also want us putting stuff up their asses. Maybe the guy will pretend he doesn't want anything up there, but he's lying. You spit on your finger and stick it on up there and, Presto! You got yourself a happy man. You can use vegetables too," Lisa said, growing increasingly animated. "You ever put zucchini up your pussy?" she asked in all earnestness.

I felt like there wasn't a right answer to this question, so I made a noncommittal grunting sound.

"Just make sure it ain't too ripe. Damn thing'll come apart inside you, and you'll have yourself zucchini pussy puree."

"Un-huh." I nodded vigorously. I didn't want Lisa thinking I didn't appreciate her counsel. She was the only person at school who spoke to me, and when the day came and all those doll-haired kids decided to let down their guard and kill me, I hoped she'd call 911.

When we got to the horse show, my father gave me five bucks and told me to stay out of trouble as he and Kitty wandered off to the tents where the horses' stalls were set up.

I didn't know where Zack was and didn't want to draw attention to myself by asking so I went about my business, ambling around the fairgrounds. I headed for the doughnut truck where a man without teeth sold me two glazed doughnuts.

The doughnuts didn't sit well, and I felt ill. I had half a joint in my pocket left over from the previous day when Lisa had gotten me stoned after school. I went to lurk behind some bleachers near one of the jumping rings and smoked the half joint. The doughnut nausea passed, and my outlook on life improved. The sun started beating down mercilessly, and though I took off my sweater I was still blisteringly hot. As I skulked out from behind the bleachers and walked, unintentionally zigzagging as if avoiding sniper fire in a parking lot, I started wondering if Lisa's joint had been spiked with something. My vision started going black at the edges, and I walked as quickly as I could to the nearest structure, where I sat down, partially shaded by the side of what proved to be a Porta Potti.

"Darlin'," I heard someone say.

Zack was staring down at me with concern.

"Honey, what's wrong?" he asked and, to my astonishment, got right down there with me in the dirt and took my hand in his.

He'd called me "honey." It didn't matter that in all likelihood he called hookers, would-be presidential assassins, and mental patients "honey."

"I don't feel very well," I said.

"You stoned?" he asked.

"Just a little."

"You're gonna be fine, little girl. Just don't smoke so much," he said. He had draped his arm around my shoulder now and was still holding my hand with his other hand.

"Thanks," I said.

"I told you I'd look out for you," he said.

With that he reached over, traced my jawline with his index finger, then leaned his mouth over mine and kissed me. He tasted like tobacco. He put his rough, callused hand down the front of my T-shirt, at first gently rubbing with his fingers, then pinching the nipple, a bordering-on-violent teasing.

At some point I became aware of people looking at us. I realized there was a possibility of the police being called since I was fifteen, and, by now, Zack's hand was down my pants. Also, there was some likelihood of my father strolling by. Although I never quite got there, Zack squinched up his face, then looked embarrassed, and, I had to guess, came. Not that I knew the face of orgasm yet, but I had thoroughly studied every sex book I could find and committed every possible detail of every possible act to memory. So I had an idea of what to look for.

"We should get out of here, Darlin'," Zack said, bashful now, not looking at me. "You gotta clean up a little, you got dirt on your pants, and your hair is a mess. There's a nice ladies' room over there," Zack motioned off into the distance. "Better than a portable toilet. You go in there and clean up. I'll see you later on."

That was the last I saw of him at the horse show.

Later Olias, the cranky horse, tried to kill the woman who was interested in buying him. He bucked her off, jumped out of the ring, and tore ass across the show grounds. My father and Kitty and I went home that night.

After school on Monday, Lisa was waiting to give me a ride home.

"Hop in, Shorty," she said.

Lisa's terms of endearment were unusual.

"I'm really not that short," I told Lisa as I slid into the passenger seat.

"Aw, don't take it hard. Guys like little girls. Makes 'em think you got a tight little twat," Lisa said.

"According to some statistics I found in the encyclopedia in the library, the average American woman is five foot four. I'm five foot three, and there's a chance I'll still grow another couple of inches," I said defensively. "What's more, the average American woman is like a hundred and forty pounds, and I only weigh one ten, but you, on the other hand, are probably closer to the average weight."

Lisa slammed on the brakes.

"Are you being a little bitch?" She screwed up her face and put it very close to mine. Behind us a car honked, narrowly avoiding rear-ending us.

"I'm just saying," I shrugged.

"You're just being a bitch. I'm womanly," Lisa said.

Lisa *was* womanly. She was taller than me and she had big breasts and a big butt and big hair, and it all hung nicely on her. But I was trying to give her a taste of her own medicine.

And then, to my astonishment, Lisa started crying. Right there in the middle of the road, with traffic backed up behind us.

"I'm a pig," she wailed.

"Oh my God," I said. "You're not, Lisa, I'm sorry. I was just being a bitch, you're right. I'm an asshole, I'm sorry, just please drive the car forward?"

"My daddy fucked me in the ass when I was seven," Lisa said through her sobs. "I started pigging out on Ring Dings so I'd get fat and he wouldn't fuck me no more."

This was more than I was equipped to deal with. I felt my mouth opening and closing.

Then, suddenly, Lisa flipped back her hair, brought her face close to mine and started laughing bawdily. "Kidding!" she screamed.

I released the breath I'd been holding for several minutes.

Lisa was still cackling as she drove the car forward.

She offered me a beer, and I turned it down.

"Since when you turning down booze?"

"I don't even like booze, Lisa. I like pot."

"Well, you got some?"

"No."

"Then shut your short face and drink up," she said.

I did as I was told.

After a brief beer-guzzling interlude, I decided to tell Lisa about Olias the cranky gelding's attempt on his potential buyer's life.

"And then he *jumped out of the ring*," I said, thinking surely this would make Lisa more interested in horses. She just looked at me and blinked.

"Does he have a really big cock?" Lisa asked.

Now she'd gone too far.

"That's my friend you're talking about. Horses are noble gentle beasts. What's more they don't talk about your pussy, so leave it alone. Stop grossing me out."

"Congratulations," Lisa said.

"For what?" I snarled.

"You said 'pussy.'"

I stared at her.

"You never said 'pussy' before. In fact I was beginning to wonder if you had one." She looked toward my crotch, and suddenly I feared she was going to stick her hand down my pants to check. I was open to experimentation but I wasn't wearing underwear, so I seized up with fear. Not wearing underwear in high school would be considered a far graver infraction than not saying "pussy," graver even than not actually *having* a pussy.

"Pussy, pussy, pussy," I said quickly, "And I *have* a pussy, and what's more, Zack Maxwell put his fingers in my *pussy* on Saturday." This was calculated to distract her from any possible genital inspection, and it worked like magic.

"He did?" she said. "Well, good for him. What else he do to you? He fuck you in the ass?"

My friend Lisa. She sure liked the ass fucking.

"No, Lisa, it was our first kiss."

"Well, he put his fingers in your pussy. Ass fucking is next."

"Really?" It sounded painful, potentially embarrassing, and, I would later learn, an example of one of the more baroque American laws, illegal in several states.

"Probably," Lisa said, nodding her head gravely, then falling silent.

About two months after my Porta Potti make-out session with Zack, my father announced we were moving to Pennsylvania.

"I'd like for you to finish out the school semester here, though," he said, sitting me down in the kitchen.

"Oh?"

"You mind staying down here while I set things up for us in Pennsylvania?"

I envisioned living in the forest, foraging for berries.

"I guess not," I said.

"Zack said you can stay with them."

"Them?"

"Him and Gloria and the kids."

"Ah," I said.

Rare is the just-turned-sixteen-year-old girl who gets to go move in with her married paramour and his wife and kids. My dad, who seemed sincerely to believe that Zack's interest in me was of a strictly paternal nature, thought this would be the best possible thing for me. To stay in one place two months longer before being uprooted again.

"Is that all right?" My dad scrunched up his face and, for the first time, looked old.

"It's fine," I said.

If I'd expected Zack to greet me with fanfare and a sound groping session—and I had—I was severely disappointed.

"Zack's in Arkansas," Gloria said that first night as I sat down to dinner with her and the three kids, all boys, all blond. "Won't be back till next week. Maybe the week after that."

"Oh," I said.

"He's never around," I told Lisa one afternoon. "I think he's got some other girlfriend somewhere."

"He's got the wife, you, and someone else too?" Lisa asked.

"I think so, yeah. And anyway, I don't count. I only made out with him that one time."

"I told you to put stuff up his ass," Lisa said, shaking her head.

"I haven't had a chance," I said, implying that I was yearning to go through with it but just hadn't found that special moment.

Lisa rolled her eyes.

Lisa and I took to hanging around together anytime she didn't have a date or an after-school job. She'd had many after-school jobs but got fired from all of them somewhere between one day and three weeks of being hired. It wasn't that she was incompetent, just that she invariably had opinions about the clientele at the beauty salon, diner, or feed store where she was working and she expressed these opinions volubly. As for Lisa's men, they were usually ten to thirty years her senior, and things never worked out. So I got a fair amount of Lisa's time, which was a very good thing since she was the only native of Georgia other than Zack who actually spoke to me. Without Lisa, I probably would have unraveled completely. The afternoons we spent driving aimlessly as Lisa recounted her sexual exploits were what kept me from sticking my head in the oven.

The school year came to an end and I started counting the days until I flew to Pennsylvania to meet up with my father. Nothing had happened with Zack, mostly because he was rarely at home. It's also possible that I'd have actually felt guilty now, what with living with Zack's wife and kids and spending far more quality time with them than with him. So I felt a little odd when, one afternoon a few days before I was to leave, while Gloria was out with all three kids and I was idling on the couch staring at a Joy Division album cover, Zack came in, snuggled up next to me on the couch, and announced that we had unfinished business.

I pictured some sort of transaction involving calculators and accounts payable books.

"Come on," he said. "Come on outside."

He led me to one of the trailers near the barn, the one where any horse people passing through town could stay.

Once we got inside, he cupped my face in his rough hands and looked at me really closely. A few months earlier, my knees would have buckled; now I just kept wondering if he was looking at my dirty pores.

He led me by the hand into a dour little bedroom. The walls were moldy, and the carpet smelled. There was an unmade bed. Zack pulled my T-shirt over my head.

Oh, I thought. He's undressing me. Something to tell Lisa.

He pushed me back on the bed and undid his pants. They barely made it down to his ankles before he launched himself at me. He yanked his Jockey shorts down and, moving the crotch of my panties aside, entered me. His eyes were a bright blue. Just as I relaxed into it, accepting his body inside mine, he came. I thought of Lisa and how she'd have ordered him to go down on her for an hour as penance or, at the very least, made herself come. But I couldn't envision either scenario.

Zack kissed me on the stomach, then pulled his pants back up.

"We better get out of here," he said.

I got up and put my clothes on.

At least I had something to tell Lisa. I started imagining how to embellish the whole thing to make it better for her than it had been for me. After all, she'd been waiting months for this.

The next day Lisa was supposed to pick me up and give me a ride to our last day of school. She never showed up, which was unlike her. She was a little mercurial, but she'd always kept her dates with me. I forlornly trudged through my final day at school, and as soon as I got back to Zack and Gloria's that afternoon, called Lisa at home.

"She ain't here," Lisa's boozy mother said.

"Do you know when she'll be home?"

"Not for a week or so," said the mother.

"A week or so? Where'd she go?"

"Hospital. She was in a car wreck."

"Car wreck? What?"

The boozy mother told me Lisa had been in an accident and was seriously injured. She eventually gave me the address and phone number for the hospital. I tried calling, but the nurse wouldn't put me through to Lisa. Later I begged Gloria to give me a ride to see Lisa before I had to fly to Pennsylvania and the next day, we drove to the hospital in Augusta.

Lisa was lying back on the narrow hospital bed with tubes coming out all ends of her. There was a huge bandage on her forehead, and her big hair was flat. She was still Lisa, though, still wanting to tell me all about her disaster. As Gloria sat in the corner of the room, completely silent, Lisa told me what had happened. She'd been engaging in one of her favorite pastimes: masturbating on the highway. She had her jeans unzipped, hand in her panties, and was touching herself while driving. It thrilled her that it thrilled the truck drivers, who could look down and see her having a go at herself, then get on the CB, telling one another about it. It didn't matter if the truck drivers in question were four hundred pounds with pelts of greasy fur covering their entire bodies. Lisa liked the thought of exciting people. Any people.

"I got extra horny," Lisa told me. "This cute guy in a pickup was watching me and he rolled down his window and started shouting dirty at me. The guy was like yelling out how he wanted to come on my tits and stuff."

I glanced over toward Gloria to see if this was making an impression, but she was just staring ahead blankly.

"And then I don't really know what happened," Lisa said, her voice getting smaller. "I sort of remember going off the road, then a big blank until I woke up with tubes down my throat."

I didn't know what to say. I had brought Lisa a Whitman's Sampler, but this seemed so paltry in the face of near death.

"I'm tired now, Shorty," she said after about ten minutes. "I appreciate you coming all the way out here, but I gotta rest. You have a nice time in Pennsylvania, and call me when you're settled."

"Sure," I said. I got up from my chair, leaned over and kissed her on the cheek.

She didn't say anything, but I saw what looked like a tear in her eye.

I never saw Lisa again or ever figured out quite what made her tick. In part she took me on just to be contrarian, since no one else would speak to me, but there was also a lot of kindness in her. She was a bighearted drunken slut and, in spite of her drinking and nymphomania, had a good mind. You never knew what would become of a girl like her. She could be a prostitute by age eighteen or she could excel at college, go to law school, run for office, and end up governing the state, her hair getting bigger by the year.

I moved to Pennsylvania where I met a wild, bawdy strawberry blond named Annie who befriended me while we were smoking in the girls' bathroom at school. She was different from Lisa, a little more refined in her tastes in men and booze. But she was the same basic type. The same bad-girl-type girl I would end up befriended by time and again through the years, one of those untamable souls who would shock me with her exploits but also be there to catch me when I fell.

Peacock's Hand

ROXANA ROBINSON

*I*n tenth grade I went away to boarding school.
This was normal in my family. My parents
had gone to boarding school, and my three
older brothers and sisters had gone; my younger sister would follow me. I went to my mother's school, on the Main Line, outside
Philadelphia. It was only an hour away from home, and the
school was familiar, so it was not frightening to go. In some ways
it was a relief.

Until eighth grade I went to a Friends' school, and so had my
four brothers and sisters: we were Quakers. My parents had converted to Quakerism before most of us were born. My father had
been an Episcopalian and a lawyer, in New York, but he had left
the church, the law, and the city to become a Quaker teacher in
the Pennsylvania countryside. He had given up a life governed by
financial concerns for one governed by moral concerns. We were

brought up to believe that material things were not important:
What was important was a person's beliefs and a sense of moral
responsibility.

My father was not only the head of our family, he was also the
headmaster of our school, which meant that there was never a
moment in which we were not exposed to his exigent gaze. For a
while I was the only one from our family at the school, and during those years my father drove me to school in the mornings,
through the countryside. In the car we did not speak. When we
reached school we separated, my father striding ahead of me up
the gravel path. After school the other children were picked up by
mothers and carpools, but I waited for my father, drifting alone
through the empty classrooms, or sitting by myself in the library,
reading. At five o'clock my father drove me home again.

When I was in the second grade I was sent to the principal's
office for whispering to the girl next to me during rest period. We
were lying side by side on mats, and I thought that she was a
friend, and we were having fun, but it turned out that she was
not, and that I was bothering her. She told the teacher, and the
teacher called me to the front of the room. She said, "Go to the
principal's office," and I understood, from the way she spoke, that
I was in disgrace.

I went alone through the front hall, down the steps to the
smaller corridor where my father's office was. The door was
closed, and I knocked on it.

"Come in," my father said, and I pushed open the door.

My father was sitting at his desk. He looked up when I came in.
When he saw who it was his expression did not change.

"Why were you sent here?" He raised one eyebrow
interrogatively.

"I was whispering during rest period." As I said it out loud it
seemed terrible.

"Go and sit on the sofa," my father said.

The sofa was shaped like a pen, with three high wooden sides. The seat was a blue plaid cushion, and along the back and sides were thick dark blue pillows, against which I did not lean. My father looked down again at his papers. I tried to keep still: The sofa was too high for my feet to reach the ground. If I moved my legs, my feet would make a sound on the wooden frame. I could hear my father's pen on the paper as he wrote. I tried not to move at all.

After a long time my father looked up at me.

"You can go back now," he said.

I got down from the sofa and went out again into the silent hall. When I came into my classroom the other children looked at me. Afterward my father and I never mentioned the incident.

Our family, the principal's family, was exposed to continual public scrutiny. We understood that our behavior reflected on our father, and that we were expected to set an example. This meant that I could never be bad. I could never side with the students, because I was, by birth, on the side of the teachers. The teachers were friends of my family; I was a member of their tribe. Also, I could not break the rules because I knew too well how pained and disappointed this made my father. Our misbehavior was terrible to him; it was true for all his students. Whenever a student committed a crime, my father's response flooded through our family like cold water. Every lapse produced a deep and private wound.

"The eighth grade boys have been smoking." It was like the apocalypse. We saw his face, we heard his voice. Every incident was a personal blow, evidence of his failure as an educator, a moral leader, and a friend. He was sickened and disheartened. He ought to have prevented this, he ought to have created a community in which this would not have happened. The repercussions of the crime echoed horribly throughout our house. My father sat silent

and frowning at the table. It was terrible for him, and so it was terrible for us. We, too, sat silent at the dinner table. When a sixth grader cheated on a test, when the seventh grade boys ganged up on someone, we all felt it.

When one of our family committed the crime, of course, it was far worse. When my older brother was discovered *selling fireworks on the school grounds*, our entire family was plunged into sulfurous gloom.

So leaving home was, in some ways, a liberation for me.

In boarding school I would not have to think of my father. I would no longer be aligned with the faculty: I did not know a single member of the faculty, and did not want to. I no longer had to set an example. I no longer arrived at school every morning with the headmaster; I no longer hung aimlessly around in the afternoons, waiting for the headmaster to leave. I had been liberated. I would not have to think about what the headmistress thought, ever. The headmistress was a wise, kind woman, but I didn't want to think about her wisdom and kindness. I didn't want her to become my friend. I wanted nothing to do with her. I wanted to sever completely my long and involuntary alliance with the grown-ups. I wanted to be on the other side.

*I*n my first year away I did nothing seriously bad. I never wanted my father to hear about anything I did at school. However bad it had been for him to learn about my crimes at his own school, it would be unimaginably worse for him to learn about them in someone else's school. I could not even consider the look on his face if he was told about something terrible I'd done at boarding school.

So I committed no crimes, though in my sophomore year I kept a cat in my room, disguised as a science experiment, for nearly a week. I was not caught for that, but soon after I was caught for something else. A friend and I decided it would be entertaining to take another girl's bed apart and remove the frame from her room. When Sally came back from classes in the afternoon, she found her mattress on the rug, neatly made up with blankets and pillows. We thought this hilarious and fell about with laughter, but Sally did not see the humor in it, and went to tell the housemother.

The school had both boarding and day students, and Mrs. Osborne, the housemother, was in charge of the boarders. Mrs. Osborne was a trim, pleasant woman with impeccable posture and neatly curled silver hair. When she was on duty she sat in the front hall, at the little mahogany desk near the front door, though she had her own comfortable office on the second-floor landing. She was in charge of the many rules that applied only to the boarding students. There were all sorts of them—regulations about clothes, lights out, study hall silence, telephone calls, and religious services, but the most significant ones concerned leaving school. We could leave school only under certain circumstances. Every afternoon, after classes were over, we were allowed to walk into Bryn Mawr, but we had to be properly dressed, and we had to be back by six. Leaving the school overnight required more serious negotiations.

When we reconfigured Sally's bed, it was Mrs. Osborne who called us into her pleasant office. We sat down carefully in her flowered chairs, but we were not alarmed. We could see Mrs. Osborne was not really angry but amused. She told us briskly that we'd upset Sally, and that what we'd done had "nu-i-sance value," giving the word three syllables. I knew, of course, from my father what nu-i-sance value meant to the school administration, so I was sort of sorry for what we'd done, but I also knew that what we'd done was funny, not serious. We were told to apologize to Sally and put the bed back together. This allowed us to reveal our cleverness in hiding it. One of the great pleasures in breaking the rules, of course, is letting people know how you've done it. We'd sneaked the frame into the dispensary, which was on our corridor, and which everyone thought was locked, but which we had learned was not. Thereafter, of course, it was. But this was not a serious event, and my father did not learn about it. It was not until junior year that I made a serious move.

By the time I became a junior, I had established a new life, separate from the old one. I had begun to believe that what happened to me at boarding school had no bearing on my other, earlier life. I told my parents very little. I knew they were not equipped to understand my new life, and that it would shock and disappoint them. The fact, which I wished to conceal, was that I was worldly and superficial, not at all a child of whom they could approve. I was neither a good student nor a good Quaker. My grades were mediocre, except in English, and I rarely went to Meeting. I was deeply interested in clothes, makeup, and boys. I did not want to listen to haunting folk songs from other countries, but to the bad, dirty, rock music on the radio. I did not want to discuss any of this with my parents.

In the boarding school the students all lived on corridors, segregated by year. The seniors lived on the grandest one, with the largest rooms and highest ceilings. It was on the second floor, over the front hall and the principal's office. Junior Corridor was above it, on the third floor. It was up under the attics, and the rooms were small. The few freshmen were put together with the sophomores, in two narrow back corridors overlooking the kitchen. When I moved up to Junior Corridor, I felt the significance. As juniors we had achieved far greater status than sophomores, but the burden of the school had not yet fallen onto our shoulders. What we juniors did, up there under the roof, was more or less our business.

In the evening, after dinner, there was a quiet study hall period for everyone. Afterward, until ten o'clock room call, there was free time. Then we could play music, go downstairs and buy ice cream, make phone calls, or wander about making noise. By that time we were usually in bathrobes and slippers. The rule was that we were not permitted to go downstairs to the main floor, where the ice cream and telephones were, wearing bathrobes and slippers. We put raincoats on over our nightgowns and traded our slippers for loafers. In our bare legs and trench coats, we didn't look respectable, we looked like young flashers. Still, those were the rules.

One evening in junior year, during this free time after study hall, as I was walking down the corridor my friend (whom I'll call Lena) came suddenly out of her room. She was wearing a quilted bathrobe and fluffy slippers. Lena was from the Midwest, and she had a square face and liquid brown eyes. Her thick hair was streaky blond, and she had a rich, choking, infectious laugh. She wore gold jewelry and rather dashing clothes. She loved boys and parties. She was good-natured, gregarious, and famously scatterbrained.

Lena was poor at French, and on the night before the French exam, I went past her room on the way to the library. She was stretched out on her bed, listening to music. I asked if she had studied for the exam. It was around eleven o'clock.

"Not yet," Lena said earnestly, "but I've been thinking about it."

That evening, junior year, Lena came barreling out of her room, looking distressed.

"Oh, God, I don't know what I'm going to do!" she wailed.

"What's the matter?" I asked.

"I'm meant to go to St. Paul's Winter Weekend, and I forgot to get permission from my parents. I'm supposed to leave tomorrow. I won't be able to go!"

We were only allowed to take a certain number of weekends

off campus each semester, and parental permission was required for each of them.

"Can't you call your parents now and get it?" I asked.

"They left for Nassau today," said Lena. "Oh, God."

"Can't you call them in Nassau?"

"I don't know where they're staying. They won't be back until next weekend. I forgot they were going until just now." Lena looked miserable. "I *have* to go to St. Paul's. Robbie asked me in October. I've been planning this for *months*. I'm all packed. What am I going to do?"

"Can't you find your parents? Doesn't someone know where they are?"

Lena shook her head. "I don't know how to find them. They went with friends, but I don't know where. I mean, if they're in a hotel or a house. I can't even remember who they went with. My mother told me but I wasn't paying attention. *What am I going to do?*"

"Does your mother know about the weekend?"

"I think so. I'm sure she does," Lena said. "I'm sure I told her, ages ago. I must have. I thought I'd get her to talk to Mrs. Osborne later, or write me with permission, and then I forgot. I'm supposed to leave tomorrow! I'm all packed! I got all these clothes! What am I going to tell Robbie? *What am I going to do?*"

Of course she had to go to St. Paul's, there was no question of that. Boys took precedence over everything, that wasn't the issue. The issue was just that one obstacle embodied by Mrs. Osborne, trim, pleasant Mrs. Osborne, with her flawless posture, her curled silver hair, her gray wool dresses, her cardigans draped neatly over her shoulders.

It seemed to me there was an obvious solution. It wasn't a question of permission, because that had already been granted by Lena's mother—it was only the question of the letter, which didn't exist, but ought to.

"I'll write you the permission," I said.

"But it has to be from my mother," Lena pointed out.

"I'll sign it from your mother," I said. "I'll copy her handwriting. You can take it to Mrs. Osborne."

The scheme appealed to me because it was so neat. It wasn't a deception, it was only a matter of providing something that had been inadvertently omitted. It seemed actually virtuous: I was helping someone in distress. Also, I liked to write, and this made me feel resourceful. It allowed me to use my skills. It was like survival in the wilderness, rubbing sticks together to make fire.

"Oh, my God," said Lena. "That's brilliant."

"Do you have a letter from your mother?" I asked Lena. "I'll need to copy her handwriting."

"Would you? My God. *My God*. That would be great!"

We had a project. We had become partners.

We went into Lena's room, where she rooted around in her desk until she found a letter. Her mother used dark blue ink and a brisk perpendicular style.

"Here's some paper," Lena said. She handed me a box of stationery from the school store. In the corner was embossed the dark green school monogram.

"I don't think your mother would use this," I said. "Do you have any plain?"

Lena did not, and we went along the corridor from room to room, explaining our situation and asking for unmonogrammed stationery. The hall prefect offered us plain pale blue sheets, and I sat down with Lena's mother's letter and began to practice the handwriting. We agreed that Mrs. Osborne wouldn't need to see the envelope, which would have been a problem, since we couldn't create a canceled stamp. Lena would take the letter to Mrs. Osborne and say it had been inside a letter her mother had sent.

I was increasingly pleased: I was saving the day. I was a hero.

As I practiced Lena's mother's hand, imitating those brisk perpendicular strokes, I thought about the letter itself. I had read Agatha Christie, and I knew all about the risks of the criminal giving himself away by being too clever. My letter would not be too clever. There would be no charming flourishes or giveaway asides. My letter would be impeccably simple: "Dear Mrs. Osborne, I am writing to give my permission for Lena to go to the Winter Weekend at St. Paul's. Yours very truly—"

"What's your mother's first name?" I asked Lena.

"Patricia. But she's called Peacock."

I looked at her. "How does she sign her letters?"

"She signs mine 'Mom,'" said Lena earnestly.

"Yes," I said. "But to other people?"

"It depends."

"But what would she say to Mrs. Osborne?"

"Probably 'Patricia.'"

"Not Pat?"

"Definitely not Pat."

"Yours very truly, Patricia Haydock."

I practiced the upright style of Mrs. Haydock (not her real name) until I could produce it easily, the words flowing out without pause or effort. Then we went up and down the hall, looking for a pen with the same dark blue ink that she'd used. We wanted authenticity. It was possible, of course, that Mrs. Haydock might have used different pens on different days, but it seemed that the greater the authenticity, the more minimal the deception. Or at least this was the way I felt, and it was my idea, and I had become proprietary.

The president of the student body, on Senior Corridor, produced a pen with almost exactly the same color blue. We took it back upstairs, and I sat down at Lena's desk and wrote out the message. "Dear Mrs. Osborne, I am writing to give my permission for Lena to go to Winter Weekend at St. Paul's School on January 24th. Yours very truly, Patricia Haydock."

Lena picked it up and studied it, frowning, intense.

"That's perfect," she said. *"It's perfect!* My God, it looks just like my mother's writing. This is perfect! *Thank you! You've saved my entire life!"*

But we hadn't finished. I eyed the letter.

"It looks too new," I told her. "It looks like it just came from the box."

"But it did."

"Handle it. Rub it with your fingers."

"It shouldn't look *dirty*, just as though it's been sent through the mail."

"Put it in an envelope. We'll hand it back and forth to each other. That will make it look used."

We slid it into an envelope and handed it back and forth to each other. After ten times we took out the letter. It still looked pristine, but we cared less: Now something was hurrying us. We felt pressed by some internal urgency. Our time was up.

"Okay," I declared. "It'll be all right. Lots of letters look like this."

"It looks fine," said Lena.

"Take it to her," I said.

"Okay," Lena said.

We had arrived at the moment.

It was like a school project: here it was, finished, the model village of the Eskimos, the family tree of the Russian grand duchesses. Here was our letter from Lake Forest. Everything about it was correct: the stationery—thick Crane's bond, pale blue—the ink—smooth medium blue—the handwriting—that brisk, cheerful up-and-down stroke, unmistakably a mother's. Unmistakably

Lena's mother's. Now Lena would go to Winter Weekend at St. Paul's. Here was the drawing together of the celestial bodies, here was the ordering of the galaxy. We had done it.

Lena kicked off her slippers, put on loafers over her bare feet, and pulled on her raincoat over her bathrobe. Letter in hand, she jogged down the front stairs to the first floor.

Mrs. Osborne was on duty that evening. Still feeling proud and proprietary, I followed Lena to the curve in the stairs and then sat down, peering furtively around the corner. I saw Lena head toward Mrs. Osborne, but that was all. I lurked there until Lena trotted back up the steps. When she reached me I stood and joined her, and the two of us kept going to Senior Corridor.

"What happened?" I whispered conspiratorially.

"Nothing!" Lena said loudly, excited. "It's completely fine! I gave it to her and said, 'Here's permission from my mother for my weekend.' She said, 'Thank you, Lena.' So that's that! *Oh, my God, I'm so relieved.* Oh, my God, this is so great! Thank you! I can't tell you how great this is! I was so scared I wouldn't be able to go!"

I swelled with pride.

It actually was great, she was right. The whole thing was great, and it had been entirely my idea and my execution. I had saved the city. I had saved the whole country. I had saved the planet; I was a hero.

Lena and I rushed up to Junior Corridor, where we stormed up and down, telling our exciting story, interrupting each other and laughing wildly, accepting praise and admiration.

It took very little time to find us out.

Mrs. Osborne had waited only until Lena and I had pounded raucously back up to the third floor. Then she picked up the phone and called Lena's mother in Lake Forest, who was not leaving for the Bahamas, it turned out, until the next day.

Lena got off lightly, since she had only lied about where she'd gotten the letter, and since her mother actually had given her permission to go on the weekend. But I, of course, had committed forgery, and Mrs. Osborne called my parents.

Then it became apparent that my new life was, in fact, connected to my old life. It seemed I'd declared myself on the side of sin. Tickling my friend on the mat at rest time had been an early indication, listening to bad rock and roll a continuation of the trend. I saw that I was doomed to a life of crime.

The Thrill of the Spill

M. J. ROSE

A few years ago, on vacation in Italy, I walked to the top of a hill to visit a seventeenth-century convent and its chapel. By the time I'd reached the oversized wooden doors, I was hot and tired.

Inside was a silent oasis of cool air and dark shadows.

According to the guidebook, this small church was where the convent nuns came to celebrate mass. Now, years later, it was a tourist destination in a remote area in the countryside where few tourists visited.

I'm not religious but I am an art lover and the chapel was a gem that boasted a lustrous altar painting of the Virgin Mary and a glorious stained glass window that washed the interior in lavender light.

To the right of the entryway, a carved wooden confessional

stood like a sentry. It might have been sacrilegious but I pulled open the door and went inside the tiny enclosure. The air smelled musty and I wondered how long it had been since anyone had knelt where I was kneeling. Putting my hand up to the decorative grille, I felt the intercrossed metal design with my fingertips and whispered the words that, although not part of my religion, were familiar to me as they are to most of us.

"Forgive me father for I have sinned."

How many nuns had knelt there and had confessed their sins to the priest on the other side of the screen?

I remember thinking about what nuns would confess.

The fantasy that came to me was a not a sweetly religious transgression but a sinfully erotic scenario—about a young nun and a priest who had met in this confessional. Invisible to each other that first Sunday, she had whispered her secrets and he had listened. Week after week she exposed more and more of herself to him, and as her soul became naked, he became aroused. Soon he was in her thrall and begged her to meet him just so he could see the face of the woman who had shown herself to him so completely.

As I began to imagine their face-to-face meeting, their touching, their passion, and their sin, I started to think about the act of confession itself and wondered why we kiss and tell? Certainly sometimes it is to unburden ourselves and unload our guilt. But that wasn't enough of an answer.

There are too many times we confess when we're not feeling all that guilty. Or not feeling guilty at all.

Is it our need for intimacy that pushes us to reveal more and more of ourselves? Our desire to be completely accepted that drives us to disclose our most private thoughts and deeds? Is it the fear of isolation that gives us the courage to open up and take the chance that we will be understood—or worse—is it the worry

that we have done something truly awful and we need reassur-
ance that it wasn't all that terrible and we will survive it.

But underneath those questions and answers were deeper
issues.

Why, that day, in Italy, did the very idea of hearing someone
else's confession excite me? And why, still, does listening to a confession feel deliciously illicit to me? And how do I reconcile the
"badness" of listening, of encouraging people to confess to me?

"*I have to tell you what I did last week.*"

My friend and I are having dinner at a chic Italian restaurant on
Manhattan's Upper East Side. I lean closer. Smile. Encourage her.

"Al and I went to a convention. His work, not mine. You know
how I hate playing corporate wife, but his biggest accounts were
there and I couldn't get out of it. Thursday afternoon, while he
was golfing with the clients, I was lying by the pool and a man
took the chaise next to me and after a while we started talking. It
was totally nothing at first. He works in the industry, but not at
Al's company."

She shifts in her seat now, and her body language signals the
two men at the table next to us that she is telling me something
she doesn't want anyone to hear and so they start to listen. I sense
their interest, I feel their eavesdropping. I revel in it. Everything
about this moment is illicit: the thrill of the confession to come,
the strangers listening, and the intimacy of the moment. If Julia
senses the men listening, she doesn't show it. Or perhaps she does
and that is why she becomes even more animated as she contin-
ues the telling of her tale.

"He ordered us drinks . . . some kind of rum punches . . . and
we drank and talked and then in the middle of something, I can't
remember what . . . he took an ice cube out of his glass and put it
up to my neck, behind my ear, and then incredibly slowly he ran

it down my neck, across my collarbone, down my arm, and then across my waist, and then he let it slip out of his fingers and it slid down the inside of my thigh."

Her lips were parted and slightly moist, and her eyes were shining as she relived the afternoon at the pool. I was held in a state of suspended animation—living vicariously through her exploits. She was offering a plate of unadulterated thrills for me to share without any repercussions on my part. Whatever her assignation had done to her—it would only entertain and excite me. I was not living out being bad by listening, was I?

Of course I was. I was cheating along with her and at the same time getting the goods without having to take any chances.

That's the thrill of listening. And it's the thrill of telling too, because you know from your own experiences that the person you are sharing your story with is responding, is accepting what you've done by the welcoming tell-me-more reaction she's offering in return.

"What happened? I know. But tell me."

I urged her on. I wanted the fix she was offering. It sparked my own memories. I slipped back to the point that I could almost, almost feel real fingers on my neck and lips on my breast.

"I spent the rest of the afternoon with him in bed. It was amazing. The whole time I kept thinking that Al might be back at the hotel, might be in our room, or walking around the grounds looking for me, and it just made it better. It made it amazing. Isn't that terrible?"

But she didn't look terrible. She looked ebullient, alive, vital, and vibrant. She looked like a bad girl.

It's a gleam. You know it when you see it. A way of tilting your head, of smiling with just the corner of your mouth, of slyly looking up from under your lashes. It proclaims that you know

who you are and what you have done and you don't care if you
get branded because of how damn good it feels.

So good you need to confess it and relive it.

At least in the moment.

Sometimes the confession takes on a life of its own.

I was at a dinner with my now ex-husband and another couple.
Cara had once worked for my ex but was now working for a com-
peting company. The two men had football in common, and it
was that time of year. We all shared a bottle of wine with dinner,
and Cara, who usually doesn't drink, did. We talked about a
recent business trip she'd taken to Amsterdam and when she
leaned closer to me, I felt a tingle of anticipation. I knew the look
in her eyes. She was going to tell me her secret. And to encourage
her, I feigned a closeness to her I did not feel because I needed her
story the way an addict needs a fix.

It's all right, I told her. I won't tell anyone. You can trust me.

I smiled. She began her tale.

"I did the most amazing thing while I was there . . . the only
reason I can tell you, is that you write about this sort of thing in
your books. I think you'll understand."

I told her that of course I would. My response was automatic.
I was already hooked. I wanted to know.

Why? My own marriage at the time was on shaky ground, not
out of histrionics and hysteria but a dull, throbbing boredom.
I was ripe for a magical mystery tour of someone else's excitement, and she provided it. And because I had learned, over time,
that the thrill of listening made me feel bad. And sometimes bad
feels so damn good.

In my teens and twenties, I'd never been afraid of acting out,
rewriting the rules, or breaking the rules. The high that came
with doing what I wanted, when I wanted, was addictive. But I'd

weaned myself from that drug when I entered into my marriage. I gave up part of me to become us. And that night, years later, I was suffering the loss of my daring younger self.

It had become easier and much, much safer to listen to other people's thrills than it was to open my eyes and see that I didn't have any thrills of my own.

"We had passed through the red-light district a few times already and that last day there I knew that if I didn't go ahead I'd lose my chance. Before our last dinner I stopped at a store and bought a cheap men's silk tie. I wore my black pantsuit to the dinner, with a simple white shirt underneath the jacket. Flat shoes. I slicked my hair back. After the event ended I took a cab to the district and en route buttoned up the shirt and put on the tie. I knew exactly which girl I wanted; I'd seen her sitting in her window. Fluffy, feminine, round.

"When I walked in she didn't even blanch. I'm sure I looked like what I was . . . a woman dressed up like a man . . . but she just gave me a tired smile and asked how she could help me. She spoke very little English, but that was better. I didn't want to talk to her. I kept on the shirt and tie, just took off my pants.

"I felt as if I was someone else. On the other side of the mirror. Looking at myself going down on a woman. I wasn't really there. And that's what made it so incredible."

Amazingly the two men still hadn't picked up on the story Cara told me; they kept talking football. I was in some kind of dreamlike state, imagining the movie running behind my eyes of the scene in the prostitute's small room in the red-light district.

I was fascinated, mesmerized. And surprised. Cara was not very adventurous.

But even more surprising than the story she told me that night was what happened to our friendship afterward. Cara stopped talking to me. She couldn't face me. When I ran into her a few weeks later, she went out of her way to avoid me.

I never found out what happened, though I tried.

Had telling me made it too real for her? Had her confession forced her to confront it in a way she hadn't before? Was I now complicit in her dangerous liaison and so a reminder of a momentary slip she didn't want to face?

The experience made me wary of hearing the stories of other friends. Cautious that even if the unburdening is a release, there might be further consequences that go beyond the initial thrill of the spill.

But it didn't matter. I accepted the risk. I wanted the rewards. Even though confessing it now isn't something I'm proud of.

"Tell me this thing you have done. It is wrong (or bad, or evil, or forbidden, or blasphemous), it may be a burden for me to hear it, but it may also reveal my own hidden desires. If I listen and respond, we might experience a sudden intimacy. It could create an emotional bond between us. It might bring us closer, allow us to be spiritually naked together. It could separate us for a time or forever. But I still want you to tell me. You still want someone to bear witness to what you did. Not your partner—he or she was complicit and part of the scenario. Someone who was not there. And I want to be your witness, your screen, let you project your mind movie onto me and see it again. You'll see it again—watch it play out in my eyes. And I will be able to live it, every illicit moment of it, as if it had happened to me."

Turn It *Up*!

LOLLY WINSTON

I'm not exactly proud of the time I called our college dorm director a chicken fucker when he asked me to turn down my stereo. And so now that I'm in my forties, I wish my best college friend, Quee, would stop *telling* this story at dinner parties.

"So we turn it down," Quee recounts to a table of grown-ups sipping lobster bisque, "and we're all doing our best Eddie Haskell, convincing him we're sorry and we'll break up the party. He's about to leave, when Lolly, who's had *way* too many beers, leans out of her room and shouts, 'Is that chicken fucker *gone* yet?' And he says, 'No, Lolly, I'm still here, and you're *busted!*' "

Quee slaps the dining room table, her eyes welling with tears of laughter. "Oh, you were *fun* back then," she says wistfully. The other guests smile mildly at the lone glass of wine I've been nursing all night.

I'm embarrassed by Quee's anecdote, and I'm also a little hurt. She seems to be implying that I'm *not* fun now. Granted, I'm not the lampshade-on-my-head life of the party anymore, but I like to think I can still have a good time.

Or have I become a milquetoast bore in my old age? After one glass of chardonnay I develop a weepy affection for everyone; after two glasses I have to go home and sleep for ten hours. I'm a grown-up now—a good girl with a mortgage, who recycles and belongs to public radio and drinks green tea and pays bills on time and deadheads annuals and even irons placemats.

By contrast, between the ages of fourteen and twenty-one I smoked pot behind the garage, shoplifted costume jewelry, cut class to drink Boone's Farm wine, trespass, and skinny-dip in the reservoir, smoked Lucky Strikes (Lucky Strike Means Fine Tobacco), hitchhiked, manufactured a fake ID, smoked codeine out of a bong, slept with boys whose last names I couldn't remember, had an abortion, wrote other students' English papers for beer funds, and ate the maple syrup I was supposed to sell to raise money for my high school.

For some reason I feel worst about the syrup transgression. I still don't get why schools make kids do door-to-door fund-raising, but our school supplied us with U.S. grade-A dark amber maple syrup in a pretty tin with a bucolic picture of Vermont on it. The stuff looked so inviting that when my friends and I got stoned after school one day, we cooked up a whole loaf of French toast, sampled most of the syrup, refilled it with the lesser Log Cabin variety, sold it to the neighbors and kept the money. Now when kids shuffle up to my door with their stale candy and too-thin wrapping paper, I place my order thinking back on that duped family who bought our bogus maple blend, wondering if they ever noticed the cloying corn-syrup taste as they tucked into their pancakes.

The only bad-girl habit I've kept over the years is playing loud music. I've yet to find a medication that works as well as Pink Floyd's "Comfortably Numb" blasted at window-rattling decibels, especially when you get to the searing guitar solo. Over the years, whenever anything terrible has happened, I've blasted that song. My college boyfriend died in a car accident and I turned it up. My mother was diagnosed with a brain tumor and I turned it up. Now, I turn up the stereo when I'm feeling sad, turn it up when I'm celebrating, and turn it up when I'm frustrated with writing. I'll take a break, close the windows, and blast the Talking Heads' "Burning Down the House," hoping to light a fire under my muse's ass. Really distressing news, such as an illness or death in the family, now calls for thunderous organ music, specifically Bach's Toccata and Fugue in D Minor.

I've loved loud music since I was a kid, maybe because my parents screamed at each other for the first twelve years of my life, until my mother finally moved out of the house. I've cranked the knob since I got my first Radio Shack record player, even blasting Judy Collins. "Bows and flows of angel hair!"

"For the love of God, turn it down!" my father would bellow up the stairs.

Now that I'm in my forties I've got tinnitus and a baby-boomer hearing loss, which I actually find a bit comforting.

"*What* is that *noise?*" my younger husband will groan when we're sitting at an outdoor café or sleeping in a hotel room.

I cup a hand to my ear and struggle to listen. "What noise?"

"You don't *hear* that?"

I shake my head. A faucet dripping, a car idling on the street, a dog barking. I'm encased in my own buffer zone.

When friends come over to watch *The Sopranos* with us, my husband apologetically explains that we have a ritual of playing the opening song "really loud for Lolly."

"Woke up this morning, got yourself a gun!" the TV growls during the opening montage. Gritty images of streets and store-fronts fly by Tony's car window as he grips the steering wheel and chomps on a cigar. Raw and thumping, the song always pushes away my worries, reminding me that no matter what I'm stressed about, nobody's going to put a cap in my ass.

Back in my college days I wasn't courteous enough to close the windows before turning up the stereo. I played the records that my older hippie brothers listened to—particularly the Doors and Cream, wanting to ensure that my fellow classmates understood that Clapton was still God. Then the Talking Heads and Elvis Costello came along, saving us from disco and the corny earnest-ness of Dan Fogelberg folk rock. Video killed the radio star, and irony saved us from sincerity, and I just wanted to turn it up even louder!

One afternoon a professor called our dorm to ask that the rock music be turned down because it was overpowering an outdoor chamber music concert in a garden across campus. Thus I was "busted" again. At our school "busted" meant you were written up and referred to the college judicial committee—a student gov-ernment body of debate team nerds and senators in training—charged with determining the penance for offenses such as drinking, smoking, cutting class, staying out past curfew, blasting music—all activities at which I excelled. After they heard your defense, the committee determined your punishment, which ranged from suspension or expulsion to the lesser call to your par-ents and a sentence of working without pay in the cafeteria. I peeled lots of potatoes, but I managed to graduate.

I didn't survive those partying years without injury, how-ever. On various drunken occasions I fell into a window well and cracked a rib, tumbled out of a shopping cart I was trying to "surf" down a steep street and broke my wrist, and incurred a concussion when a car I was riding in flipped over on a dirt road. In my senior year of college I awoke to a hangover so painful that I convinced a friend to drive me to the emergency room. The nausea, squiggles, flashes, and shakes were so spooky that I drank only ginger ale and club soda for the next fifteen years. Now it's probably a good thing I don't have a teenage daughter, because I don't think I'd allow her to wander beyond the end of the driveway, let alone out to a party.

Yet when I think back on those party-girl years, they seem to have been the happiest in my life. I was easy to please, for one thing; I thought Heineken was the fanciest thing money could buy, and homegrown pot served with International Coffee whipped up in a hotpot made for a festive gathering. I even liked my summer job working as a chambermaid. I'd wake up, get stoned, clean sand out of bathtubs, swim in Ice House Pond on the walk home, shower, and wait to find out where the party would be that night. Instead of saving cash after paying the bills, I bought reggae albums and Lancer's wine. I didn't worry about money because I was financially irresponsible.

While it makes me cringe to think of my oblivious lack of manners back then (bouncing rent checks, stealing Valium out of a neighbor's medicine chest), I miss my inner bad girl. There's something about playing hooky to go sledding on a pilfered cafeteria tray that epitomizes a fearless joie de vivre I no longer seem to possess. Maybe Quee's right; maybe I'm not fun anymore. Or maybe it was just plain easier to have fun back then—back in an era when we had little to worry about other than finals and student loans. In fact the whole country had less to worry about; we didn't have herpes, let alone AIDS. We didn't know just yet that every consumable substance other than green tea is harmful to the system. Our only dire concern was the Cold War—whether the Russians or President Reagan or some nut would *press the button*. And if we college students got to thinking about that *too* much, we just partied harder, finding someone to drive us into town to buy a keg. Then Sting came out with that dreamy song about how the Russians probably didn't want to blow up their kids any more than we did and even the Cold War didn't seem so bad.

These days I worry about everything from global warming to war in the Middle East to identity theft to bird flu. YOU SHOULD WORRY! the headlines scream. It seems you can't be a responsible adult without being perpetually freaked out. But my old habits are saving me from an ulcer: I've started turning off the news more often and punching up my car stereo. Because the truth is I'm worried about all this worrying—I'm *tired* of worrying. Recently I had a moment when I decided to give it a rest. I was at the allergist, who has determined that I'm allergic to everything except feathers. I need two inhalers, a nasal spray, and two different prescription pills just to leave the house. And still I wheeze and cough. So the doctor recommended I buy an air filter for my bedroom and protective covers for my mattress and box spring. "Why?" I asked. Was I allergic to my own *bed*?

"Dust mites," he said gravely, pulling a flyer from one of many Plexiglas holders on the wall. "These guys." He pointed to a photo that had been enlarged about 500 times to reveal the image of a prehistoric-looking gray, several-legged creature with fangs. There was a plume of debris in its wake that the caption referred to as *fecal allergens*. "They live in your mattress pad." The doc handed me a catalog of products including masks and gloves and filters and covers and blowers and every kind of boy-in-the-bubble product you could imagine. I went home and dutifully ordered the air filter and the special zip-up protective mattress covers made of microfiber fabric with a pore size of only 3.03

microns. The catalog lady said the items would take five to seven business days to arrive. When I curled up under the duvet with my book that night I pictured the dust mites and their fecal matter teeming in the mattress pad beneath me. Maybe I should have chosen the more expensive overnight shipping. I contemplated sleeping on the couch wrapped in a bleached sheet. Then I closed my eyes. I could not do it. I couldn't wedge dust mites onto my worry list—couldn't fit them between the mercury content of salmon and the San Andreas Fault. My inner bad girl piped up. *Fuck the dust mites*, she said. *If you have the time and energy to stress about your mattress pad, your life must be pretty good.* She was right. At the time the people in Basra didn't have any water, and basic human rights of the women in Afghanistan had barely been restored. Knowing this, my inner bad girl helped me make a good decision: My forties are going to be my fuck-it decade.

The dust mites can picnic on my flesh and build a strip mall in my sinus cavities, and I don't care. I'll vote and be environmentally mindful and give to charities and close the windows before blasting, "Can't You Hear Me Knocking?" I won't ever call anyone a chicken fucker again, except maybe certain politicians, and it'll be under my breath. But I will not sweat the mites. Life's precariously too short and they're impossibly too small. The next morning I chucked the four-panel color brochure dedicated to the dust mites' shenanigans. I forgot the dirty breakfast dishes, left the newspapers to curl and yellow in the driveway, put on the new Raconteurs CD, and *turned it up*.

Consider the Slut

ELLEN SUSSMAN

When my teenage niece got busted by my brother for having a boy in her bed—a boy who wasn't even her boyfriend!—she boldly defended herself: *Dad, a girl has needs!*

I was a girl with needs. Back when I was a teenager, most of us thought only boys had needs. But when a bunch of us fourteen-year-olds gathered at Jerem Gordon's house to watch Neal Armstrong walk on the moon, I found a place to lie down on the couch in front of Steven Bash. He pulled a blanket over us and slipped his hand up my shirt. He kept it there, moving it ever so slightly. Wordlessly we invented a new game. I couldn't wiggle or make a sound; if I did, everyone would know that he was feeling my new breasts. As long as I kept still, his fingers would tease my nipples, circle my stomach, dip under my pants. I loved this game, with its illicit charge, and I loved what my body did under his playful touch. My God, this was better than popcorn, better than the practice kisses my girlfriends and I shared, better than my own late-night explorations. I was on fire and I stayed that way, with my gang of friends gathered round, the blanket pulled high, and Steven's breath in my ear. Neal Armstrong and I both stepped into outer space. The world was never the same.

The other boys must have learned about our game because over the next years they each played it with me while we all crowded together in someone's basement or attic. The rules always stayed the same—I couldn't stir or moan or sigh. Containing my pleasure added heat to the fire. But I understood the real reason for stillness: secrecy. If the blanket fell to the floor, we would be exposed. The boys were never my boyfriends; they were always just friends. Maybe the other girls would have considered me a slut (though the boys were not).

My game was all about female pleasure. I don't remember touching the boy in return, though I leaned back against him and enjoyed the feeling of his hard cock pressing against the back of my legs.

*O*ne night, at age fourteen, I told my parents I was going to a friend's house. A twenty-one-year-old boy I had met in Florida during my Christmas vacation picked me up in his car. We went to Cadwalader Park and in the parking lot of the Monkey House, we climbed into the backseat and lost ourselves in a tangle of clothes. A policeman's flashlight interrupted our space ride, and the cops busted the guy for statutory rape. No, I said. He didn't do anything wrong. He had his hand down your pants, they said. Yes, I told them. I wanted him to do that.

I remember the terror I felt that night—of being caught by the cops, of being exposed in the harsh glare of the spotlight, of watching Brett fumble for his ID while the cops prepared their handcuffs. And then I felt another terror—or was it a thrill?—as I spoke the words aloud: *I wanted him to do that.* The policemen's expressions changed in an instant. I was no longer the sweet young girl being molested by a beast. I was a beast in my own right.

The cops brought us back to my house. They asked my father to press charges; for some odd reason he said no. Now, looking back, I realize that he was already dying of cancer, though I didn't know it then. Perhaps when he thought of kids making out in the backseat of a car he imagined pleasure, not prison. Perhaps he didn't want to make a fuss; he had other things on his mind.

My mother called me a slut. I remember walking down to the basement, where my brother was playing Ping-Pong with Steven Bash. My mother screamed the word—*SLUT*—and then slammed the door, which rattled in the door frame for the whole time that I stood there at the bottom of the steps, looking at the boys, who looked at me, the sounds echoing around us.

I wasn't a slut. I was cautious about losing my virginity and spent most of my high school and college years looking for love. But I also wanted a good time. I wanted the remarkable pleasure of bodies rubbing up against each other, of skin awakening under someone's touch, of the surge of energy that runs from the spot under my ear to the arch of my foot.

Consider the slut. Who is she? Myth offers a girl who wants to be popular, so she sleeps with every guy on the football team. Or a girl who's plump and pimpled; she can only believe she's beautiful if the guys keep taking her to that secluded spot behind the bleachers.

Maybe not. Maybe she's a girl who likes sex. Maybe she likes it so much that she's willing to get it instead of waiting for it to get her. Maybe she's sick of the double standard and knows that while everyone's whispering about her reputation, she's exploring new galaxies.

Consider making out. You're both clothed, cramped into too tight a space—the backseat of the car, the couch in the living room, the daybed in the attic. The boy smells like a boy, like he's just finished mowing the lawn. His hair is too long and falls in his face, making him look both shy and wicked. When he kisses you he tastes like Coca-Cola and pot and potato chips. His tongue finds your ear, and something happens between your legs, something you've never felt before. Your skin becomes electric, and his fingers send shock waves along your arms, your legs. That spot between your legs pulses as if your heart slipped from your chest to your groin. You love his skin, how it tastes, how it's coarser, darker than yours. You touch his neck, and he makes a noise from somewhere deep inside and you think: *I* did that to him. You do it again. His leg pushes between your legs, your jeans rub against his, the fabric tight against your new bikini underpants with the pink hearts. You won't take your pants off, you won't slip down your underpants; he'll never discover that you're wet, but when he presses his crotch against you, he might know how much you want him.

The Beard

MADELEINE BLAIS

When I was fourteen and my mother told me that I would be leaving my public school to enter the Ursuline Academy on Plumtree Road in Springfield, Massachusetts, for the ninth grade, I balked, worried about how strict the nuns would be. My mother assured me that I should feel honored: Only the finest young ladies, worthy of the most rigorous spiritual and intellectual training, were allowed to go to "the Academy," as she called it for short.

According to her the Ursuline nuns were cultured.

They were smart. They had traveled. To Italy! To Rome!

"They are," she proudly informed anyone who asked, "the female equivalent of the Jesuits. And the best part is that their school motto is *Serviam,* I Shall Serve, same as James Joyce."

The *best* part?

Now coed and no longer Catholic, the school still stands, under different management. I dropped by recently: a brief tour yielded stock images of scuffed linoleum and metal lockers and a gym with the same dead-sock smell of yore. It was hard to reconcile the bland generic building with the hold it had over me back then. I was the girl who had to behave because she had no choice, by dint of being a scholarship student. What made matters worse is that eventually my mother took a job as a lay teacher at the elementary version of the school, and my three younger sisters also enrolled at Ursuline, so the pressure to be a role model, that most irritating of girl fates, was intense. I went along and soon enough became the official good girl, the "designated friend," the "beard" brought in by other girls to fool their parents before the good times could roll.

When I first encountered the Ursulines at the age of fourteen, they had perfected a brilliant strategy for managing adolescent girls: They treated misdemeanors like felonies. If you can get into as much trouble as we did by allowing our knee socks to droop or neglecting to stand when a grown-up entered the room or daring to talk when we were supposed to be walking single file in silence between classes, who would ever risk anything more overtly criminal? To add insult to injury, we were the only girls in Catholic school history whose "ugly uniforms" really *were* ugly uniforms, boxy, dull, battleship-gray, without the slightest tinge of submerged eroticism.

For four years, from 1961 to 1965, Mother Mary Assumpta drilled us in Latin. How proud she was that her religious name embodied a principle of grammar, a past perfect participle: "having been assumed." She led us in cheers, involving not cute boys

and football and pom poms, as we would have liked, but, oddly,
Latin prepositions:

In, cum, sine, ab, ex, de, pro.
What do they take?
The ablative!
When do they take it?
After a give, tell, or show verb!
In, cum, sine, ab, ex, de, pro.

Mother Francis Regis, who taught French with an Irish accent,
was, like all self-respecting French teachers a bit—right now I
need the *mot juste*—let's just settle for "original." She had a secret
worldly streak we all admired. She flirted with the fathers, she
lobbied to get us into speech and drama festivals at various
schools across the state, which meant she got to stop at HoJo's
on the turnpike where she ate fried clams and—can this be
possible?—she sometimes nursed a cocktail! She used to produce
LIFE magazines from beneath the folds of her habit, with pictures
of movies stars on the cover (Marilyn Monroe! Clark Gable!), magazines she later told me she hid under the mattress in her room at
the convent lest they be confiscated.

Mother Mary Immaculata did double duty as the geometry
teacher and as the dysgraphia queen, hounding girls with crabbed
penmanship into finally loosening their grip on their pencils and
creating loops and flourishes worthy of God's eyes.

They worked hard and they meant well, the nuns. Everything
about them and the school was sincere and high-minded. Our
guest speakers had two tried and true topics, moral hygiene and
the missions in Africa. February was Catholic Press Month and
we got to sample magazines like *Saint Anthony's* and *Commonweal,*

free. Sometimes we cut loose with Catholic-themed crossword puzzles: "Seven letters, across, Proper Noun: Jack and Bobby———.

*N*ot just our prayers were rote, so were our thank-you notes.

If we got invited to Cathedral High School by a boy to a bona fide prom, above and beyond our usual prim tea dances in the middle of the afternoon, we all sent the same scripted response:

> *I want to thank you for our date.*
> *We had a lovely night.*
> *It made the moon look larger.*
> *The stars twice as bright.*

*O*ur overnight senior trip was a didactically sound excursion to the Shakespeare festival in Connecticut, a theatrical marathon in which we got to see *Twelfth Night, As You Like It,* and *The Taming of the Shrew* in less than eighteen hours, leaving no time for the middle-of-the-night exchange of gossip and information that usually makes such trips worthwhile, such as discovering the double meaning of words like "diaphragm" or learning that someone's brother at the College of the Holy Cross has been "carnally active" with a girl he isn't even engaged to.

Try as they might, the nuns could not keep us entirely insulated. Despite their micromanagement (before that word even entered popular usage), a dim sense of a larger, more dangerous, and mysterious world intruded.

We all admired our classmate, Laura, who carried herself with an air of cool so convincing that everyone wanted to be like her, including having her braces, her bad posture, and the shank of hair that forever fell across her freckled face. She did not last the whole four years because she dared to talk back.

Two or three well-off girls courted expulsion because they

thought it would be fun one spring evening to hack away at the greens at their parents' country club, enacting an oedipal revenge we admired from afar.

Once in a while someone smuggled alcohol into a tea dance, with their sugary names like "Frosted Fantasy" and "An Afternoon to Remember." We alternated pilfered sips of gin with candid nibbles of cucumber sandwiches, a combination I do not recommend.

We labored to broaden our horizons as best we could. One classmate's father was an obstetrician with an office on the first floor of their house. It smelled fleshy and pharmaceutical; the series of rooms were a warren of wipes and rubber gloves and tissues at the ready, dominated by stern tables with gleaming metal stirrups. At midnight during sleepovers we would tiptoe downstairs to make giggling raids on her father's medical texts, hoping to be titillated, but somehow the photos of syphilis in action and of newborns' bloody heads cresting in vaginas were the polar opposite of an aphrodisiac.

An enterprising girl ran her own Beatles fan club out of her basement, and someone else had gone to a folk festival in Newport, Rhode Island, and actually heard Peter, Paul and Mary, with their nice New Testament names, sing about hammers and about changing the world. We saw the movie *Tom Jones* and sensed that the way the hero tore into his chicken was a symbol for something more than just tearing into chicken, though we couldn't precisely visualize the next step. We had heard of that dazzling secular temptress Mary McCarthy, and her novel *The Group*, specifically about the "deflowering chapter," and had memorized, even if we did not fully comprehend, the words to "The House of the Rising Sun."

And even though the school was small, there was always, every year, at least one girl who got into real trouble, the serious end-of-the-world kind. She would be there one day, in French class like the rest of us, reciting set pieces:

"Dis donc, ou est la bibliotheque?"

"C'est tout droit. Tu y vas tout de suite?"

"Oui. It faut que j'aille chercher un livre."

And the next thing you know she would have disappeared overnight, banished from the school rolls, trailed by vague rumors of illness, of "pernicious anemia" or "debilitating mononucleosis," medically flavored euphemisms meant to obscure the real reason for her departure.

After we lost the second or third girl to a series of medically flavored euphemisms, a subtle crackdown occurred. Homework doubled, then tripled. The lecture topics expanded to whether or not being in a clique was a mortal sin according to Jesus, and how a polite well-raised girl would never accept a ride in a car with a boy unless there was someone else in the car to chaperone.

Occasions of sin lurked everywhere.

Desperate to experience such occasions firsthand, my friend Katie and I connived to meet boys on the sly, specifically in the parking lot of the East Longmeadow Friendly's Restaurant. To this day my idea of the worst grown-up job in the world would be to have been the guy in charge of Friendly's back then, with the constant traffic of teenagers in heat who had no intention of investing in a Big Beef Cheeseburger or a Swiss Chocolate Almond Sundae or an Awful-Awful, an ice cream drink ("Awful big, awful good") whose name was the subject of a copyright dispute and was eventually replaced with the anemic "Fribble." You could see him, the manager, frantic and cop-like, middle-aged and getting older by the minute, with a furrowed brow and comb marks in his hair, wearing a white shirt and a black bow tie, racing around the parking lot, chasing away nonpaying teens in order to maintain good relations with the family clientele, a losing battle if there ever was one.

A trip to Friendly's, especially on a school night, required elaborate alibis.

"Can you get here tonight?" Katie would whisper into the phone, promising that the boy she had her eye on had a *great* friend, who was both *cute and nice*, and they would join us at eight p.m.

My job was to show up at her house by seven in my mother's Nash Rambler (another beard: Who would ever think of it in terms of a getaway car?) and to reassure her parents as to the essential wholesomeness of our plans for the evening. We would be headed to the library to do research on the Miracle at Fatima, I would say, then stopping by Brightside, with its clumsy Depression-era name, to see if any of the orphans there required tutoring, and probably lighting a candle or two at Holy Name Church, with the intention of praying for heathens to convert, followed by a brief stop at Friendly's, provided we weren't already too exhausted.

I admired my own brilliance, the derring-do of my subterfuge: Folding in the true goal of the evening as a footnote had the cold calculation of natural outlaw.

In addition to my bona fides as a publicly pious sort, my other qualifications for the job of "beard" were that I was blessed with a clear complexion that gave me a certain Joan of Arc glow, at least in the eyes of eager parents willing to believe the best of their daughters and their friends, and that I possessed a showy vocabulary I did not mind using. There was no subject I could not make sound stuffy, possessing as I did a streak of what is sometimes called the male lecture gene. I could dullify anything, even the Bob Dylan concert held at the Springfield Municipal Auditorium on January 29, 1965, nattering on to bored parents: "For those unfamiliar with Dylan, a brief thumbnail sketch is in order. He is a young social satirist who aims scathing attacks at those institutions which he deems outdated, ridiculous, or morally wrong." Short pause to purse my lips. "At the concert, I was surprised to note that not one of his numbers dealt directly with the Negro situation, as that is one of his more prominent causes."

Sometimes I stumbled over my observations, as when I informed one father that I read incestuously, when I meant incessantly, and my pronunciations were often way, way off. To me the *h* in "vehement" was the opposite of silent, and the word "gingerly" had two hard *g*s.

I found there were certain words that parents really liked.

"Invariably" was one, especially if it led into an observation such as, "I have noticed that invariably your daughter is the first one in our crowd to remind everyone of the importance of Holy Days of Obligation."

People believe what they want to believe, and looking back, I would say Katie's parents had exhausted themselves trying to rein in her coltishness, and mine by proxy. She was quickly released into my custody simply because they could not single-handedly withstand human biology. Maybe they also wanted to be alone in their own house for a few hours.

With a set pattern at work, in which I served as a latter-day Edwina Haskell, we would beeline to our mecca, puffing, if we were really lucky, cigarettes lifted from Katie's mother's purse. Sometimes they would be there, sometimes not, those boys who were our grail. Looking back I can summon them only in outline, as vague physical specimens, often impossibly thin, with chests that went in rather than out, shy to the point of aphasia, and yet in our eyes they were deities of a minor but unmistakable sort. Sometimes there would be two or three couples in a car kissing (today this seems not only quaint, but possibly disturbed) and we would be taken, all of us, to a place we had dreamed of going but did not believe we would ever get to, at least not during our ordinary dutiful daylight lives walking single file under the stern gaze of nuns.

One night I got carried away, struck by the obvious.

I realized we didn't have to stay in the parking lot of Friendly's; we could actually drive around and tour the valley. And so we took off, Katie and I and two boys whose names I don't remember, but they were probably Tim or Jack or Jimmy, normal boys' names from the fifties, straightforward and masculine. This was the heartbreaking truth: We didn't do anything, except we took most of the night not doing it. When we got back to Katie's house, her father had stayed up waiting. He was in that uniquely conflicted parental state of gratitude that we were alive, fury that we had defied him and his wife by staying out so late. He had always struck me as a conscientious, dutiful man, partly because of the way at mealtimes he tucked his napkin in at the neck, on guard against stains and mishaps.

I ended up spending the night with Katie in her room with its cool poster of Paul Newman on the wall, and the next day I could hear them talking, Mr. and Mrs. Manahan, and I knew that my cover was no longer working. Like an aging ingenue whose batting eyelashes no longer signal flirtation but, more likely, the possibility of cataracts, it was obvious I had outgrown my role. Like most self-avowed good girls, deep down I was a would-be vamp, along the same psychological principle of reaction formation that causes every vegetarian I have ever met secretly to crave bacon. When I heard one of them mutter, "A bad influence," and the other one agree, my heart lurched with happiness, and I had to recognize that to some degree those were the words I had been courting all along.

Penises I Have Known

DAPHNE MERKIN

idling Up to the Matter at Hand

There are penises so memorable that you never get over them: JC's for instance, a perfect edition worthy of my rapt contemplation, or so it seemed to me when I lay next to him on his seventies-style platform bed in his bachelor's pad on an unmemorable Manhattan side street years ago. Others, too, that you would like to recall—the one belonging to your first lover, for instance, the guy who "cracked your geode" (as the man in the red socks, another lover in your not inconsiderable lineup, once put it)—that seem to have eluded your visual grasp, through no fault of their own. Then again there are those that linger in you, like a ghost penis, although they are long gone, such as the impressive piece of equipment that came along with the deceptively slight fellow you met on a Jewish singles weekend at the now-defunct Grossinger's, a battering ram of a penis that left you raw, a penis so inflexible and obdurate that you could hang a towel on it—which, I might add, he did.

How to talk about your personal history with penises without sounding either all Mae West–bawdy (the old "Is that a gun in your pocket or are you just happy to see me?" routine) or all fluttery and awed, like a hitherto-untouched heroine in a bodice ripper (or, perhaps, like the touched-but-hitherto-unorgasmic heroine of D. H. Lawrence's *Lady Chatterley's Lover*), by the supernal otherness of the thing? "Now I know why men are so overbearing," Constance Chatterley says of her gamekeeper, Mellors, or more specifically of Mellors's penis, which he refers to as his "John Thomas," as though it were indeed an actual third person in the room, observing the action: "But he's lovely, *really*. Like another being! A bit terrifying! But lovely really!"

The problem, for starters, even before we get to the fact that it's difficult—impossible, even—for any single manifestation of this indubitably male organ to live up to its reputation, is how to deal with the word itself so that we're not all blushing or smirking. "Penis." If you say it quickly, pass your eye over it glancingly as though it were not the quasi-scientific clunker of a word, you have accomplished nothing other than a grown-up game of peekaboo: I don't see you, big feller, bulging over there in the middle of the sentence. If, on the other hand, you give the thing its due and enunciate it fully, *pee-nus*, draw it out, acknowledge that it is an awkward coinage pretending to be at ease with itself under the enormous metaphoric burden it carries—bearing the weight of the phallocentric world between its legs—you are left having to deal with the (often incredulous) attention you have drawn by insisting that everything, but everything, is a stand-in for the phallic principle: cars, buildings, pencils, tails, fruit, revolvers, literary images. Take Dylan Thomas's "The force that through the green fuse drives the flower": It can be read as a poem about the life-giving power of a divine force or, in my view, it can be read as a poem about the life-giving force of penises, the surging motilic energy of the male orgasm.

But here I am, getting stuck in an *apologia pro vita erotica sua* before I have even begun. There are countless designations for "penis," of course, just as there are many terms for its equally klutzy-sounding female counterpart, the graceless "vagina." These designations include those one-syllable terms that sound like blunt, wham-bam-thank-you-ma'am heavy objects, such as "dick," "prick," and "cock," as well as the half-amused, half-abashed Yiddish approximations like "shmuck" and "putz." "Putz is worse than shmuck," Maggie Paley declares in her *The Book of the Penis*, which is a veritable font of information on points of lesser and greater interest, including the etymology of "penis," which is Latin for "tail" and a relatively late entry into the vernacular. She adds that the two terms "are now used almost entirely to mean jerk."

Then there are the many fancy descriptions of peckers that a certain kind of male writer delights in providing on behalf of his protagonist, such as Vladimir Nabokov's Humbert Humbert rendering his Lolita-avid penis in typically self-aggrandizing locution as the "scepter of my passion." James Joyce's Leopold Bloom, who hasn't had sex with his wife Molly in more than a decade, considers the generative potential lying dormant within his own relaxed endowment while lying in the bath ("limp father of thousands, a languid, floating flower") with a kind of endearing yet pathetic self-regard. And in Bellow's *Mr. Sammler's Planet*, Sammler comes face-to-face with a black pickpocket's "large tan-and-purple uncircumcised thing" only to find himself counterphobically fascinated with fine distinctions of color and creed: "Metallic hairs bristled at the thick base and the tip curled beyond the supporting, demonstrating hand, suggesting the fleshy mobility of an elephant's trunk, though the skin was somewhat iridescent rather than thick or rough." Not to overlook John Updike, who can always be counted on to sprinkle a few exactingly detailed, paint-by-number evocations of penises in each of his novels. In *Toward the End of Time*, there is a salute to the erect penis of the sex-preoccupied (but of course) narrator, who has masturbated himself to "full stretch" with the aid of his cache of pornography, the better to admire his own handiwork: "the inverted lavender heart-shape of the glans, the majestic tensile column with its marblelike blue-green veins and triple-shafted underside. Stout and faithful fellow! My life's companion. I loved it, or him."

As for myself, I've always warmed to "Johnson," for some ineffable reason, just as I've always warmed to "cunt" over "pussy," for a similarly ineffable reason. And the ironic—or what I take to be ironic—majesty of "rod" speaks to the eighteenth-century serving girl in me. And yet, there is something about the word "penis" in all its obdurate two-syllabled out-thereness (I'll take one penis, if you please) that seems to rise above itself, if only because the stiffly protruding quality of the first syllable ("pe") followed by the curled-up flaccidity of the second ("nis") seems to mimic the dynamic of charge and retreat that is enbodied in the piece of male anatomy being alluded to.

Then again, what is this high-minded introductory musing on the strictures of a given lexicon—or, as is more likely, an extended patch of throat-clearing—but a symptom of the larger predicament of inarticulateness that I, an ordinarily voluble creature, find myself facing when in the presence of this subject? Despite their apparent demystification, penises themselves retain an odd aura of unspeakableness. For all the huge strides we appear to have taken in our discussion of sex —mainly by making it into a discussion about body and gender—the discourse doesn't seem to have advanced much since Lytton Strachey first dropped the word "semen" into one of those Bloomsbury discussions he and his friends, including Virginia Woolf (then Stephen) and her sister, Vanessa, used to have in one another's houses on London evenings in the early twentieth century. Which is why trying to talk about penises still feels, even after Erica Jong's zipless fuck, Monica Lewinsky, and *Sex and the City*, like smashing through glass: as though one were daring to touch a precious and lovingly curated object behind its protective pane with the audacity of mere language. To talk about penises as a woman is to turn yourself into an outlaw and the conversation into smut even before we've gotten to the age-old question of whether size matters. Once and for all: it does, although in less significant and subtler ways than men think. Ernest Hemingway's infamously strutting account in *A Moveable Feast*, for instance, of being called upon to reassure F. Scott Fitzgerald that his equipment was adequate despite Zelda's ballbusting insinuations (the anecdote comes from a chapter with the insufferably coy title of "A Matter of Measurements") seems bogus on many accounts, not least of which is the suggestion that anxieties about the male-signifier-to-end-all-signifiers can be put to rest in quite so concrete a fashion. But the topic makes for easy send-up, as in the brand of condoms that offers a variety of prophylactics (the Nightcap, the Weekender, and the Extended Stay) all in boxes with the word HUGE printed on them.

Penises, it appears, deserve to be worshipped or envied (or, if need be, encouraged) but they don't deserve to be nattered on about. This is still sacred male territory and women trespass at their own literary peril. The potholes are everywhere you look, waiting to trip you up into porn or parody, or perhaps the high gutter baby talk of D. H. Lawrence. Which is not to suggest that Lawrence didn't, despite what is clearly a complicatedly ambivalent attitude toward women, manage to move the conversation more radically forward than most. There may be something laughable about the rhapsodic way Mellors and Lady Constance talk about his "John Thomas" in *Lady Chatterley's Lover*, but there is also something both daring and poignant about Lawrence's attempt to win over his straitlaced and corseted readers to the liberating effect of erotic nakedness. His late phase especially, which includes *Lady Chatterley's Lover* and the short novel *The Man Who Died* (first published, by the bye, as *The Escaped Cock*), shows him pushing beyond what speculum-gazing Kate Millett and others have decried as his worship of the phallus into a more psychologically expansive view of carnal matters.

Lawrence was singular among his contemporaries for naming women's body parts and for attempting to depict female orgasm decades before Norman Mailer and Harold Brodkey got around to trying their hand at it. It seems all the more curious therefore that Virginia Woolf, in a speech she gave to an audience of two hundred women in January 1931 (almost a year after Lawrence's death), noted that it would take another fifty years before "men have become so civilized that they are not shocked when a woman speaks the truth about her body." Whether or not we have arrived at this juncture depends, I suppose, on your sense of how shockable we remain under our contemporary posture of jadedness, but please do note that Woolf's speculation does not make mention of a woman speaking the truth about *his* body. It is as though this were a possibility not even to be hinted at except on a different planet than ours. Which brings me back to where I began, unwilling to consign myself to the outpost of raunch yet unsure whether a seat will be found for me inside the clean, well-lit rooms of polite company.

The Matter at Hand
It is to be asserted, then, that very few women talk about the specifics of penises: the too-shortness, longness, thinness, fatness,

curviness, redness, veininess, *whateverness* of them. Nice girls aren't supposed to take note of the individual penis in all its clinical details (its potential for beauty or hideousness as well as defining characteristics like length, girth, and color)—for fear, I suppose, that the whole delicate scaffolding, the prerequisite of a cock-of-the-walk confidence if a man is to be able to perform in the bedroom, would come crashing down around us.

Or perhaps it's simply that no one wants to know what her husband's or lover's penis really looks like when seen through the keyhole because it's too heavy a responsibility—like carrying around a state secret with you all the time, burning a hole in your pocket, imperiling future lives. An article I read in a woman's magazine about how to maintain strong friendships advised readers not to step over the other person's "comfort zone" and went on to cite a conversation about penis size—in which a friend of the writer's revealed in a whisper over lunch that the man she was dating and whom she would later marry had a very small penis ("It's, like, miniature")—as its first and most glaring example of an inappropriate revelation. The writer felt burdened with this indiscretion forever after and can't, apparently, see this friend alone or together with her minusculely endowed husband without feeling overcome with mortification.

Indeed, I have sophisticated female friends who to this very day continue to insist that there's no difference between one penis and the next. This claim always makes me feel morally suspect, as though I were a foot fetishist or a frequenter of bondage chat rooms—someone mired in trivial and immature considerations, measuring the circumference of a banana while everyone else has moved on to worry about global warming. And, yes, I know that on the grander existential scale, or even on the less grand functional scale, it doesn't matter all that much, but then again neither does breast size or the shape of your ass—and men never tire of discussing these. One might conjecture that while the male gaze makes us feminine, confirms heterosexual women in their sense of their own desirability by the very act of assessing it (weighing breasts like so many sacks of potatoes and coming up with ideal ratios of waist-to-hip size as if women were Barbie dolls made real), the assessing female gaze *un*makes the masculine principle in men, threatens to render them into mere part objects of desire (the breast standing in for the woman, the penis for the man) rather than whole glorious beings—He who does the Desiring. We in turn collude with men in treating the detached appraisal of sexual parts as an exlusively male prerogative by looking away and talking of the ardor or duration of men's sexual performance rather than the prescribed nature of their equipment, whether crooked or straight, daunting or drooping.

Then again, there is no way not to take notice of what is more often than not first perceived to be an absurd and even ungainly appendage—before, that is, its emblematic significance to the human race is factored in, like bonus points giving added Erector set value. Not even I, brought up in an Orthodox German-Jewish household where my mother went wild if we failed to put on robes ("dressing gowns," as we called them) could successfully overlook the penises surrounding me. It's one thing to deliberately blind yourself to the reality of your father's penis—which, with the exception of girls who happen to be brought up around nudists, is what I think most of us do. To the extent that I wondered about my father's penis, I ascribed to it my feelings about him, which would have made his penis unlikable and scary at once (albeit not scary in a curiosity-inspiring way). But it's another thing altogether to overlook the penises of three brothers, especially if you happen to have slept in the same room with two of them until you are eight years old, at which point a psychiatrist suggests to your mother that it might be better for your already faltering mental health if you slept either by yourself or in a room with your two sisters.

I don't know whether I suffered from any adverse comparisons I made between my own body and my brothers' bodies—whether, that is, I was affected by what used to go by the formal appellation "penis envy"—but I do know I felt outmuscled by them. And that I studied the crotch of their pajama pants when I thought no one was looking, intrigued by the odd way the cotton bunched up in this area—as though it contained a small cluster of grapes—while my own pajamas had to make no such accommodations. Years later I would be reminded of this disparity (and the fact that it had probably made more of an impression on me than I consciously realized) when I read one of Flaubert's tirades against the treacherous nature of women: "Women have no notion of rectitude. The best among them have no compunctions about listening at doors, unsealing letters, counseling and practicing a thousand little deceits, etc. It all goes back to their organ. Where man has an Eminence, they have a Hole! That eminence is Reason, Order, Science, the Phallus-Sun, and the hole is night, humidity, confusion." No wonder Madame Bovary gave up and swallowed arsenic.

And sometimes, it must be admitted, even *after* such calculations are made, after one has an idea of what penises can get up to, they still pose themselves as less than sublime. I think of a conversation I had not long ago, sitting around the kitchen table with my adolescent daughter and my forty-year-old Filipina housekeeper, concerning the physical noncharms of the penis. Of the three of us, I'm quite sure I was the only one who had seen an adult penis up close, and thus could draw on the evidence of my senses rather than the evidence of visual images. But no matter: My daughter and my housekeeper were in cheerful agreement as to the unregenerate ugliness of penises—the sheer aesthetic silliness of the design, as they saw it, especially when you took into account the whole picture, including the surrounding hairiness and the existence of those two undignified balls.

I listened with some amusement to their remarks, envisioning us in a bawdy scene out of Chaucer, set in a dim low-ceilinged room lit by sputtering candles rather than in my linoleum-floored kitchen awash in recessed lighting, three girls sitting around the hearth speaking the unvarnished truth about men. (I should include my friend Elizabeth—who has been conversant in her time with a shuddersome number of penises and stoutly believes they're an acquired taste—in this warm and candid circle. "If you're a visual person," Elizabeth once explained to me, "the penis is a hideous organ, which isn't to say I don't like them.") But I also felt a slight sense of unease, even foreboding, at the dismissive tone that was being taken. What, I wondered, if men (any man, the father of three across the hall, say, or the doorman who guarded us from potential marauders and always greeted us as though he was genuinely happy to see us again) knew that they were being viewed in this way—that it was even possible to size up their most prized credential with so much irreverence? I understood that my unmarried and possibly virginal housekeeper had little use for men, but how had I failed in transmitting to my daughter the necessary sense of gravitas about the subject, without which she would clearly be doomed, giving off the wrong signal, a slew of insufficiently dazzled pheromones?

It wasn't, after all, as though I were consciously trying to raise a rampaging shrew, a Lorena Bobbit, say, or, going back several decades, a maddened man hater like Valerie Solanas, who first penned the SCUM Manifesto and then shot Andy Warhol. Heaven forfend. I had loved men in my time, including my daughter's father; I had loved penises, sometimes more than the men they were attached to. Presumably I would do so again, but meanwhile I saw the line I had to adopt. It was up to me to put matters right, to defend the maligned organ. "It's actually quite nice," I heard myself say, as we all scraped the last of the mint-chocolate ice cream from our bowls. I moved gingerly from the particular to the general, trying to walk a line between a discriminating embrace and wholehearted sluttishness: "They sort of grow on you." And then, as the coup de grace, I, who had gone through life half resistant and half in thrall to men and their effect on me, especially in bed, who had resisted the "privileging" of the male sexual organ even as I marveled at its ability to transform itself from something soft and passive into something hard and driven and capable of filling you up like a stopper in a bottle, came out openly as an advocate. As my daughter and my housekeeper first stared at me and then at each other, I added: "I like them." Just in the nick of time, I retracted a bit, lest I sound like I was a come-one-come-all appreciater of penises, the sort of woman who liked all flavors of ice cream as long as they were cold. "I mean, some of them."

The Matter in Hand

Sooner or later it happens. They exert their charms, persuade you that your Hole needs their Eminence. Or if not quite that, they prove indispensable to your feeling more vivid and less alone, no longer adrift in the vastness of the world but grounded in the snug fit of the erotic moment. In my case, the pivotal "Aha!" arrived, in the manner of many belated recognitions, with a compensatory force, so that for a while in the latter half of my twenties I found myself walking around in a haze of penis longing. After holding on to my virginity until the age of twenty-five with a slightly deranged fervor indicative of equal parts fear and desire, I acted as though I had awakened to a new morning. The world seemed charged not with the grandeur of God, as the poet Gerard Manley Hopkins had it, but with the grandeur of erections. I liked the feel of a penis growing firm in my hand (it would take years before I felt truly comfortable with a penis in my mouth) and I loved the feel of an urgent penis inside me, pushing through beyond my usual barriers to the hopelessly receptive Lady Chatterley core of me. I thought they—the confederacy of penises—were close to amazing in their ability to change shape in so dramatic a way. I imagined it to be a special effect that kept happening just for me, over and over again. It was hard for me to believe that other women—scads of other women—could produce this same result.

The penises I became acquainted with were uniformly circumcised—I had wandered away from my religiously observant upbringing, but not that far—and early on I noticed small differences between one circumcised penis and another that turned out not to be so small. There were a few times I got out of bed midway because the penis in question was too big or too stocky or hazardously curved, like a scimitar. Once I fled the Plaza Hotel because a minor movie producer with a legendary reputation as a cocksman appeared not only to be hung like the proverbial horse but had a slightly glazed look in his eye, which, together with his musings on the wonders of anal sex, scared me back into my clothes. Several years later, when this same man and I went to bed in a hotel in Beverly Hills, I felt appreciative of the vigor with which he made love, his penis no longer striking me as gargantuan but rather as generous.

I remember watching him afterward as he sat naked on the edge of the capacious hotel bed, singing some ditty he had learned in military school decades earlier. He began to get dressed by pulling on a pair of red socks and for a moment, before he put on the rest of his clothes, I felt a great sense of loss. He was leaving me in my expensive room—taking his penis, which I had become fond of, with him. For a moment I thought of asking him to stay, or of asking him to leave me his penis as a memento. We women become quite attached, you know, which is both our triumph and our defeat. If I had to make a guess as to what it is that we become attached to I would end up fumbling for the right words, talking in slightly abject terms about the feeling of being filled, which sounds suspiciously as though I believed in Flaubert's antiphonal Holes and Eminences, when what I really believe in is something vaguer, something along the lines of a certain kind of need being met by a certain kind of virile understanding. Not to get too Lawrentian about it, I suppose I might say that we are all composed of psychological Holes and Eminences and that sometimes a man comes along wearing the red socks—or maybe it's really the penis by way of the red socks—you've been looking for all these years. At which point you're a goner and his penis, whatever its reality, looks like the very model you've been lusting after without even knowing it.

Reckless

SUSAN STRAIGHT

About ten times a year I get completely airborne in my vehicle while speeding over the railroad tracks just past my daughters' elementary school a mile from our house.

The feeling of the van leaving the asphalt and the metal rails perpendicular to the tires, the whole body suspended for a moment and then, in my imagination during that moment gathering itself like an animal underneath me, legs curving while flying, and then slamming back down on the other side—on the other side of the school and the plaza with our grocery store and shops—is something I cannot give up. I can't give it up even though I am a single mother with three girls who lives a near-saintly daily existence of work and driving and school runs and homework and cooking and laundry—a selfless routine many of my fellow single mothers know too well.

The fact that my car is an eleven-year-old green Mercury Villager van, with honor roll bumper stickers and dents put in the body by hit-and-run idiots, doesn't negate the fact that my car has enough power to fly up over those tracks, to fly around curves on desert highways and deserted orange grove roads.

I speed up when I see the tracks, when it's late at night and I'm alone in the van after dropping someone off for a sleepover, or picking something up near midnight at the grocery store, when I feel so lonely for my old sometimes-wild life and my gone brother that I have no other choice but to turn the radio to Van Halen or AC/DC and pretend he and I are still driving together and not giving a damn about safety or sanity or anything but the pounding music and blur outside our open windows.

Because the windows have to be open. That's how it always was.

My brother, three years younger, was the only person in the world with my exact genetic heritage. I have half-brothers and sisters, stepbrothers and sisters, foster brothers and sisters. But when my brother's thick blond hair hung to his waist, as it did for more than ten years, our grandmother mistook us for each other from behind.

All my best memories of my brother are in vehicles, speeding, predatory, or celebratory. We were just made to drive. For the last twelve years of his life, he lived as caretaker and manager of an orange grove on the southern edge of our city. There, on eighteen acres, my brother collected cars and trucks and motorcycles. He raced around with my daughters and me in a golf cart. He tied our old dishwasher and a refrigerator to junk cars named Gumby and Monkey and had demolition derbies in the vacant land near his well. When he drove alone with me in one of his trucks, taking me to see a neighbor's hundred-year-old citrus trees, we clattered down washboard dirt roads where we flew over ditches and our backbones rattled and I felt that unmatchable exhilaration.

When he came down "to the city" to see us, to kill a skunk or gopher for me or to deliver oranges to us and his true cash crop to others, people who waited all year for fringed leaves and THC levels off the charts, my brother always had a dog and sometimes a weapon, and we could hear him blocks before he arrived. Van Halen or AC/DC screaming from the cab, his tires screaming around our corner, and once he was driving down the wrong lane, hollering, "I changed my mind—I want this side now!"

He and I drove together across the country in 1983—twenty-four years ago, and I remember it every day—when he came to help me with the long drive home from graduate school in Massachusetts. He arrived by plane, and I didn't know he was carrying at least a pound of homegrown. I was twenty-two, and he was nineteen. I didn't know why the three guys next door to my apartment were looped for three days, until my brother and I packed up my Honda and I heard the laments for his California crop.

We drove to Pennsylvania, stayed with a good friend, and my brother charmed everyone in her tough city by cruising bars with her brother (only seventeen) and distributing a bit more smoky happiness. He had money. He bought gas. And I left my intellectual and very safe life behind, watching my brother take in the landscape without fear. We headed through West Virginia, and he rolled his own while I drove ninety down the interstate as if I didn't care about college and my fiancé or cops, and he played Bon Jovi's "Dead or Alive" and Jimi Hendrix's "All Along the Watchtower."

We rolled into Sandusky, Ohio, one night, and then we stayed for days in the dryland high plains of Colorado, where our father was born. We raced down miles of country dirt road through wheat fields. We met our father's father for the first time, and my brother smoked at night under a huge moose head in the den, brazenly, never afraid, and we got restless and sped off one morning and went straight through Utah and Nevada, Las Vegas, and then home to Southern California.

Nothing has ever felt that way to me again. Not driving with my husband, or my daughters, or alone.

*O*ur father loved to race cars. As a teenager, left on his own by neglectful parents, he was desperate to survive, but when he had money, he customized mufflers on old cars, adding sewer pipes and glass packs for maximum sound effect, and he street raced. He left our mother when I was three and my brother was still in the womb.

He moved thirty miles away, and later he actually worked in the pit for the Fontana Motor Speedway. I remember him mentioning Richard Petty and Mario Andretti—their rhyming names like magic when he said them with reverence. My father taught me to drive when I was sixteen and visited him once a month. He had spent his life on the road, as a salesman for everything from cigarettes to worms to screws. He'd sold things to people along routes that took him through the deserts of California and Arizona and Nevada, and all along the freeways of Los Angeles and Riverside and San Bernardino Counties. He taught me well, knowing those asphalt trails and paths and currents better than he knew most people. Between his house and my mother's, we drove in his white 1970 restored Mustang down endless gray lines of road between abandoned vineyards. He taught me never to swerve for an animal, always to stay away from the right side of trucks, and to respect the speed of the car and the traffic and not drive too slowly, which would make good drivers hate me.

*N*ow I have to drive slowly every day, as we all do in Southern California where the constant congestion of traffic is nothing like my father ever saw. And I have a van full of girls, my own and other girls—neighbors and basketball players and friends. Often my mother rides in the passenger seat, worrying aloud about every lane change and always that I am driving way too fast.

My mother never taught me to drive. She knew my father was doing so, and she didn't like to talk about him at all. My brother, who was adopted by my stepfather when he married my mother months after her divorce, never visited our father. He taught himself to drive. My brother drove fearlessly and pharmaceutically fueled, and he wrecked eight cars in his lifetime—one of mine, one of my then-husband's, one of our stepfather's, and the rest all his own. He died when his truck plowed into a palm tree at the Jack-in-the-Box near my house, in February 2003.

It was intentional. He was fleeing police who wanted to question him about a crime his best friend had committed. He didn't want to betray his friend. In every other accident, he had escaped with no more than scratches.

When I miss him more than I can stand, there is nothing to do but drive to the desert, where I can move the van at speeds up to eighty-five or so, playing "Running with the Devil" while the gold sand and smoke trees stand still in the distance near the dunes, while the other cars on the freeway are only blurry Legos around me.

Everything about it is wrong. The music is bad for my hearing. The speed is foolish. Even writing about it feels dangerous, as if I'll be paid back, and I'm afraid even as I type. I am the sole support for three children. I am a good mother and neighbor and daughter and friend and basketball team fund-raiser and teacher and aunt.

It's been embarrassing for the girls sometimes. When my youngest was in kindergarten, an especially self-righteous group of mothers would gather at the playground fence before school let out, and they'd glare and gossip when I pulled up sharply at the curb behind them, "Dirty Deeds Done Dirt Cheap" and other satanic verses blasting from the open windows.

But I love to feel my car curve near out of control on desert roads, to move my own body with the vehicle's force, to get airborne and slam down and feel the tires catch and grip and scream just a little before I have to come back to earth and responsibility and the red light on the street that leads to my house, where I will sit on the porch and love my daughters and my yard and miss my brother and our youth.

*F*rom the very first time I drove those vineyards, I loved the feeling of speed and the wheels handling perfectly, and I loved steering wheels with an immense passion. I loved their precision, when you knew them, the way they spun back to the right place of their own accord when you let them pass through loose fingers after a sharp turn, the grips tapping your fingerprints.

One day my stepfather brought home for my mother a white 1959 Thunderbird, which she never liked very much because it was so heavy and hard to handle.

But I loved it. I raced Wendell Horn, whose ancient Pontiac was named Maybelle. No one could believe a skinny white girl would race, but I did. Twice in the orange groves, where plumes of dust scoured out behind us on the dirt road, and I won. And once near our high school we raced on a two-lane road that merged into one lane before a freeway bridge. I don't know what I thought would happen when I pushed down harder on the gas as we got closer, and I was in the right, merging lane, but Wendell must have loved me (as a friend) because he let up and I surged forward.

I was already dating my future husband in high school (we met when I was thirteen), and our junior prom was held at the top of the Palm Springs Aerial Tramway. Miles of winding mountain roads, and then a tram ride to the top, where we danced and ate in a restaurant. And on the way home Dwayne was tired, and I said, "Let me drive. I like mountain roads."

He begged me to slow down, over and over, while I cruised into those curves in his mother's silver Monarch with burgundy interior. I tapped the brake when I had to, but I was sixteen and feeling for the first time how it was to float down a steep incline with a car that handled the curves. I felt myself leaning into the turns. Then I went even faster, because I liked the way the car felt when it was slightly out of control, drifting for a moment toward the edge and the curve and the air before I rubbed the brake and turned the wheel, just a little.

"Please," he said, a big bad basketball player beside me. "Come on. Slow down. Please. You're gonna kill us."

"No, I'm not," I said, grinning, and I didn't.

The first time the van went into the air my girls were with me. We were late for basketball, when we played in a Sunday-morning league, and I wasn't paying attention to the recent repairs on the railroad tracks near the school, and we hit the new bump and flew and they gasped and thought it was fun, but it gave my oldest girl a headache that lasted for hours. "I'm sorry," I told her, over and over, when we were at the gym. "I didn't realize I was going so fast."

But she knew I'd gotten a thrill from the feeling of flying, and she grinned. All her life her father had been telling her stories of my wild driving.

I'm not reckless, or mean, when I'm driving all those girls to basketball games or study sessions or school shopping. I'm extremely efficient. I'm famous for my politesse on city streets. On the freeway I'm implacable. I drive fast, about eighty when I can, and I get to where I need to go.

Like most Southern Californians, I will flow as fast as you let me. If someone is driving slowly in the fast lane, I will say it, in front of my kids or my still-scared ex-husband. The fast lane is for people going fast. Move. Get out of my way. Go on. There you go.

But I do not tailgate. Never. My father, and my drivers' education instructor, a baseball coach who put the fear of God and himself into us, taught me well.

I just drive as fast as I can when I can, and I will not be sorry for it.

*L*ast year, when I picked up my middle daughter after her prom at one a.m., my city was deserted and dark and I drove eighty up the residential hills to the rich house where she was waiting, and I played Lynyrd Skynyrd "A Simple Man" because that was my brother's favorite besides "Free Bird," and I couldn't play that because we played it at his memorial and the tears would keep me from driving fast.

And I got airborne twice, over those railroad tracks and over a speed bump.

So I will only get airborne then, when no one else is around. I will only drive really really fast in the orange groves, or on desert stretches near Cabazon and Whitewater.

I just want to remember that life, that reckless freedom, that windspeed whipping my hair into my neck, that guitar and my brother's singing, those mountain curves and my brief reign as the craziest girl everybody knew could drive and not be scared.

I hadn't driven the groves since spring, since February, actually, which is our spring. That's when the white blossoms cover the trees like stars, and the heavy smell of orange blossoms fills the air for miles, and the dirt roads are my favorite place to rush past and let the music and the perfume and my tears be my memorial to my brother.

My ex-husband lives nearer to here, and he'd told me the groves were being bulldozed for offices and warehouses, but I hadn't known the ghost house would be gone.

It was nothing but a river-rock wall and foundation, a chimney and hearth, on top of a small boulder-strewn hill overlooking miles of orange groves and facing east. My brother and I played there all of our childhoods, walked along the canals to the old foundation and imagined it was ours, that we'd rebuild it someday.

The grove was gone, and I expected that, but the whole hill had nearly disappeared. Bulldozers had demolished the wall of the river rocks, which stood in a pile nearby, and now were carving at the hill itself, striations and scrape marks on the earth, which stood like a half-eaten cupcake.

I didn't cry.

I sped through the signs that read "Construction Zone" and "No Entry" and raced along the old dirt road past the bulldozers and piles of rubble, my van scraping into gullies and getting airborne over these old railroad tracks, too. My brother and I had always ridden our bikes here, and later, raced cars. One of his friends had died on his motorcycle, hitting the train that ran this crossing. I drove until I was inside my own cloud of dust, like a giant brown dandelion around me. My brother and I had seen a dead rattlesnake here once, had seen beehives and jackrabbits and coyotes. The van fishtailed a few times on the dirt, and I jounced up the washboard road to the edge of the Box Springs Mountains, where our childhood home was on the other side, and skidded to a stop at the dead end.

On either side of me were new office buildings, for sale or rent, empty, their walls of glass windows in those two colors of green and blue that mean only office buildings. It was about 102 that day. It was Saturday. The whole place was silent except for the sprinklers on the grass, which edged the burnt-tumbleweed vacant lot. My dust cloud settled around me now, not magical but ordinary, like cake flour on my windshield. Then a roadrunner stepped out of the tumbleweeds and twitched his tail, again and again, and he headed for the sprinkler. My engine clicked, and he cocked his head at me, and I put my arm on the hot window frame and laid my head there and watched him. I never turned down the music. "Sympathy for the Devil." And he raced past me as if he didn't mind.

My Dirty Secret

ERICA JONG

Bad girls are not born but made. I grew up as a good girl—good student, good sister, good daughter, good granddaughter. It was only when, after college and graduate school, I began to enter what I laughingly called the real world that I realized there was no point in being good—if you wanted to be noticed. Bad girls were noticed. Good girls were ignored. Not wanting to be ignored, I impersonated a bad girl. My dirty secret was that I was really good. And I still am. My purgatory is to be identified forever with a bad girl I invented in my youth for the purpose of being noticed. She haunts me still.

Of course I am referring to the heroine of my first novel, the irrepressible Isadora Wing, who romped through *Fear of Flying* (1973). Born in the late sixties—during which I wrote and rewrote this book—she *had* to be bad to say all the things we needed to hear. Speaking out made her by definition bad. But speaking out about sex made her unspeakable. John Updike could write about sex and make the cover of *Time*. Philip Roth could write about sex and be collected in the Library of America. For a woman the rules were—and *still* are—different. No woman can impersonate a bad girl without being considered a bad writer.

I hardly knew this at the time. In my youth I believed the gender playing field was even. But I learned it over the years as my work was wildly misinterpreted and so was its author. I was fascinating because I was bad. I was also unpardonable. To be a bad girl means you can be sexual, outspoken, naked, possibly adored but never respected.

I love my bad girl for her honesty, but I hate her for what she has put me through. I wish I could kill her. She is my self-created monster. Or perhaps she is my conjoined twin—and by killing her I would kill myself. Since we cannot be divided, I murder her at my peril. This is the precise metaphor: Chains of flesh link all good girls to their bad girls.

Mary Shelley invented the ultimate myth of women's lives in *Frankenstein*—the monster must ultimately die not because he is evil, but because he is too sensitive. Perhaps this is why so many transgressive women poets thought of suicide as the only answer to their transgressive work.

I refuse that cliché. What's the alternative? Not to transgress? Impossible. Perhaps the only answer is to redefine what it means to be a bad girl. The pop image of a bad girl? Slutty, loud, and rebellious. Unmarriageable and a bad mother. Possibly also a murderess.

For centuries good girls were seen but not heard—impossibility for a writer. You have only to read reviews of Charlotte Brontë's *Jane Eyre* in which Jane's employability as a governess is at issue to realize that this kind of criticism has been with us for a long time. Now that women supposedly can be heard we are still constrained by stereotypes of femininity. We are ghettoized in chick lit, romance, or mystery fiction. We tread a fine line between outspokenness and aggression. We are exposed to censure that men would never suffer.

I wrote to my friend the novelist Fay Weldon that I found publishing books more exhausting than writing them. She replied that "a life spent putting one's head out of a trench waiting to be shot at, wearing a succession of carapaces to defend oneself" was indeed exhausting. Every time I go out into the world with a book, I have to be ready to run a gantlet. Some people will love the book, but others will denounce it without reading it—my fate ever since *Fear of Flying*.

Why are women writers exposed to such derision? Probably to silence us. Sometimes it works. But I refuse to let it work with me. I am an ornery cuss, a middle child, a troublemaker, a jokester. Try and shut me up and I will only be more scathing, and more determined. I have that tenacity. My father came from Brownsville and was a tough little street fighter. He played basketball and the drums and piano. He taught me to shoot baskets even though I was short. I never give up. Push me down, and I jump up like a Jill-in-the-Box. My older sister has been pushing me down all my life. If she can't stop me, you can't either. I'm tough—under my curly blond hair. Don't mess with middle me.

Women writers are often treated like women politicians, damned for being all the things they need to be in order to be heard. They must be simultaneously good and bad—strong and aggressive (bad) to be effective, but also conforming to men's notions of wife and mother (good). They must be tough and yet seem feminine (as men define it). They must be fierce yet wifelike as well. They must mother their constituents as well as their children.

Think of the career of Hillary Clinton—"the most polarizing figure in America," according to *Time* magazine. If Clinton is ever going to succeed in politics she must be allowed the same latitude as male politicians. She must be allowed to build alliances, to triangulate her positions if necessary, to make the compromises that getting elected requires. Women politicians are always chastised for competence—supposedly held to a higher standard but really laden with baggage so that they can never be elected. The double standard for male and female excellence is an inspired way of demeaning women's achievements.

Hillary Clinton may be hated for the very qualities that make her effective. Journalists praise Hillary's brain yet attack her marriage—which, in truth, they know nothing about. They praise her bipartisanship yet criticize her "triangulation." If she is deft at bipartisanship, then she must be cynical and hypocritical. If she succeeds at compromise in her marriage, she must have an ulterior motive. All the things that make her male counterparts praiseworthy make her blameworthy. This is the impasse to which the good-girl/bad-girl dichotomy has led us. Whether we choose to be "good" or "bad," we will inevitably be criticized.

Of Hillary Clinton as candidate, pundit Arianna Huffington writes: "She is the quintessential political weather vane." Huffington is clever, passionate, tenacious and no stranger to weathervanes herself. She also has her own political ambitions. Why, then, can't she concede that in a large, diverse country like ours, nobody gets elected without moving toward the political center? Yet Clinton is criticized for bending to this necessity. If we are going to have women leaders, we have to allow them to be politicians, not angels.

As with Huffington, the critics of women are often women—women who seek political success, women who maybe secretly doubt themselves and thus attack their sisters. Sometimes the enemies are women who close down their sexuality in order to succeed. Closing down means that they succeed only bloodlessly—which is to succeed at the expense of your humanity.

Elizabeth I of England may have been the first female politician to famously encounter the good-girl/bad-girl problem—which is why her story is endlessly fascinating and has remained so for generations.

We are enthralled by her youthful lustiness, her clever flirtatiousness with princes, and her ultimate decision never to marry and to virginize herself for the sake of remaining independent. Elizabeth's story embodies every woman's dilemma in pursuit of power. We will be telling it again and again as long as storytellers remain because it makes the female political paradigm so vivid.

But the good-girl/bad-girl political problem afflicts women particularly in puritanical America, where we have never managed to elect a female president—despite female political triumphs elsewhere. Eighty-five countries have elected female presidents, but not the United States, as yet.

I have experienced its literary corollary for the past thirty-five years. For as long as my work has been associated with sexuality, it has been attacked—as if sexuality and excellence could not coexist. Men are forgiven for being sexual. It is assumed that their sexual juice helps to make their work more vivid. But women are not permitted the same vividness. We embrace the bad-girl role for fear of having no role at all.

Here's another paradox: The greatest feminists have also been the greatest lovers. I'm thinking not only of Mary Wollstonecraft and her daughter Mary Shelley, but of Anaïs Nin, Edna St. Vincent Millay, and of course of Sappho. You cannot divide creative juices from human juices. And as long as juicy women are equated with bad women, we will err on the side of being bad.

What is a bad girl, after all, but a full human being? She is not the angel in the house; she is, as Tom Wolfe might say, *a woman in full*. Germaine Greer called her debut book *The Female Eunuch* in order to emphasize the desexing of women in our culture. We think this has changed today because female sexuality seems to be everywhere—on TV, the Internet, in public discourse. But the public sexuality we see is as bogus and inhuman as implanted breasts. It is not a sexuality that breeds intimacy or empathy. It is the sexuality of an inflatable doll.

The fact that many men can't tell the difference, or that they in fact *prefer* plastic to flesh, doesn't make plastic sexuality satisfying to women. Once again women's sexuality is being shaped out of deference to men's fears. Men don't like hair in their teeth: We'll get bikini waxed. They want enormous breasts: We'll succumb to surgery. They want symmetrical labia to lick: We'll have them cut and shaped. What will women *not* do to be thought clean, decorous, compliant, and good? Nothing, it seems. But at the end of the process we still can't compete with plastic dolls (or six-year-old girls). Because we age and die, we terrify.

The very notions of good and bad girls are dictated by male fears. The good girl is wife, mother and daughter while the bad girl is the object of lust. As long as men cannot integrate these two creatures, we will be condemned to impersonate them. We know we are neither bad nor good. We know we are women in full, not girls in parts. But what we know doesn't matter. It's still a man's world.

So rather than define good girl and bad girl—let's throw out the terms altogether. They will never do. We didn't make the language—but perhaps we can remake it. I don't mean saying "womyn" or "herstory" (a neologism I detest), but questioning the language dictated to us and the concepts that lie behind it. There is no such thing as a bad girl—and no such thing as a good girl. We are made of contradictions: Persephone is also Athena, and Leda may lust for the swan. Zeus may not always be potent, and Hera may not always care. We are various, polymorphous, poly-amorous creatures. We are, in fact, even more polymorphous than men. Polymorphousness is our way of being. It always has been. We transform constantly through the cycle of our lives— girl, maiden, mother, maenad, crone. We are more protean than men, more capable of metamorphosis.

The words do not yet exist for what we are. Let us coin them and write our own dictionaries. We cannot be contained in lan-guage as we find it. We talk earlier than boys and with more com-plexity. It's time for us to reject masculine simplicity and create new systems of communication. We are just at the beginning of speech. We can grunt, but when will we sing?

Contributor Biographies

Kim Addonizio

Kim Addonizio is the author of four poetry collections, most recently *What Is This Thing Called Love* from W. W. Norton. Her first novel, *Little Beauties*, was published by Simon & Schuster in 2005; her second, *My Dreams Out in the Street*, is forthcoming in July 2007. Her awards include a Guggenheim and two NEA Fellowships. She lives in Oakland, California, and is online at www.kimaddonizio.com.

Elizabeth Benedict

Elizabeth Benedict's five critically acclaimed novels have established her reputation as a writer of wit, warmth, and insight who "specializes in the subterranean currents of modern relationships, the secret motivations and betrayals that underlie everyday interactions" (*Newsday*). Her novels include *The Practice of Deceit* ("A lot of wicked fun," *All Things Considered*), the bestseller *Almost* (a "Fresh Air" and *Newsweek* best book of the year), and *Slow Dancing*, nominated for a National Book Award. She's also the author of the classic resource *The Joy of Writing Sex: A Guide for Fiction Writers*, which is widely used in creative-writing programs. She taught fiction and creative nonfiction workshops for twenty years at Princeton, the Iowa Writers' Workshop, MIT, and Swarthmore, and has written extensively for many publications, including the *New York Times, Esquire,* and *Salmagundi.* (www.elizabethbenedict.com)

Madeleine Blais

Madeleine Blais, a professor of journalism at the University of Massachusetts, is the author of three books. *The Heart Is an Instrument* is a collection of her Pulitzer Prize–winning articles for the *Miami Herald. In These Girls, Hope Is a Muscle,* a finalist in the category of general nonfiction by the National Book Critics Circle, was cited by *Sports Illustrated* as one of the top one hundred sports books. *Uphill Walkers: Portrait of a Family* received a Ken Book Award from the National Alliance for the Mentally Ill.

Susan Casey

Susan Casey is the author of the *New York Times* bestseller *The Devil's Teeth: A True Story of Obsession and Survival Among America's Great White Sharks* (Henry Holt & Company, 2005). Previously she was the development editor for Time Inc. and the editor in chief of *Sports Illustrated Women.* She also served as the creative director of *Outside* magazine, which during her tenure won three consecutive history-making National Magazine Awards for General Excellence. Her writing is frequently published in magazines in North America and Asia, including *Sports Illustrated, Esquire, Time, Fortune, Entertainment Weekly, Outside,* and *O, The Oprah Magazine.* A native of Toronto, Casey lives in New York City.

Susan Cheever

Susan Cheever is the bestselling author of twelve books including five novels, *Home Before Dark*, a memoir about her father John Cheever, and *My Name is Bill*, a biography of AA cofounder Bill Wilson. Her most recent book, *American Bloomsbury*, a study of nineteenth-century writers in Concord, Massachusetts, including Margaret Fuller, Louisa May Alcott, Henry David Thoreau, Nathaniel Hawthorne, and Ralph Waldo Emerson, was published in 2007. She has written for many magazines and newspapers including *The New Yorker*, the *New York Times*, and *Newsday*. She is a Guggenheim fellow and a National Book Critics Circle Award nominee. She lives in New York City and teaches in MFA programs at Bennington College and at the New School. Her Web site is www.susancheever.com.

Maggie Estep

Maggie Estep is the author of six books. Her debut crime novel, *Hex*, was a New York Times Notable Book of 2003. Maggie's writing has appeared in many magazines and anthologies, including *Brooklyn Noir* and *The Best American Erotica* and *Hard Boiled Brooklyn*. Maggie is the coeditor of *Bloodlines: An Anthology of Horse Racing*. She lives in Brooklyn, New York. For more information, go to www.maggieestep.com.

Jennifer Gilmore

Jennifer Gilmore is the author of the novel *Golden Country* (Scribner's, 2006), which was a *New York Times* Notable Book and a finalist for the National Jewish Book Award and for the *Los Angeles Times* Book Prize. Her work has also appeared in magazines, journals, and anthologies, including *Allure, BookForum, Nerve, The Stranger*, and *Salon*. She works in publishing and lives in Brooklyn, New York.

Kaui Hart Hemmings

Kaui is a former Stegner fellow and is the author of *House of Thieves*, a collection of stories. Her work appears in the *Sun, StoryQuarterly, Zoetrope, LA Times, Best American Nonrequired Reading,* and *Best American New Voices.* Her first novel, *The Descendants,* will be published by Random House in June 2007.

Ann Hood

Ann Hood is the author of seven novels, including *Somewhere Off the Coast Of Maine;* a memoir, *Do Not Go Gentle: My Search for Miracles in a Cynical Time;* and a collection of short stories, *An Ornithologist's Guide to Life.* Her essays and stories have appeared in many publications, including the *New York Times,* the *Paris Review, Glimmer Train, Traveler,* and *Food and Wine.* She has twice won the Pushcart Prize, as well as a Best American Spiritual Writing Award and the Paul Bowles Prize for Short Fiction. Her new novel, *The Knitting Circle,* was published in January 2007 by W. W. Norton.

Pam Houston

Pam Houston is the author of two collections of linked short stories, *Cowboys Are My Weakness* (W. W. Norton), which was the winner of the 1993 Western States Book Award and *Waltzing the Cat* (W. W. Norton), which won the WILLA Award for Contemporary Fiction. Her stories have been selected for volumes of *Best American Short Stories,* the *O. Henry Awards,* the *Pushcart Prize,* and *Best American Short Stories of the Century.* Her first novel, *Sight Hound,* was published by W. W. Norton in January 2005. She is the director of Creative Writing at UC Davis, and divides her time between Colorado and California.

Erica Jong

Poet and novelist Erica Jong has published twenty books of fiction and nonfiction, including seven award-winning books of poetry, the world-famous novel *Fear of Flying*, and her recent memoir about her writer's life, *Seducing the Demon*.

Caroline Leavitt

Caroline Leavitt is the award-winning author of eight novels, most recently the BookSense Notable book *Girls in Trouble*. A critic for the *Boston Globe*, the *Washington Post*, and *People* magazine, she is also a book columnist for *Cookie* magazine. A recipient of a New York Foundation of the Arts Award and a Goldenberg Literary second prize/honorable mention winner, she was also a finalist in the Nickelodeon Screenwriting Fellowship and was nominated for a National Magazine Award in Personal Essay. Her writing has appeared in *Salon, Psychology Today, Parenting, Redbook,* and more. She is a senior instructor in writing at UCLA online and she lives in Hoboken, New Jersey, with her husband, the writer Jeff Tamarkin, and their young son, Max.

Tobin Levy

Tobin Levy is a freelance writer and editor, currently working on a novel and splitting her time between Marfa and Austin, Texas.

Laura Lippman

Laura Lippman is the author of the award-winning Tess Monaghan series and two critically acclaimed stand-alone novels, *Every Secret Thing* and *To the Power of Three*. Her twelfth novel, *What the Dead Know*, was published in 2007. A former *Baltimore Sun* reporter, she lives in Baltimore.

Joyce Maynard

Joyce Maynard is the author of nine books, including the novel *To Die For* and the bestselling memoir, *At Home in the World*. Her most recent book is *Internal Combustion: The Story of a Marriage and a Murder in the Motor City*, published in fall 2006. Mother of three grown children, she divides her time between Northern California and Guatemala, where she runs a writing workshop.

Daphne Merkin

Daphne Merkin was a staff writer for *The New Yorker* for five years. She is currently a contributing writer for the *New York Times Magazine*, where she writes profiles and personal essays. Her work appears regularly in *Slate* and *Elle* and in a variety of other publications, including *Vogue*, *Travel & Leisure*, and *Allure*. Ms. Merkin is the author of two books: an autobiographical novel, *Enchantment*, which won the Edward Lewis Wallant award in 1986 for the best new work of fiction based on a Jewish theme, and *Dreaming of Hitler*, a collection of essays. She lives in New York City with her daughter.

Kate Moses

Kate Moses is the author of *Wintering: A Novel of Sylvia Plath* (St. Martin's Press, Anchor Books, 2003), winner of the Janet Heidinger Kafka Prize and published in thirteen languages, and coeditor of *Because I Said So: 33 Mothers Write About Children, Sex, Men, Aging, Faith, Race & Themselves* (HarperCollins 2005) and *Mothers Who Think: Tales of Real-Life Parenthood* (Villard 1999, Washington Square Press 2000), winner of an American Book Award. She lives in San Francisco.

Michelle Richmond

Michelle Richmond is the author of the novels *The Year of Fog* and *Dream of the Blue Room*, as well as the award-winning story collection *The Girl in the Fall-Away Dress*. Her stories and essays have appeared in *Glimmer Train*, *Playboy*, *Salon*, and many other publications. She lives with her husband and son in San Francisco, where she teaches creative writing and publishes the online literary journal *Fiction Attic*. She is still striving, against great obstacles, to be badder than Omarosa.

Mary Roach

Mary Roach is the author of the *New York Times* bestseller *Stiff: The Curious Lives of Human Cadavers*. *Stiff* has been published in fourteen languages, including Lithuanian, Korean, and Hungarian (*Hullamerev!*). *Stiff*'s follow-up, the bestseller *Spook: Science Tackles the Afterlife*, was a 2005 New York Times Notable Book. Roach's writing has appeared in the *New York Times Magazine* and *Book Review*, NPR's *All Things Considered*, *Wired*, and *Outside*, among many others. She is a contributing editor of the science magazine *Discover*. She lives in the Bay Area and is at work on a new book.

Roxana Robinson

Roxana Robinson is the author of three novels: *Summer Light*, *This Is My Daughter*, and *Sweetwater*; three story collections: *A Glimpse of Scarlet*, *Asking for Love*, and *A Perfect Stranger*; and the biography *Georgia O'Keeffe: A Life*. Four of these were *New York Times* Notable Books; one a *New York Times* Editors' Choice. Robinson's work has appeared in *The New Yorker*, the *Atlantic*, *Harper's*, *Best American Short Stories*, the *New York Times*, the *Boston Globe*, the *Chicago Tribune*, *Vogue*, and the *Wall Street Journal*. Robinson has received fellowships from NEA, the MacDowell Colony, and the Guggenheim Foundation. She was named a Literary Lion by the New York Public Library. She teaches at the New School and at the Wesleyan Writers Conference. She lives in New York City.

M.J. Rose

M. J. Rose (www.mjrose.com) is the author of eight novels including *Lying in Bed* and *The Venus Fix*. Her short fiction has appeared in several anthologies including Susie Bright's *Best American Erotica* and *Thriller: Stories to Keep You Up All Night*.

Elizabeth Rosner

Elizabeth Rosner is the author of two bestselling novels, both published by Ballantine Books. Her highly acclaimed first novel *The Speed of Light* (2001) won several literary prizes in both the United States and Europe, including the Harold U. Ribalow Prize and the Prix France Bleu Gironde. It was translated into nine languages and optioned for a feature film by Gillian Anderson. Her second novel, *Blue Nude,* was published in May 2006, and a related essay appeared in the *New York Times Magazine*. She is also an award-winning poet whose chapbook, *Gravity*, is currently in its thirteenth printing. She lives in Berkeley, California. Her Web site is www.elizabethrosner.com.

Susan Straight

Susan Straight has published six novels, including *Highwire Moon* (Anchor Books) which was a finalist for the National Book Award in 2001 and won the Gold Medal in Fiction from the Commonwealth Club of California, and *A Million Nightingales* (Pantheon Books, 2006). She has also published numerous essays and short stories in magazines such as *Harper's,* the *Nation,* the *New York Times Magazine, WEST, Family Circle, Salon,* and many others. She was born in Riverside, California, where she lives with her daughters.

Ellen Sussman

Ellen Sussman's novel *On a Night Like This* (Warner Books, 2004) became a *San Francisco Chronicle* Bestseller and has been translated into six languages. She has published a dozen short stories in literary and commercial magazines; her essays have appeared in various anthologies. She has received fellowships from Writers at Work, Wesleyan Writers Conference, and Virginia Center for the Creative Arts. Her Web site is www.ellensussman.com.

Katharine Weber

Katharine Weber is the author of the novels *Triangle, The Little Women, The Music Lesson,* and *Objects in Mirror Are Closer Than They Appear*. Visit her Web site at www.katharineweber.com.

Lolly Winston

Lolly Winston is the author of the *New York Times* bestselling novels *Happiness Sold Separately* (Warner Books, 2006), and *Good Grief* (Warner Books, 2004). *Good Grief* was a number one BookSense Pick and has been translated into fifteen languages. Winston holds an MFA in creative writing from Sarah Lawrence College. Her feature stories and essays have appeared in *Glamour, Redbook, Family Circle, Lifetime, New Woman,* and other publications. She has published short fiction in the *Sun,* the *Southeast Review,* and *Girls' Night Out*. She lives in Northern California.

BAD GIRLS

Edited by Ellen Sussman

BAD GIRLS

Edited by Ellen Sussman

A NOTE FROM THE EDITOR
OF *BAD GIRLS*

I've just come home from my first book club meeting about *Bad Girls: 26 Writers Misbehave*. At one point in the evening, the fine women who were gathered in someone's living room began to recount their own bad girl stories. One woman had worked as a stripper while in her twenties and never told a soul. Another had had a summer affair with both a man and his son—neither one knew of the other romance! A very refined woman used to break into her ex-husband's house in the middle of the day and steal mementos from their marriage. Oh my god. The women howled with laughter. The discussion lasted far past 9 PM when all good girls go home. And once the shock of these confessions wore off, the real conversation began. Why do women act out? What does it take for us to break out of our role as dutiful wife, daughter, mother, working woman—and cut loose? What do we feel afterwards—celebration or regret? This was far better than any book club meeting I'd ever attended!

At the beginning of the evening the host of the book club asked me why I had decided to put together an anthology of essays about bad girls. I told her that I had started writing personal essays three years ago, after a lifetime of writing fiction, and that I found the process very rewarding. And when I looked at the many essays I had written over a three-year period I realized they all shared one common thread—they were about my bad girl escapades. Why, I wondered, did I keep coming back to that theme? Why, in fact, have I spent much of my life rebelling and acting out? The questions interested me—and I almost immediately thought: What would other writers have to say about this?

And so I asked them. I asked writers with reputations for being bad girls: Erica Jong, Pam Houston, Kim Addonizio, Maggie Estep, Kaui Hart Hemmings. I asked writers who were good girls but had a few secrets they might share: Roxana Robinson, Madeleine Blais, Elizabeth Rosner, Lolly Winston. I asked well-known writers like Joyce Maynard and Susan Cheever, and emerging writers like Michelle Richmond and Tobin Levy. They all shared my enthusiasm for the subject. And they were all willing to dig deep—what it is about women, our society's rules, and our wild defiance.

Then came the real fun. Once the book was published the readers began to respond. My email inbox is flooded with notes from readers who not only want to tell me how much they loved the book, but they want to add their own thoughts about this meaty topic. They sometimes even share their own tales.

Now the book has begun to appear on the book club circuit. Last night I got a first taste of what that experience is like. The women began their discussion by talking about the essays that most moved them—sometimes they loved an essay and sometimes they were furious about an essay. All of it led to fascinating discussion about the questions I wanted to raise: what does it mean in our society for women to break the rules? And in the end, the political is personal. We ended the evening by sharing our own stories and sharing our own insights. And man, did we laugh.

DISCUSSION QUESTIONS

1. We'll start easy. Which is your favorite essay? Why?

2. Which essay shocked you? Upset you? Enraged you? Excited you? Talk about it. Sometimes we learn the most from our strongest emotional response to what we read.

3. Are bad girls born or made? A few of the contributors claim they were bad from birth—some claim that they aren't very bad by nature. What do you think?

4. Kim Addonizio writes about a one-night stand, Caroline Leavitt and Maggie Estep write about their affairs, Tobin Levy writes about her sexual wish list. Why do women often act out sexually? Is the bedroom our battlefield?

5. Both Kaui Hart Hemmings and Lolly Winston write about the phases in their lives—from bad girl to wife and mom, or from bad girl to middle-aged worrywart. Both of them seem determined to claim something important from their bad girl days—their gutsiness, perhaps, or their disdain for the rules. Do bad girls grow up and become good girls?

6. Elizabeth Rosner rebels against the rigid rules of orthodox Judaism, especially the ones written for women. Madeleine Blais writes that at her Catholic school "occasions of sin lurked everywhere." Mary Roach imagines a priest she can lust after. How does religion bring out the bad girl in us?

7. Sometimes "badness" is hard to define. Is Pam Houston misbehaving at her father's funeral? Is Laura Lippman fighting for her rights at work or behaving like a pest? Can we interpret Joyce Maynard's decision to end her silence about her affair with J. D. Salinger as a bold attempt to reclaim her own story? What's so bad about that? (Just ask her critics!)

8. Ann Hood describes how she reinvents herself through lies; Susan

Straight speeds down a country road in homage to the brother she lost; Susan Casey cuts out on family Christmas in search of something more personally meaningful. These might be looked at as small transgressions. What are the ways in which we misbehave in order to find ourselves? Is acting out a way of looking in?

9. Is "bad" really a feminist issue? Elizabeth Benedict wants her boyfriend's perfect daughter to boldly use the F-word. Daphne Merkin dares to talk about the penis. Erica Jong asserts: What is a bad girl, after all, but a full human being? Are these writers (and maybe even the women you know) striking out against the rules of society that still don't give women the freedom they need?

10. OK, fess up. You've got a few secrets. Bring to the book club meeting a list of three things your book club friends would never guess about you.

MORE NORTON BOOKS WITH READING GROUP GUIDES AVAILABLE

Diana Abu-Jaber	*Arabian Jazz*
	Crescent
	Origin
Faith Adiele	*Meeting Faith*
Rabih Alameddine	*I, the Divine*
Robert Alter	*Genesis**
Rupa Bajwa	*The Sari Shop*
Christine Balint	*Ophelia's Fan**
	*The Salt Letters**
Brad Barkley	*Money, Love*
Andrea Barrett	*Servants of the Map*
	Ship Fever
	The Voyage of the Narwhal
Rachel Basch	*The Passion of Reverend Nash*
Charles Baxter	*Shadow Play*
Peter C. Brown	*The Fugitive Wife*
Frederick Busch	*Harry and Catherine*
Lan Samantha Chang	*Inheritance*
Leah Hager Cohen	*House Lights*
Michael Cox	*The Meaning of Night*
Abigail De Witt	*Lili*
Rachel DeWoskin	*Foreign Babes in Beijing*
Jared Diamond	*Guns, Germs, and Steel*
Jack Driscoll	*Lucky Man, Lucky Woman*
John Dufresne	*Deep in the Shade of Paradise*
	Louisiana Power and Light
	Love Warps the Mind a Little
Tony Eprile	*The Persistence of Memory*
Ellen Feldman	*The Boy Who Loved Anne Frank*
	Lucy
Susan Fletcher	*Eve Green*
Paula Fox	*The Widow's Children*
Judith Freeman	*The Chinchilla Farm*
Betty Friedan	*The Feminine Mystique*
Barbara Goldsmith	*Obsessive Genius*

Mary Roach	*Spook**
Josh Russell	*Yellow Jack*
Kerri Sakamoto	*The Electrical Field*
Gay Salisbury and	
Laney Salisbury	*The Cruelest Miles*
May Sarton	*Journal of a Solitude**
Susan Fromberg Schaeffer	*Anya*
	Buffalo Afternoon
	Poison
	The Snow Fox
Jessica Shattuck	*The Hazards of Good Breeding*
Frances Sherwood	*The Book of Splendor*
	Night of Sorrows
	Vindication
Joan Silber	*Household Words*
	Ideas of Heaven
Marisa Silver	*No Direction Home*
Gustaf Sobin	*The Fly-Truffler*
	In Pursuit of a Vanishing Star
Dorothy Allred Solomon	*Daughter of the Saints*
Ted Solotaroff	*Truth Comes in Blows**
Jean Christopher Spaugh	*Something Blue**
Mary Helen Stefaniak	*The Turk and My Mother*
Matthew Stewart	*The Courtier and the Heretic**
Mark Strand and	
Eavan Boland	*The Making of a Poem**
Manil Suri	*The Death of Vishnu**
Barry Unsworth	*Losing Nelson**
	*Morality Play**
	The Ruby in Her Navel
	*Sacred Hunger**
	*The Songs of the Kings**
Brad Watson	*The Heaven of Mercury**
Jenny White	*The Sultan's Seal*

*Available only on the Norton Web site: www.wwnorton.com/guides